ADVENTURES IN SINGING

A Process for Exploring, Discovering, and Developing Vocal Potential

Second Edition

Clifton Ware

University of Minnesota

Boston, Massachusetts   Burr Ridge, Illinois   Dubuque, Iowa
Madison, Wisconsin   New York, New York   San Francisco, California   St. Louis, Missouri

**This book is dedicated
to the memory of
Roy A. Schuessler (1912–1982)**

*A Master Teacher who strove to
free the spirit and light up the mind.*

McGraw-Hill

A Division of The McGraw·Hill Companies

**Adventures in Singing:
A Process for Exploring, Discovering, and Developing Vocal Potential**

Copyright ©1998, 1995 by The McGraw-Hill Companies, Inc. All rights reserved. Printed in the United States of America. Except as permitted under the United States Copyright Act of 1976, no part of this publication may be reproduced or distributed in any form or by any means, or stored in a data base or retrieval system, without the prior written permission of the publisher.

This book is printed on acid-free paper.

2 3 4 5 6 7 8 9 0   QPD   QPD   9 0 9 8

ISBN 0-07-068308-5

This book was set in New Caledonia by A-R Editions, Inc.
The editors were Cynthia Ward and Chris Freitag;
the production supervisor was Annette Mayeski.
The cover was designed by Karen K. Quigley.
Project supervision was done by The Total Book.
Quebecor Printing/Dubuque was printer and binder.

Library of Congress Cataloging-in-Publication Data

Ware, Clifton.
    Adventures in singing : a process for exploring, discovering, and
  developing vocal potential / Clifton Ware. — 2nd ed.
      p.   cm.
    Includes bibliographical references (p.) and indexes.
    ISBN 0-07-068308-5
    1. Singing—Methods.   I. Title.
MT825.W18   1997
783'.04—dc21   96-6612
                                                                       MN

http://www.mhhe.com

Contents

SONG ANTHOLOGY

Background Information

Group Songs

Folk Songs and Hymns

Art Songs and Arias

Musical Theater Songs

Preface

Adventures in Singing is an instructional package including a textbook with song anthology and an audiocassette and compact disc of song accompaniments. Although intended primarily for beginning voice students, these materials will be useful to anyone interested in learning about the singing process or exploring new vocal repertoire.

Some of the major features and advantages of the text are (1) *methodical voice-building techniques,* beginning with the speaking voice and progressing to more challenging singing tasks; (2) *foundational preparations,* including an introduction to how the voice works; and (3) *self-assessment questions* at the end of most chapters to help the student think through the material discussed. Specifically, suggested exercises are provided in conjunction with discussions related to the vocal process (how the voice works) and basic performance skills. The subject matter is systematically presented, beginning with the preparation of the mind and body (relaxing and energizing), and continuing with the discussion of vocal skills such as breath management, vocal-fold vibration, resonance, diction, coordination, and performance.

Every attempt has been made to offer a comprehensive and well-balanced anthology of songs suitable for most beginning (and intermediate) level singers taking voice class and/or private lessons. Although most medium-key selections may be sung by either male or female students, a few songs have been added for high and low voices, partially replacing songs previously offered in two keys. Standard song repertoire representative of musical historical periods, nationalities, and languages are included. Information provided in the Song Anthology includes guidelines used in selecting songs, background and interpretive comments on all songs, and International Phonetic Alphabet transcriptions and literal translations of foreign language song texts.

Serving as a learning aid for students lacking strong musical skills, the audiocassette and compact disc of piano accompaniments provide a low-volume level instrumental rendition of the vocal line. When using a stereo playback system, it is possible for the singer to adjust dynamic levels of either the voice line or the accompaniment simply by manipulating right (voice line) or left (accompaniment) stereo channels. Moreover, foreign language texts are recited prior to the playing of the song accompaniment.

Adventures in Singing is perhaps unique in its general emphasis on holistic learning, providing greater potential for self-improvement in the process of learning how to sing. Topics stressing this holistic approach include positive mental attitudes, the role of a "vocal athlete," and constructive learning habits. The overall objective is to assist the student in achieving effective and lasting results, both as a vocal performer and as a human being.

Acknowledgments

Major influences in my life and career have been teachers and students—teachers with whom I have studied and students from whom I have learned. Since 1980 this text has been developed and class-tested by more than 4,000 students at the University of Minnesota. Their comments and continuing feedback have shaped the form, content, and methods of these instructional materials.

Beginning with voice lessons at age 15 an[d] continuing through the present, I am indebted to several teachers/mentors whose e[ncour]agement and instruction kindled within me a desire to become an artist-teach[er]. principal mentor was Roy A. Schuessler, who helped me gain, during the se[cond dec]ade of my teaching career, a broader and more profound understanding of th[e] voice, both its function and its intimate connection to personality. This book in his memory and as a testament to his continuing legacy.

Following the death of Professor Schuessler, n[ew work] with Harris Balko (University of Wisconsin–Superior) began with in[vestig]ations into Italian singing technique. I am greatly appreciative for th[e follow]ing pedagogical discussions and teaching demonstrations I have share[d with] Balko—and for his expert "vocal ear."

The publisher and I would like to thank the follow[ing] insightful review of *Adventures in Singing*, 2/e: Mark Bendert, [ ] Francis Brockington, Wayne State University; Dr. J. Van Horton [arks,] Humboldt State University; Elizabeth Rice, Georgia [ ]ne Thomas, Iowa State University.

Several other people have played significant roles in [ ] wife Bettye helped through her computer skills, reading an[ ] songs, editing piano accompaniments on several songs, an[ ] ments for the audiotapes. Her personal contributions, enc[ ] support helped me to complete this ongoing long-term project[ ]

I was fortunate to secure the assistance of Deirdre ("D[ ] pathologist at the University of Minnesota Hospital's ENT Clinic[ ] ical and scientific consultant. Lawrence Weller, who teaches voi[ ] University, graciously read the manuscript and offered criticism rela[ ]

The Song Anthology involved the expertise and collaboration of se[ver] als: Steve Norquist, a musicology consultant on vocal literature; Lawre[n] arranger of several songs; Barry Brahier, Tracey and Keith Bradshaw, Dan Ne[ ] and Paul Siskind, all of whom contributed to computer editing of music examp[les] and the Song Anthology. A-R Editions, Inc. engraved the final music that appears in the book. The song accompaniments, performed by Bettye Ware, were processed by Nick Kereakos, electrotechnician at the University of Minnesota.

I also wish to express appreciation to the following reviewers, who provided helpful evaluations of the first and second editions in various stages of draft:

Adventures in Singing would never have made it to the public without the professional expertise of Paul Nockleby, my agent and general editor. I also wish to thank key persons of McGraw-Hill's College Division, especially Cynthia Ward, who served as chief facilitator of the project throughout the publishing process. Other key persons include Kate Scheinman, who served as project supervisor and coordinator, copy editor Michelle Lulos, and all of the people who worked behind the scenes to make this publication a reality.

I wish to express my genuine thanks for the collective effort of everyone associated with producing the first and second editions of *Adventures in Singing*. I hope this improved version will continue to assist singers in the technical and artistic development of singing.

Clifton Ware

Cliiton Ware is resident tenor, coordinator of vocal instruction and instructor of applied voice, vocal pedagogy, and vocal performance at the University of Minnesota in Minneapolis, where he also serves as chair of the Roy A. Schuessler Vocal Arts Center in the School of Music.

The author's accomplishments and honors include a D.M. degree in vocal performance from Northwestern University, former executive leadership positions as president of the National Opera Association and the Minnesota Chapter of the National Association of Teachers of Singing, and listings in several *Who's Who* publications.

Dr. Ware has performed extensively: more than fifty principal and supporting roles in opera, operetta, and musical comedy; more than seventy major works with orchestra and chorus; and more than twenty individually programmed recitals. As tenor soloist he has performed with more than sixty major musical organizations in the United States and Europe. He can also be heard in recordings of Britten's *St. Nicolas* (MHS) and *Paul Bunyan* (Virgin Records).

As an author, Dr. Ware has produced *Voice Adventures* (Harmony Publications, 1988), which has been revised and expanded into *Adventures in Singing*, 2d edition, a beginning-level voice text and song anthology with audiocassette or CD accompaniments. His latest project, *Basics of Vocal Pedagogy: The Foundations and Process of Singing* (McGraw-Hill, 1998), is the first in a series of three beginning-level textbooks; the other two entitled *Basics of Solo Vocal Performance* and *The Process of Teaching Singing* are in progress.

Although Dr. Ware enjoys the challenges of working with students at all levels of vocal development, his teaching involves mostly undergraduate and graduate voice majors. His interest in teaching beginning-level voice students is sustained by supervising voice class teaching assistants in the School of Music. The writer has seventeen years of experience teaching voice class through the extension program of the university.

Dr. Ware collaborates with his wife Bettye, a private instructor of piano, organist, and keyboard accompanist, in numerous music-related projects. The couple, parents of three adult sons, shares a strong interest in developing a balanced, healthy lifestyle.

CHAPTER

Preparing for the Journey

Four Questions for the Journey

Before starting any journey we need to set a destination, arrange an itinerary, and pack appropriately. While the study of singing can be a lifetime journey toward mastery or a short trip of exploration, even a short trip requires that we consider four important questions: (1) "Why do I want to take this trip?" (2) "How much time and effort can I commit?" (3) "What resources do I have or need to assist me?" and (4) "Who will be my companions?"

Why Do I Want to Study Singing?

Like other worthwhile endeavors, singing requires preparation. In addition to native talent and abilities, it helps greatly if there is a firm personal commitment that's motivated by a strong and lasting desire for learning. Thus, the most beneficial first step is to give an honest answer to the question, "Why have I decided to undertake the study of singing?"

When students are asked this question on the first day of class, a variety of responses are offered, such as: (1) "I've been told I have a pleasant voice, so I thought I'd like to develop it"; (2) "It fulfills a graduation requirement"; (3) "It was the only course open when I was free to attend"; (4) "I'm extremely shy and want to gain confidence as a performer"; and (5) "I have vocal problems that need correcting."

Though each answer represents a valid motivation for enrolling in voice class, voice teachers are most heartened by the rationale: "I really enjoy singing, and I want to get better at it." Teachers appreciate this upbeat response because dedicated, self-directed student "travelers" tend to make steady progress toward their desired destination, while enjoying every step along the way.

How Much Time and Effort Can I Commit?

The second most important decision involves the amount of time and effort you can commit to the learning process. Studies show that a distinctive characteristic of high achievers is an ability to clearly articulate realistic, worthwhile, prioritized goals that serve to order and channel efforts in a step-by-step game plan. Obviously, voice study must be balanced with other worthwhile commitments—personal, academic, and professional. Since singing demands considerable organized effort in the development of various skills, making steady progress will largely depend on time spent in disciplined study and practice, including the following activities:

1. **Reading and Review.** Read, re-read, and review the assigned text chapters until the contents are fully assimilated, which should take approximately one or two hours per week, or per chapter.

2. **Vocal Warm-Ups and Exercises.** After checking with your instructor for recommendations regarding appropriate vocal and physical exercises, making sufficient progress will require a minimum of twenty to thirty minutes per day (five to six days per week).

3. **Songs and Performance Study.** Time must be allotted for systematically studying and practicing songs, including reading texts aloud dramatically, studying the music, and listening to tapes.

4. **Learning from Model Singers.** For the purpose of hearing a variety of singers representative of all levels of development, some time should be spent weekly listening to professional recordings and attending classical vocal solo performances (recitals, oratorios, and operas).

5. **Writing and Reflecting.** Maintaining a daily or weekly journal of brief entries about your vocal activities and experiences—personal goals, learning outcomes, thoughts, and feelings—will help you organize, motivate, assimilate, and evaluate your learning.

After consulting with your instructor and mutually determining how much time you can afford or need to spend, fill in your total weekly commitment to voice study below:

Activity	*Time Allotment*
Class attendance	
Reading and studying	
Voice technique and performance	
Other activities	
TOTAL TIME (WEEKLY)	

A weekly involvement of several hours may seem excessive, especially for avocational students. However, since repetitious, routine practice is necessary for building appropriate automatic muscular responses in any intricately complex performance art or sport, you must realize in advance that there are no shortcuts in learning to sing well.

What Resources Do I Bring to the Class?

Resources for the class consist of two kinds: (1) internal or subjective know-how and (2) external or objective equipment. Among one's internal resources are the levels of proficiencies already attained, the so-called state of learning readiness. Voice classes often include students with widely ranging expertise and experience, from individuals who have practically no formal musical training to those who have varying degrees of musical and/or vocal training. Relatively inexperienced singers should not feel apologetic for lack of training, but rather think of singing as a series of adventures into ever steeper, more challenging terrain—with the prospect of enjoying some beautiful vistas ahead.

In addition to vocal experience, you have personal resources acquired through experience or education that contribute in some way to the composite personality you present to others when performing, including

1. **general attitudes and beliefs** about singing, and in particular, your personal vocal image and identity

2. **memories**—positive and negative—from childhood to the present, of teachers, friends, and relatives that help determine vocal self-esteem

3. **cultural experiences** (concerts, theater, television) that have favorably impressed you with the musicianship, style, and technique of singers

4. **knowledge and skills** gained from previous musical study or music activities, from extracurricular activities such as speech, drama, and athletics, and from nonmusic course work in a variety of related areas (literature, history, arts)

We also bring to voice class some inborn resources—talents, endowments, and abilities—that may either enable or burden us, depending on the attitude we take toward them. The all-important question is, "What will you do with the unique vocal instrument you have inherited?" One goal of voice study is to help identify your uniqueness, and to start you down the road toward self-fulfilling potential.

To save time and maximize efforts, the aspiring vocalist also needs certain tools. In addition to the personal resources you bring to voice class and the acquired instructional materials (text, song anthology, audiotape, notebook), the following basic tools are suggested for voice study:

1. **Rehearsal Space.** A pleasant, quiet, private room with favorable acoustics

2. **Pitch-Producing Instrument.** Preferably a well-tuned piano, although a guitar or pitch pipe can also be used

3. **Mirror.** Preferably a full-length mirror, for observing posture, breathing, muscle tension, mannerisms, and facial expressions (a penlight could also prove to be useful in viewing the inside of your mouth and throat)

4. **Portable Cassette Tape Recorder/Player.** For use in lessons and practice sessions to record vocal progress and song accompaniments

5. **Other.** A music stand and **metronome**, the former to hold your music high enough to be viewed without strain, and the latter to help indicate and maintain the suggested tempi of songs

Who Will Be My Companions?

The remaining issue in preparation for the course is: "What are the roles of my fellow students in the learning process?" As you and your classmates will discover, a community of learners can serve as an effective support system for exploring and developing each student's vocal potential.

The competition factor, always present in the classroom, can and should be a healthy stimulus toward individual improvement. One of the most valuable aspects of the voice class experience is observing and hearing others perform, effectively providing a yardstick for measuring individual progress. Observing others in the act of discovering and developing their voices inevitably helps everyone develop higher performance standards. Almost every facet of the singing process—vocal technique, musicianship, musical and vocal style, and performance skills—is enhanced in a group-learning environment.

Finally, the power of social interaction and interdependence in the typical classroom cannot be underestimated. When each student comes to the class with a positive attitude and an open mind, learning is greatly enhanced for all. As social animals, we thrive on the synergy of working with our peers. With the motto "one for all, and all for one" as a guiding principle, voice class can function as a support group for promoting the welfare and edification of all members.

Preparation Assessment Exercises

Exercises 1-1 and 1-2 will help you assess your learning readiness and establish some useful criteria for vocal study. Writing is suggested as the most effective way to reflect, organize, and express your thoughts.

Exercise 1-1   SOME FUNDAMENTAL QUESTIONS AND PERSONAL VOCAL HISTORY

Give some careful thought to answering these questions: (1) "Why am I taking this course?" (2) "What do I expect to learn?" (3) "Who has especially encouraged or discouraged me in my voice use?" (4) "Who are the singers I most admire and why?" (5) "How do I feel about my voice?" (6) "What is my impression of what others think about my voice?" (7) "Do I truly enjoy singing and performing, or does it frighten me?" Using these questions as guidelines, write a personal vocal history, tracing your development from earliest recollections to the present.

Since it is impossible to sing well without recognizing effective singing, students should listen frequently to audio and video recordings of reputable classical vocal artists, especially singers of similar voice type. Some examples of well-known model singers include: Dawn Upshaw and Kathleen Battle, sopranos; Fredrica von Stade and Cecilia Bartoli, mezzo sopranos; Roberto Alagna and Jerry Hadley, tenors; Thomas Hampson, baritone; and Samuel Ramey, bass/baritone. Even better, attend some live performances of opera, oratorio, and recital that feature local model singers. The more you listen and observe, the more equipped you will be to evaluate any singer's artistry and vocalism.

Exercise 1-2   LISTENING AND OBSERVING

Attend a live performance or listen to a recording of a model singer. Ask yourself such questions as: "What makes this voice and performance unique?" "How does he or she differ from the other singers I have heard?" "What are my reasons for liking or disliking this voice?" "Can I understand every word, and do I get the meaning of the text?" Write an evaluation, commenting on such factors as: (1) *presentation*—general effectiveness, posture, and mannerisms; (2) *vocal tone*—intonation, quality, consistency, and range; (3) *musicianship*—rhythm, pitches, phrasing, and style; and (4) *diction*—pronunciation, clarity, and textual expression.

CHAPTER

Getting Started

The Vocal Process: How the Voice Works

The human **larynx**, or voice box, evolved from a mechanism designed by nature for protection (keeping foreign matter out of the lungs), and for thoracic pressure (lifting, defecation, and childbirth), to an instrument capable of wide-ranging oral and verbal expression. Since singing is an exaggerated extension of speech and, like speech, requires the development and coordination of many complex skills, our appreciation will be enhanced if we consider speaking and singing as the products of a single instrument.

All musical instruments, including the voice, have in common three elements for the production of sound: (1) an actuator, (2) a vibrator, and (3) a resonator. In addition to these three elements, the human voice includes a fourth: an articulator. The balanced coordination of these four elements results in functionally efficient vocal tone. Since the impulse behind all intentional vocalization is mentally based, we must also consider the decisive role of the brain/nervous system as the motivator of the vocal process.

What follows is a brief outline describing the five steps in the vocal process (Fig. 2-1), listed formally or conceptually (in bold) and functionally (in italics, as *physical cause > musical effect*).

Figure 2-1   **The Vocal Process**

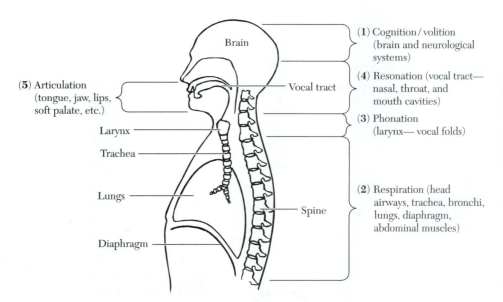

(**5**) Articulation (tongue, jaw, lips, soft palate, etc.)

Brain

Vocal tract

Larynx

Trachea

Lungs

Spine

Diaphragm

(**1**) Cognition/volition (brain and neurological systems)

(**4**) Resonation (vocal tract— nasal, throat, and mouth cavities)

(**3**) Phonation (larynx— vocal folds)

(**2**) Respiration (head airways, trachea, bronchi, lungs, diaphragm, abdominal muscles)

1. **Volition** *(Motivator > Mind-body connections)*. The brain and neurological system send commands to and receive messages from the body, resulting in muscular responses that control various aspects of the vocal process.

2. **Respiration** *(Actuator > Breath energy)*. The muscles and organs of breathing (trachea, lungs, bronchi, diaphragm, ribs, and abdominal and back muscles) act in coordination to control the inhalation and emission of air, the fuel for vocal tone.

3. **Phonation** *(Vibrator > Creation of fundamental tone)*. The larynx, or voice box, consists of folds, muscles, **ligaments**, and **cartilages** that coordinate airflow, resulting in vibrating **vocal folds** and a fundamental "buzz-tone."

4. **Resonation** *(Resonator > Enhancement of tone)*. The combined resonance cavities, principally the throat, mouth, and nose, act as acoustical secondary vibrators for enhancing the fundamental buzz-tone. On a larger scale, the experience of singing in a shower (secondary vibrator) illustrates the effectiveness of a resonant chamber for voice enhancement.

5. **Articulation** *(Articulator > Shaping of tone into recognizable speech sounds)*. The organs of speech (tongue, jaw, cheeks, teeth, lips, **hard** and **soft palates**, and dental ridges) coordinate in producing all of the sounds normally associated with human verbal communication. The only natural instrument equipped with an articulator, the human voice has the capacity to produce a seemingly infinite variety of sounds.

Individuals will vary in their degree of technical control over elements of the vocal process. A malfunction in any one of the parts will affect overall coordination and, hence, the final vocal product. For example, a singer might exhibit efficient breath functioning but inefficient phonation, resulting in an inadequately resonated tone. Another vocalist might be phonating well, but due to inadequate airflow the voice will again be deficient in resonance. The ultimate objective in both speaking and singing is a balanced coordination of the four physiological elements of the vocal process: respiration, phonation, resonation, and articulation.

From Speech to Singing

Although speech and singing are functionally analogous, dynamic singing requires more energy and a more exaggerated manner. Singing simple folk and popular songs can be compared to ordinary conversation, but full-voiced singing used in **opera** and **oratorio** is analogous to dramatic acting and speaking (sermons and public speeches). **Recitative** and *Sprechstimme* (types of speaking set to musical pitches) are hybrid forms of speech and singing. Since speech and singing are so closely related, we begin with a consideration of speech before launching into singing.

Our initial step is to find the voice's natural, comfortable, and efficient speaking-pitch range, a task that can be hampered by a person's acquired speech habits. For instance, many people talk at lower pitch levels, possibly because of social and cultural conditioning. In some cultures, for instance, young men may believe that lower-pitch-level speaking is "manly," while women may think of a lowered voice as more "sensuous."

For those who have sung in choirs or studied voice, it is possible that well-meaning choral directors or voice teachers have unknowingly assigned voice classifications incompatible with your natural vocal abilities. Having your voice type incorrectly or prematurely classified can create an incongruity between your *acquired* and *natural* vocal images that could become increasingly difficult to reconcile in future years. For this reason an exploration of your natural tessitura is an important first step in the process of learning to sing.

Exercises for Exploring Speaking Range

The following techniques can help you explore and discover your natural speaking range, particularly if you can arrange to tape-record them for critical listening.

Exercise 2-1

Check your natural uninhibited sound pitch levels by crying, laughing, coughing, yawning, and speaking "um-hum," or whatever expression you use instead of "yes" when responding to a close friend's question. These involuntary, uninhibited, unsophisticated sounds are clues for determining your natural vocal range.

Exercise 2

With a friend or teacher at the piano, explore the comfortable extremes of your vocal range, beginning with the lowest pitches where the voice begins to "fry" or "crackle" and moving to the highest pitches (in the lighter-head mechanism). (**Vocal fry** is caused by insufficient breath flow and extremely relaxed folds on the lowest audible pitches). A range of approximately two octaves is typical for most people.

Exercise 2-3

Using normal speaking voice, locate your present speaking level by talking in normal quality while checking pitch levels on a pitch-producing instrument (piano, guitar, pitch pipe). Use such phrases as "My name is (*fill in*)," "I like to sing," or "How are you?"

Exercise 2-4

Experiment with a higher speaking level by reading one stanza of a song using your current speaking level. Then gradually move to higher pitches with several successive readings, noting where your most comfortable, least stressful range lies.

Speech levels will vary according to individual differences in **vocal range** (low to high pitches), **timbre** (color), and **volume** (loudness). Given the octave difference between male and female voices, as a rule most people should speak about a fourth to a fifth (pitch intervals) above their lowest singable tone, which allows spoken cadences to occur without hitting "gravel" or "frying."

Exercises for Improving Speech

The singing voice can be enhanced with the following speech improvement techniques.

Exercise 2-5

Repeat some short phrases (such as in Ex. 2-3) in a higher than normal voice. Note that it takes more breath energy (airflow or breath support) to speak in a higher range.

Exercise 2-6

Use extreme speech variation (inflection, emphasis, stress) by shifting pitches from high to low in an animated, exaggerated manner. An easy way to exaggerate speech is to mimic persons who appear "out of their minds," that is, insane, crazed, drugged, or drunk.

Exercise 2-7

Create an enthusiastic, "heady" sound with an awareness of sensations in the *mask* (the area around the eyes and bridge of the nose). The tonal sensation must be very light and in the head. Men get this feeling when singing head voice (less so in falsetto), while women can easily experience the same sensation when using their lighter, high-voice mechanism.

Exercise 2-8

Allow this light feeling to grow dynamically by increasing airflow, especially in higher ranges of speaking. The feeling of exaggerated excitement will help in achieving extra airflow, as when exclaiming: "**W**ow, **w**hat a **w**onderful day!"

Exercise 2-9

Read selected texts aloud in an exaggerated, oratorical manner similar to that employed by Shakespearean actors. Eventually this technique can be expanded to a form of *Sprechstimme* (*atonal* or declamatory vocal style) and also can be applied when singing the more tonal, speechlike singing form known as *recitative*.

From Speech to Singing Exercises

Synthesize all the above five exercises through the following "Speech to Singing Exercises." For example, repeat a short phrase, "Oh, what a beautiful morning," at four levels of increasingly higher dynamics, progressing from normal speech to full-fledged singing. Use the following progression of voice levels.

Exercise 2-10   CONVERSATIONAL

This is normal speech of a casual nature, similar to what you would use in a quiet, small room with low background noise.

Exercise 2-11   ELEVATED

This level is used with a small to moderate-sized audience, as in an average classroom with some background noise. This level of speech will probably suffice when speaking in voice class, such as when making introductions and comments prior to performing, and reciting song texts.

Exercise 2-12 DECLAMATORY

This is an oratorical manner of delivery you might use in a large room or an out-door space with large audiences present, the same as used with Shakespearean dia-logue or evangelistic preaching.

Exercise 2-13 RECITATIVE/*SPRECHSTIMME*

This is an exaggerated, operatic-like speech form or singing style based on either tonal (recitative) or atonal (*Sprechstimme*) pitch organization.

Getting Started with Physical/Vocal Exercises

Now you are ready to work on fundamental vocal technique. The following exercises are distilled and condensed from more detailed directions included in later chapters and are designed to get you started quickly and safely on your way to singing. We begin with general stretching exercises accompanied by vocalized tone, using a "lip-buzz/hum." The "lip-buzz/hum" is produced with vibrating lips when air is blown through them, similar to the imitation of a pow-erful motorcycle engine revving up or the vigorous sound you make when exclaiming "b-m-m-m-m, it's cold outside."

Exercise 2-14 UPWARD STRETCH AND FULL CIRCLE DRAW

Reach upward, first with one hand, then the other, stretching up on tiptoes. While stretching your arms upward and drawing broad circles in the air, simultaneously emit random, rising and falling pitches using a lip-buzz/hum ("bm-m-m-m") or a hum, with a chewing action to loosen the jaw and tongue. Next, with hands remaining together in up-stretched position and feet spaced approximately 2 feet apart, slowly draw a large circle from left to right in vertical relationship to the floor. Starting at the top position and, on a high pitch, sing with a lip-buzz/hum from high-to-low-to-high (or low-to-high) as you draw a full circle. Now repeat the exercise in reverse, drawing a right-to-left circle. In drawing the full circle you will bend over at the waist as your hands almost touch the floor.

Exercise 2-15 RAG DOLL STRETCH

This is a useful technique for achieving a state of relaxation and stretch of the body.

1. Begin by lifting and stretching your hands overhead while taking a deep full breath.

2. Next, let your arms swing gently forward and downward, leading your head and upper body into a bent-over position, with your arms and head dangling loosely and knees bent. While falling let the air escape quickly with a voice-less lip-buzz.

3. While bent over and dangling loosely, hum a few "m-m-m-m's" as though expressing great delight over a yummy meal. Notice the head vibrations result-ing from the hum in the upside-down positioning of your head.

4. Gradually and slowly start to straighten up, beginning with the knees (but not locking), then the buttocks, up the spinal column to the shoulders, neck, and head, finally lifting the arms upward as though you're reaching for the sky. When you reach a full-stretched position, observe the position of your chest, which should be fully expanded with a high breastbone (**sternum**).

5. Next, drop your arms while keeping your elevated chest position. The feeling you should aim for is an upward buoyant stretch, as though you're being gently pulled by a rope or wire attached at the crown of your head. A loose, dangling feeling of hanging from the crown of your head would also be effective imagery. At the same time your feet should be firmly planted on the ground approximately 8 to 12 inches apart, and your knees should remain flexibly unlocked.

If all has gone well up to this point, you should have a correctly aligned body for singing. Congratulations—you're looking like a singer!

Exercises for Coordinating Breath, Phonation, and Resonation

At this early point we want to establish initial awareness of (1) a solid breath connection (respiration), (2) a clean vibration of the vocal folds (phonation), and (3) head sensations (resonance). Once these three elements are in place, we will be ready to build a voice based on healthy, efficient vocal technique. Though the coordination of these three elements is the goal, we need to look at each separately.

Exercise 2-16   BREATHING CHECK

1. Begin by standing in the tall stretched position achieved at the end of the "Rag Doll Stretch" Exercise (Ex. 2-15), with a lifted chest and expanded rib cage. Place your right hand open on your lower abdominal area (gut) with the thumb tip located on your navel. Experts who work with relaxation techniques speak of "centering" oneself by concentrating on a point approximately 2 inches below the navel. This is approximately where the focus of your breath expansion and energy should be felt when singing or expelling air.

2. Now place your left hand flat on your upper abdominal area (stomach area or **epigastrium**) with the tip of your little finger touching your navel and right thumb tip. In this position you will be able to experience the effects of deep breathing.

3. Blow out as much air as possible, emptying the lungs. Hold this position for a few seconds before taking a full, deep breath. Allow the rushing intake of air to fill your torso completely in a downward and outward manner. If you are doing this exercise correctly, you will observe your hands moving outward as a result of the air moving in. It is important that you relax the lower abdominal wall rather than hold it in.

4. You can now experiment with breathing. With relaxed jaw, closed teeth, and slightly parted lips, slowly suck the air in (4–5 counts), suspending it (1–2 counts), and hissing it out slowly (10-plus counts) until most of the air is depleted. Then allow the breath to be sucked in, causing the lungs to be filled with air.
   Observe that when exhaling or blowing out, the action of the abdominal muscles is inward and upward, the opposite of when inhaling. If everything is working correctly, you should be ready to explore the connection of vocal tone and breath.

A *focused tone* is largely the result of vocal-fold vibration and is produced by the vocal folds coming together (**adduction**) their full length when air passes through them. (The opposite of adduction is **abduction,** the term used for open vocal folds, as when breathing.) Any opening in the folds will result in air escaping, and the resulting tone will sound "breathy." Conversely, too much pressure on the folds will result in a "pressed" or "tight" phonation. Therefore, the trick is to allow the vocal folds to vibrate naturally in response to airflow.

The lip-buzz/hum technique discussed earlier illustrates the phonation principle very well, for when one blows air while humming, the results are similar to the action of airflow through vibrating vocal folds. This exercise is best accomplished with a full flow of breath and loose articulating organs. Use a very contented, exaggerated sigh from a medium-high to medium-low pitch range, such as an interval of a fifth or an octave.

Exercise 2-17   SIGH GLIDE

Another technique similar to the lip-buzz/hum is a "sigh-glide." Use plenty of airflow to vocalize a descending pattern such as an interval of a fifth or an octave. This technique is initiated with an "h" as the following exercises (Exs. 2-17a,b) demonstrate:

Exercise 2-17a

B-m-m-m
Hah ___
Whee _
Whoo _

Exercise 2-17b

B-m-m-m
Hah ___
Whee _
Whoo _

Exercise 2-18   MOANING AND WHINING

An effective technique for achieving a clean vocal-fold vibration is to effect a relaxed body state and emit a healthy, moderately loud "moan" or even a slight "whine." If you avoid pressing or tightening the tone and use adequate airflow, you should experience a more clearly focused vocal tone.

The term *tone placement* is often used referring to physical sensations experienced by singers when the tone seems to be produced freely and easily. The most important aspect of tone placement is that it must be concentrated primarily on *head sensations*, not in the mouth or throat. This is not to say that one does not use the mouth and throat when singing, for they are of great importance in allowing a fully resonated tone. However, one must not try to *make* things happen in the mouth and throat, for the tendency will be to create unnecessary tensions that will interfere with freeing the voice.

Head or nasal resonance, sensations of vibrations in the mask, is best achieved by using a combination of consonants. Because humming uses the nasal consonant "m," it is a technique frequently used by teachers. In addition to the hum, you can use "ng" as it occurs in such words as *sing* and *song* and *hung*. Although both sounds are useful for helping induce nasal resonance, the "ng" is usually preferable. Of course you must learn how to vocalize these consonants correctly, for it is easy to misuse them. That's why it's essential to have a qualified listener (teacher) give proper feedback.

While striving to "place" the tone, you should never attempt to drive, force, or "stick" the tone in the head: Just *allow* it to be there. Furthermore, it is essential that you learn to let go totally of control mechanisms (tongue, jaw, throat muscles) when using these exercises. In other words, effect the attitude of someone who is surprised, spellbound, or dumbfounded. Furthermore, avoid monitoring or adjusting the tone according to your hearing. Rather, trust the process and *allow* it to happen.

Exercise 2-19   DEVELOPING NASAL RESONANCE

Before vocalizing, check that the blade of your tongue is touching only the hard palate of your mouth, not the soft palate, and that it is arched in a position for an "ee" vowel. Now begin by saying "um-hum," with your tongue in the position of "ng" rather than "m." Next, intone the "ng" slowly on a descending sliding interval of a third, fourth, fifth, and an octave (Ex. 2-19a). Now, try the "ng" on specific pitches such as 5-4-3-2-1 (Ex. 2-19b). Finally, sing it on a 1-5-4-3-2-1 (Ex. 2-19c) pattern, taking care to connect the 1 to 5 interval with a slight sliding pitch, or **portamento**, upward.

Exercise 2-19a

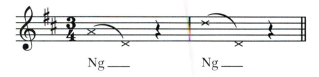

Exercise 2-19b

Exercise 2-19c

Once you have achieved a well-focused tone both in head resonance and at the vocal folds, you will automatically have a good breath connection as well.

That's why many teachers prefer to concentrate initial efforts on phonation and resonation before spending much time on "breath hook-up." The main thing to remember is that the voice is carried on a *flowing air stream* (without breathiness), and you must always be aware of using sufficient airflow as the foundational support for the voice.

Getting Started with Learning and Performing a Song

Since students will probably begin learning and performing songs in the first few sessions, the following brief introduction to learning and performing a song is provided. Detailed information can be found in Chapter 11.

Song Study

The first step in learning a song is to find one suitable to your present talent and experience. The Song Anthology, found in this book, provides a wide range of possibilities from which you and your teacher can make an appropriate selection. It helps the learning process if you are enthusiastic about the song selected, so try to find one that will challenge and inspire you when working on it.

Since hearing others perform a particular song is a good way to become more familiar with it, try to listen to a recording of the song performed by a reputable vocal artist. Another listening exercise is to hear your class members sing through it in unison as a song-study project. Learning a song is greatly facilitated when more than one person is studying and performing the same song in class. Increased exposure and instructive comments by the teacher and classmates serve to enhance and hasten learning.

If you have limited keyboard skills, you can use the supplemental audiotape or CD to help familiarize you with the song. Better yet, if you have a tape recorder, you can use it to record the song as it performed (solo or group) in class.

The most efficient approach to song learning is to separate the song into components, each of which can be mastered independently before integrating them into a final memorized product. This means (1) studying and reading aloud the text for meaning and clear pronunciation of all words, (2) learning the melody and rhythm accurately, (3) using appropriate dynamics (soft, loud, accents), (4) making decisions on phrasing and breathing points, and (5) interpreting and communicating the song's meaning or intent.

Song Performance

In vocal performance the singer assumes an acting role, with the responsibility to present a song's musical and dramatic content as intended by both the composer and the textual source (poet, author). This means that your presentation should mask, to some extent, your own personality as you become the person interpreting the song's special meaning.

With your body language you are expected to command attention to your presence when entering (you should normally enter stage right, with your accompanist following slightly behind), walking to the "crook" of the piano while maintaining a very tall but comfortable body alignment. When you reach the crook of the piano, you should recognize the audience and their applause with a sincere "thank-you" bow. Calmly, slowly, and firmly make all introductions—

your name, the title of your song, the composer (and textual source), and your accompanist. Although you will have many technical things to think about such as breathing, tone quality. words, pitches, rhythm, and dynamics, your primary artistic responsibility will be to concentrate on delivering the song's meaning.

After the mood is established, subtle signals such as posture, breath, and focus will let your accompanist know you are ready to begin. Throughout the song your entire body should appear relaxed, particularly fingers, hands, and arms, although your concentration should remain constant, especially during piano interludes. Be absolutely focused on your performance until the *final note* of the song. Depending on the nature and mood of the song, pace your "return to reality" by keeping your concentration for a few seconds following the song. When the applause begins, graciously take a solo bow—hands loosely by your side, and bending slightly at the waist with the top of your head pointed toward the audience—followed by a duo bow with your accompanist. Exit stage right followed by the accompanist.

Plan to spend time practicing in front of a full-length mirror for self-observation. While practicing, ask yourself: "Do I have any peculiar mannerisms: eye blinking, brow furrowing, finger twitching, hand and arm conducting, body swaying, or chest heaving?" In addition to mirror study, using a video camera to catch your foibles can be very instructive. Because of frustration caused by seeing yourself in a new and potentially unfavorable light, you may be reticent to observe yourself in a mirror or on a video screen. Fortunately, experience teaches us that the more we use these viewing learning tools, the more comfortable we will become in using them for self-evaluation.

Expanding the Mind

Learning to sing, like any worthwhile endeavor, occurs first in our *imagination*—a mental faculty that previews or images future experience and guides us as we bring it into being. But imagination cannot work alone. Because emotion and thought precede action, our *attitudes* also determine *what* we decide to see and *how* we interpret what we see as we undertake any activity. For example, a half-filled glass will be seen negatively by some people as being half empty, while others will consider it half full, a positive interpretation.

Furthermore, imagination and attitudes are filed away in our *memory*, which provides us with the ability to recollect past experiences—scenes, words, feelings, tastes, and smells. Thus, imagination, attitudes, and memory are important ingredients in "possibility thinking," the ability to create a mental idea of a positive future outcome. For example, in order to become successful singers, we must first believe in the possibility and then commit to a vision which will inevitably become more clear as experience and expertise is gained. Since a vocal journey begins inwardly with the identification of our inner resources, we begin by exploring aspects of imagination, attitudes, and memory.

The Roots of Your Vocal Self-Image

Part of what we bring to voice study is our vast storehouse of memories and conditioned responses called *habits*. As noted already, the habits we bring to speech and singing are largely influenced by other people, greatly influencing our ability to imagine (image) new outcomes. If we were to pinpoint the major influences on our vocal personality, we would list parents, relatives, friends, colleagues, media figures (including singers and entertainers), teachers, and other significant personalities. In most cases our voices reflect our origins—cultural, social, and familial.

As you begin to explore your vocal roots, you'll probably find a striking resemblance between your own vocal mannerisms and those of your parents or siblings. By listening attentively to them, you will probably hear echoes of yourself. Moreover, by listening to or recalling the voices of childhood and teenage friends, you may hear speech patterns and vocal characteristics which you have assimilated. Males, in particular, mimic voice mannerisms of their peers, especially during adolescence when the voice pitch changes from high to low and they experience their new rumbling masculine voices. Young female voices change more slowly, almost imperceptibly. But as their chest voices gradually develop, they too enjoy exploring their emerging vocal powers. Often the vocal habits of a lifetime stem from this period of intense youthful experimentation and exploration.

For better or worse, it is during the impressionable years of adolescence that we are likely to develop a taste for a particular vocal style, usually of a popular genre. Pop singers, while exemplary in some ways, may be less than ideal models of healthy, efficient voice use. Generally speaking, professional pop singers and particularly "hard-rockers" lack adequate vocal resources and training yet remain very influential as singer role models. Occasionally we must take deliberate steps to unlearn their strong influences on our vocal personality.

As a way of appreciating the impact of voice apart from visual effects, let us look at some realistic situations in which a person's voice is a major factor in determining our opinion of him or her. For example, how often have you had telephone conversations with people you have never seen before and formed impressions of them based solely on their speaking voices? When listening to people on a radio call-in show, do you visualize callers according to their voices? Usually, we tend to match particular voice qualities (high, low, soft, loud, smooth, rough) with faces and personalities we think suit the people to whom we are listening or speaking. Frequently, when we eventually make first-time visual contact, we are surprised that the mental image we've fashioned bears little resemblance to their actual physical appearance.

Indeed, it's not only *what* we say, but also *how* we say it that determines the perception others have of us. To continue exploring your vocal image, ask yourself these questions: (1) "What do I think of my voice?" (2) "What do I think others think about my voice?" (3) "Are my impressions compatible with others' views?" (4) "Am I aware of voice changes associated with the state of my general health or mental attitude?" After giving careful thought to answering these questions, it should be apparent that you are recognized and judged by your speaking voice—its tone quality, dynamics, expressiveness, and general state of health. Dr. Morton Cooper, well known in the Los Angeles area as "voice doctor to the stars," writes in his popular book *Change Your Voice, Change Your Life:*

> Though your voice image is probably a new concept to you, it is one of the most vital, pervasive, meaningful, and controlling factors in your life. It pertains to sound and persona. It designates the way your perceive your own sound and the way you perceive others' sounds, as well as the interpretive judgments you apply to those sounds. (Cooper, 1984, p. 5)

We are entering an area of discussion that will involve delving into areas of psychology and, more specifically, into the role of the mind and its constantly interacting relationship with the body. Although we will not pursue this subject in depth, we will take a cursory look at some topics related to the mind/body connection.

Personal Vocal Perceptions

Voice study can be approached on several levels. One level is *visual* (seeing), or imaging a mental picture to project an idea, thought, or emotion. A second level is *aural* (hearing), which affords immediate feedback on the tone produced. For singers, hearing is perhaps the most readily accessible monitoring device, but unfortunately it is not the most dependable. A third level is *kinesthetic* (feeling), or developing awareness of physical sensations associated with body movement, tension and relaxation of muscles, and even vibrations of acoustical energy generated by vocal responses. Giovanni Battista Lamperti, a famous nineteenth-century vocal teacher, emphasized the importance of feelings over listening when he said: "Do not listen to yourself sing! Feel yourself sing! When internal conditions are right and ready, the singing voice appears, not before!" (Brown, 1973, p. 16). A fourth level of investigation is *analytical* (thinking), or learning intellectually how the voice functions physiologically and acoustically.

Because of the way the human body is constructed, it is physically impossible for us to hear our voices as others do. Upon hearing our recorded voice for the first time, we often react to the vocal sound in disbelief and disorientation. "That can't be me, I don't sound like that!" is a typical response. Developing an ear for our true vocal sound and hearing ourselves as others do require the assistance of a good-quality tape recorder. Without such an impartial listening source, we hear our voices primarily through internal head-bone conduction and reflected external sound waves, which presents a distorted impression at best.

Paradoxically, the individual's perception of his or her sound is often perceived almost in an opposite manner from the way it is externally perceived by others. Since this factor of *inverted imagery* has application in all areas of singing, it must be kept in mind if the singer is to make steady progress. For this reason, the voice student must have confidence in the instructor's assessment and faithfully execute the instructor's recommendations.

The relevance of the inverted image, or *theory of opposites*, can be further explained by viewing an illustration of the "pendulum analogy" (Fig. 3-1). The pendulum at rest (*center*) illustrates a coordinated vocal process while the polarities or opposites of movement represent the singer's shifting vocal quality in varying degrees to right and left of center. For example, a singer who is tight-voiced (*extreme right*) might be well-advised to work toward the other extreme, namely vocal relaxation or breathiness (*extreme left*), in order to counteract tightness caused by excessive muscle tension. It is possible such a singer may believe his or her voice is full and resonant, when in fact it is tight and tense. By thinking and working for a more breathy quality, the singer will probably make a vocal compromise, with the tone becoming more balanced in the middle of the two extremes.

Opposites: Coping with Contradiction

One perplexing issue confronting students is coping with what appear to be contradictory concepts or instructions. For example, in the process of learning to sing, the student needs to reconcile contrasting vocal characteristics, such as brilliance and warmth, lightness and heaviness, intensity and relaxation, words

Figure 3-1
The Pendulum Analogy

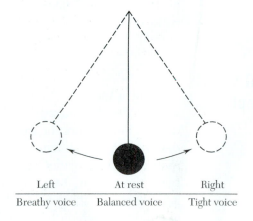

Left	At rest	Right
Breathy voice	Balanced voice	Tight voice

and tone, vowels and consonants, releasing and focusing. To be instructed to do something that conflicts with previous instruction can be confusing: for example, when first encouraged to "relax and let go," but later told to "energize and intensify."

A philosophical explanation for this paradoxical situation is that opposites represent the extremes of reality which must be integrated and balanced in everything we do. Extremes or opposites of thought and action are manifested in a multitude of ways: between **classicism** (rationalism) and **romanticism** (emotionalism) within the western European tradition; between "yang" (active, positive) and "yin" (passive, negative) in Chinese philosophy; or between science and art, form and content, idealism and realism, product (ends) and process (means). Rather than being distraught when coping with opposites, we must simply accept the fact they exist and then strive to reconcile and integrate them throughout the learning process. As English jurist, philosopher, and reformer Jeremy Bentham (1748–1832) said, "The mark of a first-rate mind is that it can maintain two contradictory ideas at one time."

The Two-Part Brain and Two Intelligences

Perhaps we are capable of reconciling opposites because the human brain is naturally equipped to handle such a complex task. Since the early 1960s brain research has shown that two distinct regions of the cerebral cortex function independently by processing information differently. Theoretically speaking, the two hemispheres in the brain help us understand how we are able to learn and perform complex physical and mental skills, including singing (Campbell, 1986).

The two lobes of the human brain are normally referred to as the left and right hemispheres. The *left hemisphere* processes information by sorting and ordering individual components and is dominant in analytical/rational functions, such as speaking, reading, timing and rhythm, logical thinking, conscious mind processes, and controlling the right side of the body. The *right hemisphere* perceives stimuli holistically, contextually, and intuitively and is dominant in controlling visual-spatial relationships, pitch discrimination, imagination, creativity, expressiveness, and the left side of the body (Edwards, 1979). Although the brain is composed of two equally important hemispheres, most tasks require cooperative alliance. This is especially the case with dynamic singing, which requires coordinated use of complicated intellectual, verbal, muscular, and vocal skills.

Strongly related to the right/left brain connection are two types of intelligence, both of which are important in learning and executing tasks. The familiar type of intelligence is associated with "smartness" and is typically measured by traditional IQ (intelligence quotient) tests. Goleman (1995) has labeled the other *emotional intelligence,* which is measured by such personal qualities as self-awareness, self-motivation, persistence, empathy, social deftness, altruism, and compassion. Such emotional qualities play a predominant role in determining how people of moderate IQ are capable of achieving outstanding accomplishments, all the while coping effectively with life's normal ups and downs.

The Two Aspects of Self

Another illustration of opposites can be found in comparing our external lives with our internal lives. Our external life involves what we do in the world, the way we present ourselves to others, and how we interact with our environment. Our internal life involves the mental and emotional self, the way we feel and think about everything we experience. One way to view these two realms is as "game boards" on which we play continuously.

In external games we work to overcome obstacles that interfere with external goals, for example, doing whatever is necessary to perform well and gain success. In internal games we struggle with inner obstacles that block our goals, for example, gaining self-confidence by overcoming self-doubt and fear. By eliminating or minimizing internal obstacles, we can more easily achieve external goals, effectively reconciling and integrating these two opposites.

In the realm of vocal performance, the external game is to overcome all external obstacles associated with the performance of a prepared vocal work. The internal game is to overcome the mental and emotional obstacles we might encounter through the learning and performing process, including the anxiety known as *stage fright*. As with most activities requiring complex skills, the main way to reduce anxiety is to reconcile and balance it by focusing our mind on the external goal or task at hand (an expressive rendition of the song's message for the benefit of listeners) rather than self-conscious concerns ("What are people thinking?" or "How do I look?" or "Am I singing well?"). In this as in other situations, our thoughts govern our actions.

Extending the analogy further, the game of opposites can be described as a contest between two aspects of self, one the external/nurtured self and the other the internal/natural self. The former represents all that we have become through the influences of civilization. And the latter represents the innate, instinctive, spontaneous, childlike self.

Personality integration requires connecting our internal and external selves, the states of *being* and *doing*. In the ideal world, people nurtured from birth to adulthood within the context of a creatively stimulating learning environment develop the requisite knowledge and skills to play both external and internal "life-games" effectively. In the real world personal growth without negative influences is rare indeed, perhaps even impossible.

For additional information, see *The Inner Game of Music* (1986) by Barry Green with Timothy Gallweh, and *A Soprano on Her Head* (1982) by Eloise Ristad, both highly recommended for delving into these topics.

Learning Modes   Of course *how* we learn is just as important as *what* we learn. Research within the past two decades has increased our understanding of individual differences in how people select, comprehend, absorb, and use the raw data of experience. This subject is fully addressed in numerous publications, including Wesley Balk's *Performing Power* (1986) and Dawna Markova's *The Art of the Possible* (1991). Only a brief summary of the major learning/expressive modes—visual, auditory, kinesthetic, and analytical—is presented here.

1. **Visual Mode.** The visual learner receives input through the eyes and the inner window of the mind's eye. Experiences are processed through sight and visual images, such as visual details, colors, visions, maps, lines, lists, views, perspectives, drawings, doodlings, writings, graphic images, diagrams, charts, movies, television, photographs, and wardrobe. Visual output involves transferring ideas to visible form, as in writings, paintings, or film.

2. **Auditory Mode.** The auditory learner receives input through the ears, and experience is processed through sounds and words, by means of conversations, innuendo, vocal tones and inflections, music, spoken meanings, poems, stories, debates, speeches, noise, radios, tape recorders, and lectures. Auditory output involves using sounds and words to express consciousness. As might be expected, most singers tend to be more developed in this mode than in the others.

3. **Kinesthetic Mode.** The kinesthetic learner receives input through hands, skin, and muscles. Experiences are collected in smell, movements, actions, touch, feelings, textures, awareness of physical space, temperature, pressure, use of energy, and internal images of feeling and movement. Kinesthetic output involves activity using the hands and body—running, walking, dancing, playing, working, and so forth.

4. **Analytical Mode.** In addition to the three principal learning/expressive modes, some psychologists refer to a fourth mode—analytical—which is associated with reason, logic, analysis, ideas, and abstract thought. People who are highly intellectual will use these rational thinking tools both in receiving input and for expressing output.

Whether three modes or four, it is relevant for singers to be aware of the role each mode plays in learning and expression. Can you identify your primary learning/expressive mode from the above descriptions? Although most people have a dominant mode, all people use all three modes with varying degrees of competency. Even though it is a rarity to be equally proficient in all three modes, such proficiency would be ideal for singers, who must be equally skilled in imagination (visual), voice (auditory), and acting (kinesthetic) ability in order to become consummate vocal artists.

The Goal and the Journey as One

As with any challenging long-term task, the road that leads to success for a singer will be more interesting and rewarding if the focus is on process (means) rather than product (end). Focus on process means that our energy is concentrated on the journey rather than merely the destination. There is very good reason for such an emphasis on the journey/process. In Eloise Ristad's words, "If we put our energies only into getting to our destination or reaching the goal, we block our sensibilities along the way" (Ristad, 1982, p. 80). In other words, if we are single-minded in our pursuit of a far-off goal, we may fail to enjoy the views and activities along the way.

One of the major impediments on the road to learning is impatience. Because of eagerness to reach the destination, beginning students are often tempted to look for shortcuts or quick results, without application of disciplined mental and physical effort. Experience suggests that when the student learns to enjoy the journey, that is, the process of learning with the detailed routine of practice, real progress begins. In place of an instant-voice mentality, the cultivation of a long-term perspective will help prepare the learner for slower but steadier development.

You should be forewarned that even the most patient, enjoy-the-process approach inevitably will include learning plateaus, which are periods when little or nothing appears to be happening. Fortunately, frustration can be avoided and long-lasting results achieved by using plateaus as learning time for consolidating and internalizing muscular and mental responses through purposeful repetitious practice. If you patiently wait and plug away, the next growth spurt will probably take you by surprise.

Being process-oriented also means being continuously aware of your feeling state in the present moment. Consciousness of body/mind status helps you to focus attention on what's happening in the present rather than the past or future. This intense state of concentration, often referred to as "flow," is easily acquired once you are deeply involved in an enjoyable activity that results in an optimal experience. Frequently, under such ideal conditions, your absorption in a challenging activity is so intense that nothing else seems to matter and time appears to stand still. When thinking of the activities you most enjoy, you surely will recall similar sensations associated with intensely experienced accomplishments. Wouldn't vocal study be more rewarding if you were to truly enjoy the many hours spent in preparation for performance?

By now it should be clear that learning to sing well, technically and artistically, takes considerable effort and time. Although learning cannot be rushed, one can certainly enhance the process by consciously working to make singing an enjoyable long-term pursuit. George Leonard, instructor in the martial art of aikido and author of a powerful little book entitled *Mastery: The Keys to Success and Long-Term Fulfillment*, addresses this topic with these words of wisdom: "We fail to realize that mastery is not about perfection. It's about a process, a journey. The master is the one who stays on the path day after day, year after year. The master is the one who is willing to try, and fail, and try again, for as long as he or she lives" (Leonard, 1992, p. 140).

To summarize some of the major points made thus far, effective learning requires willingness to make constructive personal changes. To make consistent, steady progress, the serious learner must give attention to the three "P's" of personal growth: PRACTICE, PERSISTENCE, and PATIENCE.

The Singer as Risk-Taker

Although conscientious singers must be willing to take calculated risks in their pursuit of excellence, they also must allow room for the possibility of failure or imperfection. The typical perfectionist struggles constantly in the pursuit of goals, primarily due to a subconscious fear of failure. Consequently, he or she sometimes ends up procrastinating or shirking responsibilities. In stark contrast to the fear of failure, there is also the fear of success. Although difficult to comprehend, some people unconsciously sabotage their own efforts, presumably because they are unable to handle the high expectations associated with success. Do either of these tendencies fit your personality profile?

The achievement of any worthwhile endeavor requires the investment of time and energy and a willingness to take some calculated risks. Participants in all kinds of competitive performance activities, including sports, dance, and music, are typically strong, individualistic people with a strong degree of risk tolerance. The risk-taking thrills sought by singers are usually connected with major challenges of learning and performing extremely difficult vocal repertoire, for example, full-length song recitals or major opera roles.

Process-oriented risk-takers are continuously aware of their feeling-states, a constant awareness of mind-body status that helps focus attention on the present rather than the past or future. Under ideal conditions this enjoyable state of intense concentration is often referred to as *flow*, when absorption in a challenging activity becomes so intense that time appears to stand still. Singers, for example, frequently report being so caught up in performances that "it was over before I knew it."

One of the most impressive books on this subject is *Flow: The Psychology of Optimal Experience* (1990) by Milhaly Csikszentmihalyi of the University of Chicago. The author describes individuals who have self-contained goals, are seldom anxious, never bored, intensely involved with what is happening in the present, and capable of turning potential threatening situations into enjoyable challenges. His rules for developing characteristics of a self-directed person (similar to those of the risk-taker) are:

1. **Goal Setting.** An inner decision, not dictated by external sources, is made to set realistic goals, and a system of action is planned for the purpose of accomplishing one's desires and objectives.

2. **Immersion in Activity.** Opportunities for expansion of the self are balanced by the level of skills one possesses in dealing with the activity.

3. **Attention and Concentration.** When one is totally focused, self-consciousness ceases, resulting in a sustained involvement in the activity.

4. **Enjoyment of Immediate Experience.** Although any activity can be a source of joy, determination and discipline are required to bring it about.

Voice/Movement Improvisation Exercises

What follows are voice/movement exercises which involve making a vocal sound in conjunction with a corresponding physical movement. For example, a voice/movement event occurs when a person exclaims, "Oh!" in a surprised manner, simultaneously clasping his or her cheeks with both hands.

The primary purpose behind these physical/vocal exercises is to explore uninhibited vocal expression, a product of the whole person in a perfectly synchronized mind/body coordination. As it encourages spontaneity of expression without judgment, the mind/body exercise also helps free individuals from their inner judges. In other words, there is no right nor wrong, only that which happens spontaneously in the act of connecting the voice with body movement. Enjoy making a fool of yourself in a spirit of fun and play while doing these exercises.

Exercise 3-1   MIRRORING

This exercise can be used in at least three situations: (1) as an individual working in front of a mirror; (2) as a couple with each person taking turns leading; or (3) in a group with a selected leader, such as the instructor. In all cases, the idea is for someone to take the initiative in producing a unique motion exercise which is mimicked by the other. All the while, everyone simultaneously sings a mutually agreed upon vocal phrase. In order to keep the exercise uncomplicated, the phrase might be limited to simple vocal scales and arpeggi. These phrases may be sung on a vowel such as "ah" or the lip-buzz/hum in progressively higher keys.

Exercise 3-1a

Exercise 3-1b

Exercise 3-2   PASSING AN OBJECT

This exercise is best done with the group, standing in a circle. Someone describes an imaginary object that is then passed from one person to another while using voice and movement until it has come full circle. For vocal reasons, describe objects that require a healthy use of the high-voice mechanism. For example, something described as "small, round, and lightweight" will elicit a higher voice than something described as "heavy and sticky." Each person is free to experiment vocally and physically, as long as the action reflects a genuine response to the imaginary object.

Exercise 3-3   TWO-PART

The group again forms a circle. Each person performs a two-part maneuver, one part while moving two or three steps into the middle of the circle, and the second part while returning to the original position. Each consists of a different voice/ movement exercise, such as a part one (inward) voice/movement and a part two (return), a contrasting voice/motion. After the individual finishes, everyone mimics the exercise in unison. Try not to plan ahead as to what you will do. The fun of the exercise is in experiencing the freedom of unconscious, spontaneous action. Go with the flow!

Exercise 3-4   PASSING ENERGY

Form a circle and act out passing "energy" (like a slow-moving electrical charge) throughout the group from one person to the next. The energy enters each person at the point of physical contact and then passes to the next person through contact with any part of the body (finger, elbow, knee, foot, toe, head, hip). The energy source can be slow, fast, or variable, but it must be profoundly felt and vocally expressed as it progresses through the body.

Exercise 3-5   GIBBERISH

Gibberish is a form of made-up speech that can mimic any language but usually sounds more like a form of eastern European languages (Russian, Polish) with lots of consonants. To add an extra improvisational dimension, it can be applied to any of the above exercises. Making up a story in gibberish requires a bit more skill, but it provides a big challenge for those willing to work at it. Begin by sketching out a scenario. For example, a young man and woman get into an escalating argument that becomes even more aggravated as innocent bystanders join in the fracas, with the outcome left to chance. Now, if you really want to complicate the exercise, sing it! Speaking and singing in nonsense gibberish can be great fun, especially if you're a daring and skillful performer.

Voice and Self-Assessment

The following personal assessment exercises are questions that you can answer either mentally or in writing. You can choose to answer them singularly or in a more general journal format.

Your Vocal Image.   Assuming that your singing is in a developing stage, what image do you have of your basic singing voice? Is it pleasing and satisfactory to you? Do you wish it were more like someone else's? If so, whose? What feedback have you received from others regarding your singing? Have you ever been discouraged from singing because of anyone's criticism? Do you have an idea of what you'd like your voice to sound like? What are some vocal qualities or characteristics you desire as long-term goals? In terms of the pendulum analogy, does your voice tend toward one of the extremes (breathy or tight) or more toward the balanced center?

Your Vocal Roots.   To explore your vocal roots, make an audiotape of yourself reading a text (poem, article, quotes) aloud using your normal speaking voice. Repeat the experiment with grandparents, parents, siblings, other relatives, and friends. In each case, describe the speaker's mannerisms as related to inflection, accent, pitch level, rate of speed, and phrasing. Make observations regarding both similarities and dissimilarities of your voice characteristics with those voices you have studied. What conclusions have you reached?

Your Ability to Cope with Change and Contradictions.   Can you think of some opposites other than those discussed in the text? If so, can you relate them to the process of learning how to sing? Do you consider yourself open-minded, or are you reticent to accept new information? Are you really willing to make changes in your vocal technique, or do you feel set in your ways? Can you make some differentiation between both your external and internal games and your external and internal self using concrete examples? Are you aware of the external forces or influences that helped shape your personality and who is ultimately in charge of your life?

Your Mental Attitude and Singing Personality.   Which of the learning modes (kinesthetic, visual, auditory) do you perceive as your dominant mode? Which mode or modes need developing? Do you truly enjoy most of the activities you undertake or do you tend to be bored? Which activities do you most enjoy, and why? Do you think of yourself more as one who works only toward reaching a goal, or as one who also enjoys the process leading to the goal? Do you really like to sing because it's fun or because you think you should due to external pressure—parents, friends, teacher? Are you a person who plays it safe, or are you willing to take calculated risks in order to have a meaningful personal growth experience? Are you willing to share your inner thoughts and emotions ("bare your soul") with others as a communicative vocal artist?

C H A P T E R

Energizing the Body

The Vocal Athlete

The pursuit of high-level vocal performance requires a mind/body coordination level like that of accomplished Olympic athletes. Like athletic bodies, singers' bodies (their "vocal instruments") need comprehensive conditioning for strenuous performing requirements. This is why serious-minded singers often think of themselves as "vocal athletes" in training.

A figure skater executing a triple-axel leap has mind/body coordination comparable to a singer executing a "vocal leap" in a difficult aria. In both cases, performance expectations are extremely high, and great results require (1) setting specific goals and objectives—short, medium, and long range, (2) setting high standards of excellence for technique and artistry, (3) committing to regular self-disciplined effort and training, and (4) consistently producing a high level of physical energy for any given task.

Admittedly, your motivation to study singing may not correspond to that of an "Olympic-level singer," but your level of energy is one measure of how far you will be able to go on your vocal journey. What is energy and how do you get it? A composite definition is offered by Charles T. Kuntzleman in his book, *Maximum Personal Energy:*

> Energy is your zest for working, playing, loving—living. It is the biological power or force within you—your physical capacity for living and your mental attitude toward your capacity for living, In practical terms, you have "energy" if you can get through your working day with enough resources to meet unexpected demands, and still enjoy life. (Kuntzleman, 1981, p. ix)

Because energy is so crucial in athletic singing, we will discuss the energy building blocks of (1) fitness and exercise, (2) diet and nutrition, and (3) rest, relaxation, and recreation. Then, we will look at some strategies and exercises to build and maintain reservoirs of energy for dynamic singing.

Fitness and Exercise

Anyone trying out for a school-organized sport knows that getting in shape is expected. Since our bodies were designed by nature to be efficient, energy-producing mechanisms, we must engage in various kinds of physical activity regularly in order to develop peak performance ability.

The danger of a sedentary lifestyle is that prolonged physical inactivity leads to body weakness—inefficient lungs, a weaker heart, less pliable blood vessels, and loss of muscle tone. With the body's capacity for delivering oxygen lessened, an overall weakened condition leaves the body vulnerable to illness and disease. In turn, symptoms indicative of low energy levels and physical fatigue can only be alleviated by sleeping, resting, and avoiding negative, artificial stimulants such as caffeine.

According to medical experts, the best type of physical conditioning for overall fitness is aerobic exercise. *Aerobic,* which literally means "with oxygen," is any activity that maintains a pulse rate in excess of 100 beats per minute for 20 minutes or more. Since oxygen economy is the key to physical endurance, the main benefit of aerobic exercise is the creation of a strong system of support for oxygen transport throughout the body. Exercise is virtually the only way to ensure that every cell in the body is furnished life-producing oxygen and that impurities are flushed out.

The minimum weekly requirement for achieving optimum effect is 20 to 30 minutes of aerobic exercise at least three times per week, preferably on alternate days. The safest and most sensible form of outdoor aerobic exercise is brisk walking for more than 20 minutes. Other popular forms of aerobic exercise include jogging, swimming, bicycling, and cross-country skiing. Also, as part of a goal to adopt a physically active lifestyle, regular household tasks (lawn mowing, leaf raking, snow shoveling) can be incorporated into an overall exercise plan.

In addition to aerobic exercising, everyone can benefit from judicious application of muscle stretching, calisthenic, and weight-lifting exercises to build muscle flexibility, strength, and tone.

Before undertaking any vigorous exercise program, it is important to have a thorough physical exam by a physician, which includes blood pressure monitoring and an electrocardiogram (EKG). It is usually recommended to begin an exercising routine cautiously, perhaps with muscle stretching and short walks, gradually increasing activity as the body is ready. Here is a rule for exercise as well as singing: Always listen to your body and it will tell you what you are able to handle at any given time. The goal is to make physical conditioning a lifelong priority. Getting the most out of life—and your voice—begins with a serious commitment to maintaining a healthy mind and body.

Diet and Nutrition

The word *diet* in this discussion refers to a program of food consumption based on nutritious food and drink. Diet also means eating healthily to produce the energy needed for leading a vigorous lifestyle. Although weight control is often a fringe benefit, it is not the primary objective.

Fad diets, for example high-protein/low-carbohydrate diets that emphasize one or two specific food sources, are sometimes dangerous and should be avoided. In contrast, a well-balanced intake of all major food groups on a daily basis will satisfy normal nutritional needs. A healthy diet is based on a variety of the major groups: vegetables, fruits, grains, and meats. Although vegetables and fruits are nutritionally superior when fresh, canned foods are acceptable when packed in natural juices (or water) and free of excessive preservatives. As a general guideline for nutrition, seek out the natural state of any food source (e.g., fresh apples versus applesauce).

Rest, Relaxation, and Recreation

Everyone needs rest time to recharge the body's "energy batteries," particularly during stressful times when energy levels are low. A typical student's schedule is often irregular and intense. Due to heavy academic loads, part-time jobs, extracurricular activities, and socializing, hectic schedules often lead to accumulated stress, leaving little time to catch up if you get sick or behind in obligations. The result can be an occasional "crash" or "burnout," when the body says "I've had enough" and shuts down for a day or longer. What can you do under such circumstances?

First, set priorities based on what is truly important in your life. Then be sensible in applying yourself so that you can accomplish realistic goals. A "mission statement" can help you define fundamental principles which will in turn help you clarify goals and objectives. Stephen R. Covey, author of the book *The Seven Habits of Highly Effective People* (1990), provides guidelines in a workbook format.

The most significant rest period is the customary six to eight hours of daily sleep required by most people. Studies have shown that the more regular and peaceful the sleeping period, the more the body is revitalized. Because sleep requirements vary considerably among individuals, each person needs to learn how much sleep is required for optimum functioning. Whatever amount of sleep, it should be scheduled into a daily time-management program.

For most people, relaxation (quiet time) and recreation (play time or recreation) are prerequisites for a sense of wholeness. Any activity that diverts the mind from other stressful activities and sets the stage for regeneration is salutary. Rather than waiting for a "crash time," consider scheduling regular recreational or hobby pursuits.

As proof of the strong link between rest, nutrition, and exercise, it is scientifically documented that we actually require less sleep—and gain energy—when we increase physical exercise and consume nutritious food and drink. Pertinent information on the subjects of nutrition and the fitness can be found in a series of publications produced by the Pritikin Longevity Centers in Santa Monica, California, and Downington, Pennsylvania, including *The New Pritikin Program: The Premier Health and Fitness Program for the '90s* (1990) by Robert Pritikin. Another excellent source on nutrition is the "Life Choice Diet," by Dean Ornich, M.D. Much of the information discussed above is derived from these publications. [See Ornich (1993).]

Care of the Singer's Instrument: Voice and Hearing

Although the first line of defense for warding off vocal problems is to maintain overall good health, you can still become ill and develop voice problems. Most singers have been vocally incapacitated at one time or another due to fatigue, illness, and self-abuse or -misuse. Mild bouts of vocal fatigue are common among active voice users, especially when undergoing stresses that lead to a general run-down condition.

Susceptibility to vocal fatigue is a highly individual matter, closely related to your emotional, mental, and physical health. For this reason it is difficult to draw clear-cut guidelines applicable to all vocalists. For example, almost everyone has observed some "iron-voice" singers who are capable of sustained aggressive vocalism in spite of consistent mistreatment of their bodies and voices. On the other hand, some singers abide by all the rules of vocal health and yet are unable to ward off vocal problems. For whatever reasons (genetics, lifestyle, personality), some people tolerate stress better than others. Fortunately, by recognizing strengths and weaknesses and developing effective coping strategies, you can partially compensate for both natural and acquired limitations.

How does a singer know when there's a voice problem needing attention? In most cases, the problem comes about after a short-term upper respiratory illness, such as a cold or flu, or following excessive or abusive voice use. Some tell-tale vocal symptoms to listen for are (1) marked disturbance in high pitches and soft-toned singing, (2) intonation problems, particularly flat pitch in register transitions, (3) "breaks" or sudden jumps from the upper end of the middle register into the head register, and (4) less resonance and "ring" in the tonal quality. Affected singers might also experience (1) a lowering of pitch in the speaking voice, (2) difficulty with singing in the middle to upper vocal ranges, (3) a hoarse tonal quality marked by roughness and difficulty with phonation, and (4) a need to remove a perceived obstruction from the throat by constantly clearing and coughing.

Since the human body is composed primarily of water, maintaining a humid living environment (40–50 percent humidity) and drinking 7 to 9 glasses of water daily to replenish reserves is highly recommended. Dehydration leads to unhealthy vocal conditions (including increased, thickened mucous flow) and precipitates infections. When the indoor environment becomes very dry, you should carefully consider using a properly functioning steam humidifier or vaporizer, taking care to keep it free of mildew, mold, and bacteria.

You should also be aware that certain weaknesses in voice production might possibly indicate positive developments. Occasionally, when feeling vocally tired or experiencing a peculiar soreness, it may be that new muscles are being used for the first time. Since the larynx, like any other body part, can feel tired or sore before it "gets in shape," such reactions are to be expected when first experimenting with new vocal techniques. As you gain rest, increase vocal stamina, and improve skills, discomforts should disappear within a reasonable time-frame. However, should symptoms persist, it might be time to reevaluate your technical approach and try another method.

Since singers rely on their hearing for feedback and for fine-tuning the voice, being aware of aural health and knowing how to prevent excessive hearing loss are important. The Environmental Protection Agency estimates that more than 20 million people are exposed to injurious noise levels every day and 16 million suffer impaired hearing due to genetic damage, disease, or excessive loud noise. No age group is immune to "noise pollution," and there is growing evidence that young people today are experiencing greater hearing loss than previous generations.

In order to protect yourself against hearing loss, you should (1) reduce the number of hours per week of exposure to loud noises (90 decibels or more), including music; (2) wear ear protection devices whenever possible (plugs or muffs); (3) have a periodic hearing examination by an audiologist or otologist if hearing damage is suspected; and (4) consider using a hearing device if hearing loss is severe.

General guidelines for maintaining a healthy vocal instrument are summarized succinctly in the box entitled "The Do's and Don'ts of Vocal Health." These pointers should prove very helpful in safeguarding your voice, hearing, and overall health.

Physical/Vocal Exercises

One of the perplexing "opposites" issues confronting singers is that of tension and relaxation. Every physical function involving muscle use is dependent upon **muscular antagonism,** a balance of muscle tension and relaxation between **agonist** (prime mover muscle group) and **antagonist** (opposing muscle group). This may be confusing if we are accustomed to thinking of *relaxation* as a positive term and *tension* as a negative one. Muscular antagonism refers to the natural muscle opposition that occurs in physical activity, as when one set or group of muscles contracts while an opposing group relaxes. For our purposes, we will think of *relaxing* as a state of releasing negative, interfering muscular

The Do's and Don'ts of Vocal Health

Do

- Consume a variety of nutritious foods, beverages, and vitamins

- Attain and maintain physical fitness with regular aerobic and muscle-toning workouts

- Obtain sufficient rest, sleep, and recreation

- Maintain a humid living environment (40–50 percent humidity)

- Maintain body hydration by drinking 7 to 9 glasses of water daily

- Use efficient vocal technique in speech and singing

- Use the voice judiciously

- Wash hands frequently

Don't

- Inhale or ingest harmful substances such as caffeine, alcohol, recreational drugs, tobacco, and polluted air

- Pursue an overly stressful lifestyle

- Make physical contact with persons who have contagious diseases

- Work or live in noisy, polluted environments

- Speak too much or too loudly, especially in noisy environments

- Scream or clear the throat too much

- Use over-the-counter preparations for colds and allergies, especially antihistamines

activity and *tensing* as a state of excessive muscular activity. Our objective will be to find acceptable ways to release those excessive tensions that often block mental, physical, and emotional energies.

The warm-up techniques listed below are designed to assist you with a systematic approach for developing a balance between relaxation and tension. Whenever possible, a full-length mirror (or video camera/playback equipment) should be used to aid self-observation when doing these exercises.

General Exercises

General exercises include the two warm-ups listed in Chapter 2: Exercise 2-14, "Upward Stretch and Full Circle Draw," using the lip-buzz hum on sliding, random pitches; and Exercise 2-15, "Rag Doll Stretch." Begin with these exercises in preparation for the specific exercises that follow.

Specific Exercises

Exercise 4-1 TENSION/RELEASE

As though lifting a heavy weight, stretch arms and hands out in front of you; tighten and release. Spread arms straight out to both sides; tighten and release. Pull shoulders up to ears; tighten and release. Make a distorted, tense facial expression and release.

Exercise 4-2 SHOULDERS

Lift shoulders to ears, hold, and drop. Rotate forward, then backwards two full turns. Notice the expanded rib cage and the elevated chest position that result when shoulders rotate to a backward position.

Exercise 4-3 NECK AND HEAD

Stretch gently and slowly to left and right by looking over your shoulder, each time holding the position 4 to 5 counts. Then, while looking straight ahead, tip your head toward your left shoulder, then right shoulder, and then forward for 4 to 5 counts per position. Affect a "dumb-jaw" look by letting it drop open when you lean your head left and right.

Exercise 4-4 JAW

Begin with the dumb-jaw look, feeling absolutely no facial expression other than stupidity. (For most singing, notably in the speaking ranges, jaw drop should not be exaggerated. However, for high-note singing, there must be a considerable jaw drop.) Now, let your jaw drop from the joint where it connects with the skull. Feel the space at the joint when the jaw is "unhinged." Yawn contentedly with the jaw stretched comfortably. Chew slowly and with exaggeration. Check under the chin (from chin to larynx) for muscle tension. Move the jaw side to side (with the tongue following the jaw's motion). These exercises will help you discover tensions and create flexible, articulating organs. (*Note:* Grinding and clicking sensations in the jaw, especially if there is pain associated with it, should be checked by a physician.)

Exercise 4-5 TONGUE FLEXING

Stick the tongue out as far as possible, roll it around, then side to side, and finally up and down. While gently holding the chin in a relaxed, downward position with your index finger, sing the vocal exercises (Exs. 4-5a,b) 1-2-3-4-5-4-3-2-1 and 1-3-5-8-5-3-1 on the syllable "yah," with the tongue sticking out on the first, top, and last pitches.

Exercise 4-5a

Exercise 4-5b

Yah ____ yah ____ yah.
Lah ____ lah ____ lah.

Now sing "lah" on the same exercises, this time allowing the tongue to act as a valve cover for the mouth. In other words, extend the tongue up to initiate "l" and then down to lie relaxed in the mouth, lolling out on the upper lip. Roll an "r" as in "r-r-rah."

People who are tongue-tied may experience some minor difficulty with these exercises. Examine the connecting membrane underneath your tongue. If the membrane connecting the underside of the tongue to the bottom of the lower dental ridge comes more than halfway up to the full extended length of the tongue, you may have to adjust the way you articulate certain consonants, such as "l" and "d," especially in high-range singing.

Allow the tongue to lie as relaxed and flat as possible, with the rounded tip slightly touching the backside of the lower dental ridge and teeth. The tip of the tongue should never be pointed, pushed back, or curled up when sustaining vowel sounds. Any extraneous tension in the tongue will be felt and heard in the vocal tone, especially if the back of the tongue is tense. In general, the entire articulating mechanism should be flexible and agile for producing speedy, clear articulation.

Efficient Body Alignment

Correct alignment of the body is extremely important in setting up the right conditions for coordinating the vocal process. Since physical carriage reveals much of your personality through "body language," movement courses, such as modern dance, provide excellent training for the vocalist who desires to move with an attractive, graceful physical appearance. Valuable insight into proper body alignment may also be gained by investigating the Alexander Technique, a body awareness method utilizing principles of efficient body movement. A reprint of F. M. Alexander's book *The Use of the Self* (Centerline Press, 1984) is a prime source of information. Although we have worked on body alignment in earlier exercises, the following suggestions will further help you in developing a flexible, dynamic posture.

Exercise 4-6   ESTABLISHING EFFICIENT BODY ALIGNMENT

1. Start with the "rag-doll" exercise (Ex. 2-15) to create a spinal stretch from the bottom to the top of the body. Beginning at the feet, slowly straighten up from the bottom upward: first to the knees; second to the buttocks and waist; then vertebra by vertebra upwards to the top of the neck and head.

2. Back up against a wall, allowing as much body surface as possible to touch the wall. Relax all over. Place one hand behind you in the small of your back and the other hand behind your head for a cushioning effect.

3. Assume the stance of an athlete ready for action, vital and balanced with feet planted firmly on the floor. You should feel weighty, yet buoyant.

4. Place feet apart 6 to 8 inches with one slightly in front of the other for total balance. For most persons, the left foot will be placed slightly forward of the right foot.

5. Keep the knees flexible and unlocked.

6. Tuck the posterior slightly to avoid a swayback and to balance the pelvic area.

7. The abdominal area remains relaxed on inhalation and the lower abdominal area remains firm (but not tight) on exhalation.

8. The chest remains comfortably high but *not* pushed out and upward in the manner of a soldier at attention (see Fig. 4-1). Instead, the rib cage is slightly expanded outward.

9. The shoulders hang loosely and relaxed with arms dangling at the sides of the body.

10. The neck is held in erect position, but not rigidly.

11. The head is balanced on top of the spinal column so that it can roll easily in any direction. A good analogy of this flexible balance is a bowl turned upside-down and balanced on the tip of a pencil.

Vocal Athlete Assessment

Caring For Your Voice.   How do you feel about your genetic endowment? What physical limitations have you observed or have been pointed out to you by others that might have a bearing on your vocalism? Have you experienced any vocal disorder due to illness, or misuse and abuse? If so, how have you dealt with the problem? If you have an ongoing affliction [for example, allergies, asthma, temporomandibular joint (jaw hinge-joint) problems or hormonal imbalance], does it affect or incapacitate you as a singer? Do you recall any major changes in your voice due to physical growth and aging, such as the typical voice change that occurs during adolescence? If so, do you recall your thoughts and feelings about the change and how you used your voice? Is your daily professional activity

Figure 4-1
Incorrect and Correct Body Alignment

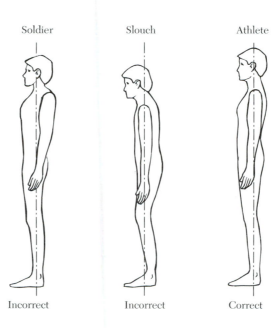

| Soldier | Slouch | Athlete |
| Incorrect | Incorrect | Correct |

"voice-intensive"? If so, do you take care to use your voice according to techniques discussed in this book? Are you frequently exposed to loud noise or sound? If so, do you take precautions to protect your hearing?

Caring For Your Body.   How would you classify your eating habits? Do you eat balanced meals (major food groups) regularly, primarily for nourishment and nutrition? Have you ever dieted to lose or gain weight? Is your present weight normal for your height, body type, age, and sex? How would you classify the physical activity quotient of your life? Are you sedentary, somewhat active, moderately active, or very active? As a vocal athlete, are you a spectator, a "bench warmer," a sandlot player, an amateur player, or a professional? What type of physical activity do you do on a regular basis? Does your exercise program include a variety of physical activities, including aerobics and muscle-stretching, toning and strengthening? Are you aware of your posture and the way you "carry yourself" throughout each day? How do you visualize your health in five, ten, twenty, and thirty years? Are you satisfied with the way you treat the vehicle in which you will journey the rest of your life?

CHAPTER

5 Developing Breath Management

The Role and Benefits of Breathing

Each day the typical adult completes more than 20,000 breath cycles, exchanging approximately 10,000 liters of air in the process. For healthy adults the normal involuntary at-rest inspiration-expiration cycle lasts about four to five seconds, with the inspiratory segment taking about one second, and the expiratory segment taking about three seconds.

Although breathing is, for most purposes, an automatic function, we are able to exercise some degree of voluntary control. Yoga practitioners are able to regulate their pulse rate, metabolism, and brain activity through direct control over their breathing. Athletes, particularly swimmers, weight lifters, and long-distance runners, rely on their aerobic training and breath control to accomplish feats requiring physical strength and stamina. Since vocal athletes are also highly dependent on their respiratory capacity, they must maximize their ability for taking in air and managing it effectively.

Some of the potential benefits of conscious self-regulated breathing include increased physical strength, heightened awareness, acute concentration, and total relaxation. One special benefit of the singer's practice of deep breathing is an increased output of *endorphins,* the same hormones released in aerobic exercise that produce a relaxation response.

An understanding of the respiratory mechanism and its functioning will help you develop and maximize your breathing in all facets of your life, including singing.

The Anatomy and Physiology of the Respiratory System

For study purposes, the anatomical structure of this highly efficient "breathing machine" can be organized into four principal components: (1) skeletal framework, (2) head airways and larynx, (3) sub-laryngeal system (trachea, bronchi, lungs, diaphragm, and rib cage), and (4) musculature.

Skeletal Framework

The underlying bone structure of the respiratory system consists primarily of the *torso* (body trunk), except the head airways. The *spine,* or backbone (Figs. 2-1 and 5-2), is the main pillar of the breathing mechanism and is composed of twenty-four *vertebrae,* graduated in size from the smallest in the neck to the largest in the small of the back. The twelve ribs (Fig. 5-2), or *costae,* are somewhat semicircular and the upper seven of them connect with the breastbone (sternum) in front, forming an imperfect circle. Because they do not reach the sternum, the very short eleventh and twelfth ribs are known as "floating ribs." Since the *rib cage* serves as the housing for the lungs and diaphragm, the importance for keeping it expanded in singing will become more evident as we proceed.

Head Airways and Larynx

The source of energy or fuel in respiration is the very air we breathe. The passage of air into the body begins in the head airways (Fig. 5-1), and continues through the **pharynx** (throat), the *larynx*, the *trachea*, and the *bronchi*, into the lungs. The two head airways, both of which are used in singing, are in the nose (*nasal cavity*) and mouth (*oral cavity*).

For quick breaths and exhalations—as during heavy physical exertion and fast, loud, singing—mouth breathing is more efficient than nose breathing. When done properly, the advantages of mouth breathing are: (1) volumes of air can be inhaled more quickly and (2) more interior space is formed by lifting and arching the soft palate, relaxing the articulating organs (tongue and jaw), and lowering the larynx. The combined result is a vocal tract effectively prepared and aligned for singing. Since the nasal passages are equipped to filter, moisten, and warm the air as it enters the body, one should try to breathe through the nose whenever feasible, especially when time permits slower breathing. The sensation of correct inhalation is a "cool spot" high in the back of the throat at the level of the soft palate. After achieving this initial breathing position, one simply maintains the established "gesture of inhalation" throughout the singing process.

The valving action of the larynx allows for the movement of air in and out of the lungs with the opening and closing of the **vocal folds.** When the folds are open, air is allowed to pass in either direction—in or out. When the folds close during such acts as holding one's breath (swimming underwater or lifting weights), the air is effectively "dammed" by the folds' closure. This valved adjustment of the folds during singing retains and slows the exit of air at a pace partially determined by technical facility, dynamic levels, vocal range, and length of musical phrases. (The role of the larynx is more fully discussed in the next chapter.)

Figure 5-1
The Breathing Mechanism

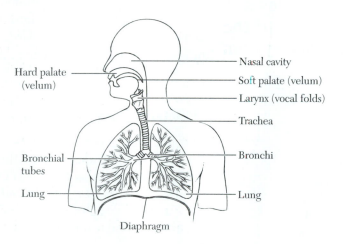

Hard palate (velum)

Nasal cavity

Soft palate (velum)

Larynx (vocal folds)

Trachea

Bronchial tubes

Bronchi

Lung

Lung

Diaphragm

Sub-laryngeal System

Air movement from the larynx to the lungs passes first via the **trachea** (windpipe), a flexible, cylindrical, cartilaginous pipe resembling a vacuum hose, to the two **bronchi** (branches) within the lungs. From there the bronchi further subdivide into millions of ever-narrowing **bronchiole** that terminate in approximately 7 million *alveolar sacs* (air cells) where carbon dioxide and oxygen are exchanged.

Because of their elasticity and spongelike characteristics, the *lungs* (air sacs) increasingly expand as more air is inhaled. However, like rubber balloons, the lungs exert a force that shrinks them back to their original size. This elastic recoil process works in opposition to the expansion of the rib cage. When elastic recoil forces are greater than the muscular forces that expand the rib cage, the lungs recoil. As the lungs recoil, air is expired (exhaled). The volume of expired air is directly proportionate to the amount of air inhaled, which is the body's way of equalizing inside and outside air pressure. You can observe this phenomenon by taking a series of increasingly larger breaths, then noting the proportionately larger volume of air expelled each time. The volume of air moved in and out of the lungs depends on the air needs of the individual at any given moment.

Respiratory Musculature

The **diaphragm** (Figs. 5-1 and 5-2), the second-largest muscle in the body and the single most important muscle in the process of inhalation, is responsible for 60 to 80 percent of increased air volume. Separating the **thorax** (chest cavity) from the **viscera** (abdominal cavity), the diaphragm serves as both the floor of the chest cavity and the ceiling of the abdominal cavity. Unlike most skeletal muscles (which exist in pairs, one for either side of the body), the diaphragm is a single muscle which spans the entire thoracic cavity. During inhalation, the diaphragm flattens to resemble the shape of a salad plate, forcing the abdominal organs downward and forward, distending the abdominal wall, and creating a bulge in the **epigastrium**—the triangular part of the abdomen located at the base of the sternum, directly below the ribs. At rest it resembles an upside down salad bowl with two irregular domes (Fig. 5-1), the right side of which is slightly higher than the left.

Two muscle groups called **intercostals** (Fig. 5-2) attach to the ribs, filling the gaps between the ribs with muscles and membranes. Their main purpose is to aid in inhalation and exhalation and to help create a constant air pressure below the vocal folds for voice use, which is accomplished by coordinating and balancing the action of the inspiratory and expiratory muscles.

The **external intercostal muscles** raise the ribs to expand the rib cage. When we inhale, contraction of the external intercostals causes the rib cage to expand simultaneously vertically (up and down), horizontally (side to side), and anteriorly-posteriorly (front to back).

In contrast, the **internal intercostal muscles** use a contracting, recoiling expiratory (expulsion of air) muscle action to lower the ribs, effectively causing the rib cage to collapse and decrease in size vertically, horizontally, and anteriorly-posteriorly. Singers try to resist this collapsing process by maintaining a high chest position and expanded rib cage.

The abdominal wall ("belly") muscles (Fig. 5-2) are used for expiration and to support or steady the tone when speaking and singing, which is accomplished by providing opposition to the recoil forces of the lungs and diaphragm during expiration. These powerful vertical and oblique muscles cover the entire upper and lower abdominal region. You will experience their actions during breathing and when using the singing exercises introduced at the end of this chapter.

Summary of Respiratory Action

During normal breathing the action of the diaphragm and abdominal muscles during a complete inspiration-expiration cycle can be described in four phases: inspiration, suspension, expiration, and recovery (Fig. 5-3).

Figure 5-2
Rib Cage and Muscles of Breathing

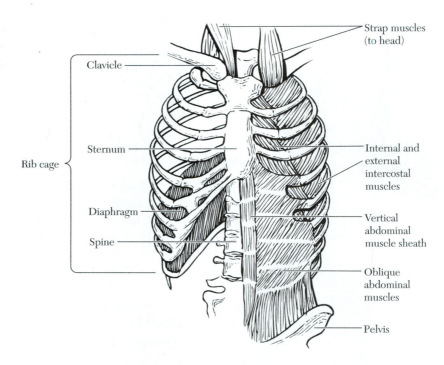

Figure 5-3
Air Movement during Inspiration and Expiration

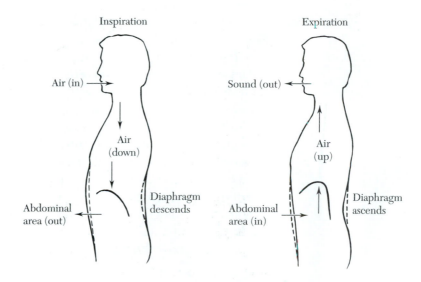

Adventures in Singing

1. **Inspiration.** When oxygen is needed, the diaphragm contracts and rib cage volume is increased, assisted by the external intercostal muscles. Inhaled air enters through the mouth or nose, passes through the pharynx, larynx, trachea, and bronchi, filling the expanding lungs. At rest, **inspiration** (**inhalation**) takes approximately one second and consists of the following action (both literally and figuratively) based on simple observable responses:

   In   air enters through the mouth and/or nose into the pharynx
   Down air moves downward through the larynx into the trachea, bronchi and lungs; diaphragm descent expands rib cage and abdominal wall
   Out   abdominal organs and lower abdomen distend and the lungs expand within the rib cage

2. **Suspension.** There is a brief suspension period when recoil forces overcome the muscular forces of rib cage expansion, and the process reverses direction. This usually lasts less than a second but could last considerably longer if the muscles of inspiration (mainly external intercostals) are held in a contracted state to check the recoil forces.

3. **Expiration.** This action is the reverse of inspiration and at rest lasts approximately three seconds. **Expiration** (**exhalation**) consists of the following actions:

   In   the lungs recoil inward, drawing the rib cage with them; abdominal muscles return to their resting state, or are contracted, and the abdominal viscera moves in and up
   Up   the diaphragm recoils upward, reducing the volume of the rib cage and increasing pressure in the thorax
   Out   air is expelled from the lungs, first through the trachea and then through the larynx and vocal tract, either silently or with vocalized tone; the length of this phase lasts approximately fifteen to twenty seconds for singing and one to five seconds for normal speech

4. **Recovery.** Finally, there is a moment of relaxation for all muscles involved in the breathing process, before the breath cycle begins anew.

Methods of Breathing

There are three principal ways people can breathe: high torso, middle torso, and low torso. But, the most efficient method is a combination of both the middle and low torso. We will consider these "from the top down," from the least to the most desirable.

High torso breathing involves shoulders and upper chest. This is the "breath of exhaustion" and is observed, for example, in sprinters who have just run 1,000 meters at top speed. In this type of breathing, the shoulders and chest pump violently to move air quickly in and out of the respiratory system. The breath of exhaustion is definitely not conducive to effective vocalism, as it leads to tensions in neck and throat muscles and unsteady tone production.

Middle torso breathing involves expansion of the ribs (primarily sideways and partly forward), but neglects lower abdominal breath-related action. This "corseted" manner of breath control tends to create an overly pressurized, tense breathing system causing restrained airflow and strained vocal quality, especially in high-range singing. This Victorian manner of breathing was encouraged by a voice culture that used the admonition "hold in those tummy muscles," particularly when working with young women.

Low torso breathing involves greater use of low abdominal muscles. In this method the diaphragm fully descends for a relaxed and complete breath. In middle torso breathing the lower abdomen is pulled in, while in low torso breathing these muscles relax and release. Low torso breathing is widely practiced in disciplines of meditation and concentration, such as yoga. Another low torso breathing method overemphasizes forced breathing activity in the lower abdominal area. While deep breathing is beneficial for singers, excessive "pushing-down-and-out" muscular effort should be avoided.

Middle/low torso breathing involves a combined use of the **costal** (rib) and low abdominal muscles. This is the best possible breathing technique and is achieved through a combination of middle and low torso expansion which includes: (1) an elevated, expanded chest and rib cage to provide space for full lung expansion; (2) a relaxed lower abdominal expansion, resulting from diaphragmatic distension which causes downward lung expansion and inhalation; and (3) a broad back expansion, the result of an expanded rib cage and lower abdominal muscle release.

Breathing and Breath Management Exercises

Many of the following exercises are most effective when done with the assistance of a full-length mirror. When performing these exercises, unless otherwise noted, place one hand over the upper abdominal area (epigastrium) and the other over the lower abdominal area in order to feel the muscular movements involved in breathing. The lower abdominal area lies below the navel. Think of the navel as the center of the combined areas.

Breathing Exercises

Exercise 5-1 BLOWING OUT

In the standing "singer's posture"—hands clasped behind your head, chest expanded, and feet evenly spaced—begin by blowing out (exhaling) as much air as possible. When air is expelled, hold for a few seconds (five to six) until you feel a strong need to breathe. Then let the air rush in, filling every nook and cranny of available space. Observe the physical sensations associated when performing this exercise.

Exercise 5-2 LYING DOWN

Lie flat on the floor on your back and place both open hands over your entire abdominal area. Breathe in and out in a slow, relaxed manner, observing the rise and fall of your abdominal area with each breath you take. Continue the exercise with the addition of a weight (such as a large book) placed on the upper abdominal area. Next, try lying on your stomach while breathing slowly and deeply.

Exercise 5-3 PANTING

Pant like a dog at varying rates, from fast to slow, and notice the outward-and-inward action of the high-middle-low abdominal area. Let your tongue rest loosely on your bottom lip with the jaw dropped comfortably.

Exercise 5-4 SITTING AND LEANING

Sit erect on the edge of a chair with your legs spread comfortably and with your feet resting flat on the floor. Lean over slightly, and place your elbows on your knees. You should be facing the floor at about a 45° angle. Take slow and relaxed breaths at first, then pant at various rates, with your hands feeling the sensations of your body's mechanism in the lower torso.

Exercise 5-5 STANDING

Stand erect with legs spread as far apart as possible and with hands on waist in reversed position (thumbs forward). Like a "toy water bird" or mechanical toy, bend over slowly at a 45° angle from a fulcrum point at the bottom of the pelvic area (not at the waist). Breathe slowly, gradually increasing the breathing tempo as you pay attention to the action of the breathing mechanism.

Exercise 5-6 BENDING

Spread feet slightly, stand erect, then bend over at a 90° angle with hands on your ankles. Breathe as described above but be particularly aware of expanding a full breath; this will be evident by a sensation of tightness in the back below the ribs. This exercise can also be done by placing your forehead on your hands at the edge of a table while bending over in the same manner.

Exercise 5-7 BENDING AND BLOWING OUT AN INTENSE FLAME

Assume the same position as in Exercise 5-6 above. Hold your right (or left) index finger approximately four to five inches from your mouth and pretend you are attempting to blow out an intense flame emanating from your fingertip. Use a vigorous breath for three to four seconds. Observe the action of the abdominal area and rib cage.

Exercise 5-8 SNIFFING

Take a slow deep breath while breathing through the nose for five seconds. Then sniff in extra air to fill the lungs completely and to reach your full lung capacity. Next, while maintaining the sensation of inhaling, hold your breath with expanded abdominal muscles (not at the larynx) for a count of five. Finally, release the breath on a hiss for approximately ten counts until all air is expelled.

Exercise 5-9 CHEST EXPANSION

Thoracic-rib expansion can be accomplished with the following exercise, which is an exaggerated form of the morning-stretch upon awakening. Begin by extending both of your elbows horizontally, straight out on both sides and parallel to the floor, with fingertips slightly touching the chin. Next, swing the elbows upward vertically, as high as possible above the head. Then begin slow, slightly circular rotations backward, all the while keeping the elbows pulled backward (like a bird's wings) so as to expand the chest and rib cage. The hands will part as the arm/elbow rotation broadens.

Breath Coordination and Management

Most singers are concerned about having enough air to complete long, difficult phrases. Sometimes a singer will compensate for this concern by overcrowding the lungs with more air than is needed, causing bottled up sensations. Ideally, a singer will have a mental concept of all phrases ahead and will have planned appropriately measured breaths to complete each phrase. Whenever it is impossible to make it through an extended phrase, however, a singer has the option of taking additional breaths at opportune moments. Judicious **catch breaths** will usually not harm the phrasing, as long as the singer concentrates on the musical/textual intent of the phrase, that is, "carrying over" or "connecting" the textual and musical idea.

Frequently, the excitement and "performance jitters" of a performance cause a singer to burn more oxygen than normal, resulting in a seemingly inexplicable loss of breath. If you have difficulty getting through a specific phrase during rehearsals, it might be prudent to consider "working in" some extra breaths as a safeguard.

Relaxed breathing involves the rhythmic expansion and relaxation of the upper abdomen/epigastrium. Two muscle groups work in opposition to one another (the principle of **muscular antagonism**), with the lower abdominal muscles being active and the diaphragm remaining relatively passive. Airflow rate varies, depending on the demands of the sung or spoken phrase and the resistance of the vocal folds at the laryngeal level.

It is best for beginning students to concentrate first on acquiring a relaxed yet energetic flow of breath. The eventual goal is to find a "balanced pressure" (breath suspension) between inhalation and exhalation when sustaining a tone. You can get an image of balanced muscular coordination by placing the back of one hand into the palm of the other and applying equal pressure with both hands. When using abdominal muscle support, be aware of the tendency to tighten muscles rigidly. At all times the abdominal muscles must be flexible enough to respond to external manipulation. To demonstrate this, sing a sustained tone on "Ah," and press your fist inward on the epigastrium with regular pulses. You should hear and feel the tone changing from soft to loud (**marcato**) dynamic each time you press inward (see Fig. 5-3, expiration).

Be aware that coordinating exhalation muscles requires contradictory muscle actions. For example, when the lower abdominal muscles firm up and move inward to expel air during exhalation, the epigastrium area (under the sternum and lower ribs) bulges outward, the degree of "bulging" determined by how aggressively the abdominals thrust. This partially helps explain the controversial issue of whether one "supports" by "pushing out" or "pulling in." In reality, both pushing and pulling occur simultaneously, for when the lower abdominals are activated inwardly, the epigastrium automatically reacts by distending. Though it is possible for a singer to achieve similar results by using either method, the preferred method is to allow an inward movement of the lower abdominals when singing. These muscular actions can be experienced while singing marcato (stressed notes) exercises (see Exs. 5-16a,b).

Breath-Tone Coordination Exercises

Exercise 5-10   HISSING

Inhale a full breath, then allow the air to exhale slowly with a hissing "sh" or "s" sound. Increase the dynamic level gradually and notice the corresponding increase in airflow.

Exercise 5-11   DEEP BREATHING WITH TONE

Use the deep breathing exercises presented earlier, especially Exercises 5-1, 5-2, and 5-3, this time with normal vocalization. Place hands on the abdominal area to feel the breathing action.

Exercise 5-12   ABDOMINAL MUSCULAR RESPONSE

Establish the proper sense of muscular support by softly grunting, sobbing, or calling out "Hey" or "Hi" as if to someone across the street, using the higher pitches of the head voice. Be aware that occasionally the natural response of these muscles is the opposite of the singing response. For example, they might go "down-and-out," not "in-and-up" as in healthy singing. Since these same muscles are used for evacuation of body wastes and other natural functions, singers must train them to work in an opposite movement but with the same intensity.

Exercise 5-13   BREATHE-SING

Place hands on your abdominal area, assume the correct posture, and relax. Perform the following exercises in an exaggerated panting manner (breathe—movement out; singing tone—movement in). Do this on a comfortable pitch and in moderately slow tempo, first with grace notes and then without them.

Exercise 5-13a

Hah ⌣   hah ⌣   hah ⌣   hah ⌣   hah ⌣

Exercise 5-14   HOOK-UP MANIPULATION

Spread both hands over the middle-lower abdominal area and sing *vocalises* and phrases from songs that place sufficient demands on your breathing. Feel the outward action on inhalation as well as the inward and upward action when singing. Help the breath connection or "hook-up" by hand manipulation if necessary. If there is a pulling or sucking sensation when the breath releases during singing, it is probably a good indication that airflow is free. At the beginning it is fairly normal to experience a need for more breath. This sensation will change gradually as a balanced coordination of the vocal process is achieved. In any case, avoid pushing downward or outward during exhalation.

Exercise 5-15   BOUNCE-JIGGLE

Bounce or jiggle your entire body by repeatedly rising on the balls of your feet (lifting, and then dropping your heels) quickly during vocalization on a single pitch. A more vigorous and rapid bounce will exaggerate the effect.

Exercise 5-16   PULSATING AND STACCATI

Pulsating and staccati exercises will enable you to realize and develop a proper sensation of support in the coordination of breath and tone. The action of both the lower abdominal and back musculature will also be experienced when doing these exercises. Various combinations of rhythmic patterns and keys may be used, in addition to the ones illustrated below. The idea is to move from slow to faster pulses as your technique allows.

   The following pulsating and staccati exercises are to be sung on "ah" and other vowels, with marcato [<>] and staccato [•]. Marcato requires a stressed, strong emphasis while **staccato** requires a light, detached execution. The contrasts between slow, vigorous, loud laughter, and faster, lighter, higher-pitched laughter will give you an idea of these two types of singing.

Exercise 5-16a

ah   ah   (etc.)

Exercise 5-16b

Breath Management Assessment

Breathing. Have you had respiratory problems such as asthma, allergies, or bronchitis? If so, what effect did illness have on your voice? Are you ever conscious of your breathing during activities such as sleeping, public speaking, walking, jogging, and singing? Normally, do you breathe low and full, or high and shallow? How do you breathe when you are under physical or mental stress? Are you aware of your posture, chest, and rib-cage positions throughout the day? Do you understand the physiology of breathing as discussed in this chapter? Do you think your body type affects your breathing habits? What sensations do you have when breathing deeply and fully? How would you describe your sensations when breathing during singing? Are these sensations different from those you experience when you are speaking?

Breath Coordination and Management. Can you perform all of the exercises listed according to the muscular responses discussed—the outward and downward movement upon inhalation, and the inward and upward movement upon exhalation? Do your muscles respond immediately when singing staccati or marcati exercises, or is there sluggishness in muscular response? Are you aware of your body's energy level during singing? How long can you sustain a specific pitch at a moderately loud dynamic level? Do you have trouble singing complete musical phrases without taking frequent breaths? Do you take most of your singing breaths through your mouth, your nose, or a combination of mouth and nose? Can you perform the pulsating exercises (Exs. 5-16a,b) with relative ease, or are they somewhat difficult to execute?

CHAPTER

Producing Tone

Characteristics of Vocal Tone Production

Phonation, or laryngeal vocal-fold vibration, is the result of complex interactions of the vocal folds' muscular and elastic properties working in combination with airflow to produce tone. Three conditions occur simultaneously in phonation: (1) recoil of the lungs and diaphragm, sometimes combined with action by the intercostal and abdominal muscles, causes air to flow through the space between the two vocal folds; (2) muscular forces within the larynx draw the vocal folds close together; and (3) airflow through the narrowed space causes the vocal folds to vibrate together very rapidly, anywhere from 50 to 2,000 vibrations or cycles per second!

When breath is expelled from the lungs and passes through the vocal folds (lips), the folds part slightly, allowing a tiny puff of air to escape. The folds immediately close, then reopen, allowing another puff of air to escape in a continuously repeating cycle. Airflow at fast speed in these cycles produces high pitches while airflow at slow speed produces low pitches. For example, 440 vibrations of the folds produce the pitch A_4, while 880 vibrations produce A_5, an octave higher. Vocal-fold adjustments of length and thickness also play an important role in producing pitch. Commonly referred to as "hook-up," this coordination of airflow and vibrator is an interaction that occurs in all wind instruments.

The following exercises will give you a better idea of how the vocal folds vibrate:

Exercise 6-1   PAPER BLOWING

Hold two sheets of notebook paper in a vertical position in front of your mouth and blow forcefully between them. You will observe that, contrary to what you might expect, the sheets of paper do not separate perceptibly as air passes between them. Instead, they vibrate together in much the same manner as the vocal folds vibrate when air passes between them.

Exercise 6-2   LIP BUZZ/HUM

Next, blow air through your lips as though you are exclaiming, "Bm-m-m-m it's chilly today." You will discover it as possible to emit a tone throughout your full vocal range provided your lips are loose and the breath flow is adequate. This lip-buzz/hum ("bm-m-m-m") exercise is a visible illustration of what occurs when the vocal folds vibrate. It is also an excellent general vocalise for voice building, establishing at least five helpful objectives: (1) consistent breath flow; (2) freedom of the jaw, tongue, and lips; (3) efficient humming; (4) head placement sensations (in the mask); and (5) range extension.

Exercise 6-3   TRUMPET MIMICKING

Perhaps you have experimented with mimicking trumpet sounds by tightening your lips and blowing through them. If so, you are aware that the more the lips are tightened and the airflow is increased, the higher the pitch. A brass instrumentalist uses this technique, adding to the final effect by adding a mouthpiece and full instrument (resonance chamber) to enhance the quality and volume of tone. By scrolling a sheet of paper into a cone shape (small on one end and large on the other), you can improvise an instrument that will produce a similar acoustical effect.

Anatomy and Physiology of the Larynx

The **larynx,** a cartilaginous framework situated at the top of the trachea, serves as a housing for the vocal folds. Its three primary functions are to (1) keep food and other foreign matter from entering the lungs through the trachea by closing the epiglottis, (2) retain the inhaled air to provide back pressure (torque), known as *thoracic fixation,* for such activities as lifting heavy objects, giving birth, or defecating, and (3) produce vocal tone.

Larynges of humans and animals are extremely diverse, and in all cases voice size and overall pitch levels are fundamentally determined by laryngeal dimensions. For example, the human male larynx is approximately 20 percent larger than the female. Although all healthy human larynges share general anatomical characteristics, each larynx will be as uniquely formed as an individual's facial features.

The basic framework of the larynx (Fig. 6-1) consists of three major parts: (1) hyoid bone, (2) thyroid cartilage, and (3) cricoid cartilage. During childhood and youth, the horseshoe-shaped **hyoid bone** is the only true bone in the larynx, but with increasing age both the thyroid and cricoid cartilages gradually **ossify** (become more bonelike). The **thyroid cartilage,** shaped like a shield, is commonly thought of as the **Adam's apple.** It is more prominent in males because of its larger size and its increased protrusion at the front of the cartilage. The **cricoid cartilage,** which resembles a signet ring, connects to the thyroid above and the trachea below. You can actually explore the dimensions and shape of your own vocal instrument by using your fingers to gently feel your larynx. Begin at the very top with the hyoid bone and slowly work downward to the thyroid cartilage, the cricoid cartilage, and finally the trachea at the very bottom.

Figure 6-1
The Larynx Viewed from the Front, Back, and Left Side

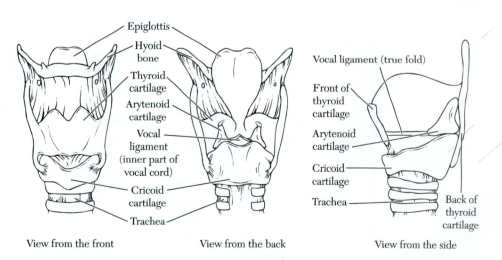

View from the front   View from the back   View from the side

Two bilateral, pyramid-shaped **arytenoid cartilages** (Fig. 6-2) are located at the top portion of the cricoid cartilage. The arytenoids are the attachments for muscles whose functions are to open and close the **glottis** (space between the vocal folds) during breathing and phonation and to assist in adjusting both pitch and loudness. The arytenoids are capable of a number of movement patterns, depending on which muscles are contracting. The degree of vocal-fold closure determines the quality of voice that is produced—from the extreme of whispering (breathiness) on one end of the vocal spectrum to the extreme of phonation that is tight, pinched, or pressed on the opposite end.

Attached to the inside of the thyroid notch is the **epiglottis**, a leaf-shaped cartilage that functions as a cover for the glottis. It folds over the vocal folds during swallowing to protect the folds and keep the lungs from ingesting foreign matter.

The musculature associated with activity of the larynx can be divided into two parts: (1) the **intrinsic (internal) muscles** that have points of origination and connection to points of attachment on or within the framework of the larynx and (2) the **extrinsic (external) muscles** that originate from a point on or within the larynx and connect to another part of the body, such as the jaw or sternum.

Intrinsic bilateral muscles adjust the vocal folds and cartilages for four basic movements: (1) *abductors* for opening, (2) *adductors* for closing, (3) *tensors* for lengthening and thinning, and (3) *relaxers* for shortening and thickening (Zemlin, 1988). The extrinsic bilateral muscle system, commonly referred to as **strap muscles,** stabilizes and anchors the larynx in a suspended position within the neck and throat. In addition, intrinsic tongue muscles connecting to the larynx and hyoid bone are also capable of affecting laryngeal adjustments. It is easy to understand why undue tensions in any of these muscles can adversely affect the quality of vocal tone.

The action of the vocal folds can best be viewed from an overhead view. Figure 6-2 shows the inner structure of the vocal folds, with both illustrations (open and closed) split down the middle to show a fleshlike representation on the left and a schematic representation on the right. Fig. 6-3 reveals the vocal folds as viewed with a laryngeal mirror. Both figures present the folds in open position (*illustrations on right*) and closed position (*illustrations on left*). In this normal overhead view, the *false folds* lie above the *true folds*. These false folds are activated only by severe vocal utterances, such as harsh coughs or gagging reflexes, which protect the airway to the lungs. Separating the true folds from the false folds is a **ventricle** (cavity or open space), which is difficult to see from an overhead viewing.

Figure 6-2
The Physical Structure of the Vocal Folds Viewed from Above

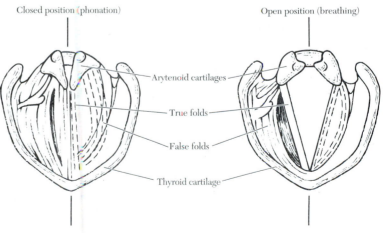

Closed position (phonation)   Open position (breathing)

Arytenoid cartilages

True folds

False folds

Thyroid cartilage

Front of thyroid cartilage (Adam's apple)

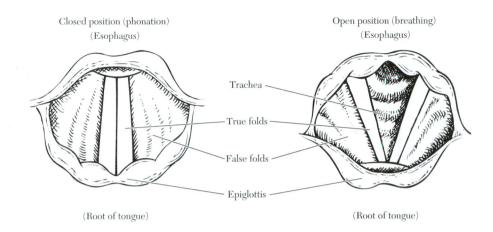

Figure 6-3
The Vocal Folds Viewed from Above during Laryngoscopic Examination

Closed position (phonation)
(Esophagus)

Open position (breathing)
(Esophagus)

Trachea

True folds

False folds

Epiglottis

(Root of tongue)

(Root of tongue)

Three Types of Tone Production

In addition to innate reflex systems, singers must learn to control vocal tone production through voluntary "prephonatory tuning," which is based on *proprioceptive memory,* the ability to mentally image, sense, or hear a desired tonal result in advance. In other words, the kind of vocal tone produced is the direct result of the singer's intentions. For this reason, a pop-oriented singer will tend to sing any vocalise or song using a production based on familiar tonal images.

From the extreme of breathiness—such as whispering—on one end of the vocal spectrum, to the other extreme—tight, pinched, or pressed phonation—on the opposite end, the type of tone production is the product of both the force and the duration of vocal-fold closure during each vibratory cycle. There are essentially three types of normal phonation: (1) aspirate (lax, breathy), (2) pressed (tense, tight), and (3) coordinated (balanced, blended). In addition, there are abnormal types that are the result of physical abnormalities or vocal misuse and abuse.

Sustained Phonation

The three types of sustained phonation that characterize a person's general vocal production are briefly summarized below.

1. **Aspirate (Lax) Phonation.** This hypofunctional (low energy) vocal production uses variable airflow combined with a weak adductory force of the vocal folds. The perceived result is a "breathy voice," characterized by noisy airflow and flutelike tone quality.

2. **Pressed (Tense) Phonation.** This hyperfunctional (high energy) vocal production uses high subglottal breath pressure combined with a strong adductory force of the vocal folds. The perceived result is a "tight voice" characterized by a stressful-sounding tone, including "crackling."

3. **Coordinated (Balanced) Phonation.** This balanced vocal production, known as "flow phonation," uses moderate levels of subglottic pressure and vocal-fold adductory force. This optimal pattern of vibration allows a moderately large airflow with little air turbulence or interference. Flow phonation also allows a relatively large amplitude of vocal-fold vibration, resulting in ample loudness, yet with greatest efficiency of energy use.

Singing with balanced phonation is often referred to as singing "on the breath" or on the "gesture of inhalation." When the singer maintains a sensation of inhaling throughout the act of vocalization, the throat remains in a comfortably open and stretched position. As the throat opens, the **soft palate** (**velum**) is lifted and creates what is often referred to as the "arched tone," a sensation of vertical stretch that enlarges the throat (pharynx) and lowers the larynx to create a larger resonance chamber. One should imagine initiating singing with a light stroke on the thin edges of the folds, avoiding a heavy, pressured use of the full body of the folds. Another way of approaching the coordinated onset is to think of it as "imploding" rather than "exploding" air at the vocal-fold level. Some experts recommend singing with only the air accumulated at the vocal folds at any given moment.

Three Types of Vocal Onset

Closely related to the three types of sustained phonation are three corresponding ways to initiate and release tone. Thus, hypofunctional (breathy) singers will tend to use aspirate onsets, while hyperfunctional (pressed-tone) singers will tend to use glottal onsets. Singers with efficiently produced voices will generally use a balanced approach for both onsets and sustained phonation.

In singing, the manner in which a tone is initiated often depends upon technical, stylistic, textual, and dramatic considerations. For example, when initiating tone on a vowel, one may choose to use an **aspirate** (soft) onset for relaxed expressions, or a **glottal** (hard) onset for explosive expressions. For example, the exclamation "Oh" can be used either in a breathless, surprised way as in "Oh, how beautiful it is" (aspirate), or in a tense, angry way as in "Oh, you don't say" (glottal). In most of our vocal expressions, the healthiest, most efficient vocal onset will require a medium approach, or coordinated (balanced) onset. These three primary ways of initiating (**onset**) and releasing vocal tone are explained below.

1. **Aspirate (Soft) Onset.** Anytime one uses an "h" to initiate a tone, an aspirate onset results, as when speaking such phrases as: "*H*ow are you?; *H*e is here; *W*ho are you?; and *W*here is she?" This kind of onset can relax the larynx and encourage an easier vocal production. William Vennard (1967) actually suggests singing with an imaginary "h" to encourage an easily flowing vocal tone.

2. **Glottal (Hard) Onset.** The glottal onset is created when breath pressure builds up below strongly adducted vocal folds and explodes them apart. A light glottal onset (hiatus) is normal for clear articulation of many initial vowels in words, and is especially needed in certain languages, such as English and German. In contrast, the Italian and French languages minimize the use of glottals. Frequent use of glottal onsets tends to encourage pressed phonation.

3. **Coordinated (Balanced) Onset.** As in flow phonation, balanced onset is an ideal combination of airflow and vocal-fold adduction, which is depending upon dynamic adjustments of the inspiratory-expiratory muscles, vocal folds, and resonators.

Three Types of Vocal Release

Because the end of one tone influences the onset of the next, the release of a tone is as important as its initiation. The three ways to release a tone correspond to the three vocal onsets: (1) aspirate (soft) release, (2) glottal (hard) release, and (3) coordinated (balanced) release.

1. **Aspirate (Soft) Release.** Aspirate release occurs when the vocal folds do not close completely during each glottal cycle, resulting in a breathy

tone quality. Usually caused by the collapse of the breathing mechanism and a subsequent loss of "hook-up," the soft release lacks intensity and is often very weak.

2. **Glottal (Hard) Release.** Glottal release is epitomized by the "terminal grunt" one hears when big-voiced opera singers end a loud high note. Although it has its place as a dramatic device in performance situations, the glottal (hard) release is out of place in soft-to-moderately-loud dynamic levels and in low-to-medium pitch ranges.

3. **Coordinated (Balanced) Release.** Accomplished singers strive to end most phrases with the same consistent tone quality sustained throughout the phrase. This requires a coordinated or balanced release, with the vocal folds under neither too much tension nor too little. A coordinated (balanced) release can be experienced by laughing in a relaxed, hearty manner.

Characteristics of Efficient Vocal Tone

What are the properties of an efficiently produced vocal tone? Aesthetics of tone quality vary from expert to expert, but most agree that a good tone will include the following:

- A unique vocal quality that seems natural to the person producing it. (Artificiality or unnatural tendencies are usually sensed by the listener.)

- Freedom from observable extrinsic and intrinsic muscular strain and tensions in the face, neck, limbs, and torso.

- Tonal clarity and accuracy. Out-of-tune singing is one of the best indications that something is not right.

- A self-starting and self-stopping elasticity, with the ability to sing varying dynamic levels on a sustained tone.

- Ample volume level with a ringing, forward-in-the-mask focus, particularly when increasing airflow for louder dynamic levels.

- A timbre best described as having both bright and dark tonal characteristics (**chiaroscuro**), that is, brilliance and ring plus warmth and richness.

- Flexibility and agility in fast-slow movement, in soft-loud dynamics, and in low-high range.

- A vibrato pattern of 6 to 8 pulses per second.

Exercises for Developing Efficient Phonation

The objective in phonation is to synchronize breath pressure with vocal-fold vibration. This is accomplished by adjustments of the vocal mechanism which avoid excesses in either breath pressure or vocal-fold tension. Efficient phonation includes a sensation of singing on the breath. The following exercises are sequenced so as to allow a dynamic vocal adjustment to occur.

Exercise 6-4   BREATHING AND HOOK-UP

Begin by reviewing the breathing exercises in Chapter 5, especially Exercises 5-3 and 5-13, with emphasis on the outward and inward movements of inhalation and exhalation in conjunction with tone production.

Exercise 6-5   SIGH OF CONTENTMENT

Using the panting exercise in slow motion, take a relaxed, deep breath, and release it in a contented, but not breathy sighing manner on "H-h-h-h hah." Also, the feeling of an incipient sneeze can help set up the proper physical sensations.

Exercise 6-6   SLIDING SIGH

Repeat the above exercise, this time adding a vocalized tone to the relaxed, comfortable sigh on a descending one-octave sliding-pitch scale. At this point don't be too concerned about pitch accuracy.

Exercise 6-6

Hah _____
Whee _____
Whoo _____

Exercise 6-7   DESCENDING VOCALISES

Having established the "contented sigh" technique, you can experiment with various modifications. The following **vocalises** (vocal exercises) employ descending musical patterns for developing the head voice and are especially helpful in countering tight-voiced production. These exercises should be sung lightly in an enthusiastic manner with a vibrant, nonbreathy intensity; you should begin in the speaking range and gradually move into the upper range. As you progress in coordinating phonation, the "h's" may be minimized or eliminated altogether.

Exercise 6-7a

Hi   there!
Hel - lo!
Whee ___
Whoo ___

Exercise 6-7b

How ‿ are you?
He ‿ is here!
Whee _____
Whoo _____

Exercise 6-7c

How _ are _ you?
Who _ are _ you?
Whee _____
Whoo _____

The vocal hook-up effect is achieved by the following staccati (•) and marcati (<>) exercises, which require coordinated control of the respiratory and phonatory systems. Here you need to vigorously apply breath energy at both soft and loud dynamic levels. But be careful not to push, blow, or force air through the folds when doing these exercises. Feel free to raise or lower the keys throughout your comfortable singing range. Start by reviewing the breath/sing exercise (Ex. 5-13). This exercise should be practiced at first with softer dynamics (**mp**), gradually increasing to louder dynamic levels (**mf**).

Exercise 6-8   STACCATO EXERCISES

Sing some light staccato exercises on five-note scales and octave **arpeggi,** raising the key higher with each repeating **scale** and **arpeggio.** Although "ah" is the preferred vowel, you are encouraged to use the other major vowels "ee," "ay," "ah," "oh," and "oo," either singly or in combination, according to your proficiency level.

Exercise 6-9   MARCATO ATTACK

Sing the same five-note scales and octave arpeggi with a marcato pulse, this time perhaps a bit slower to accommodate the extra stress of each note. This will necessitate a more energetic use of the breath and greater activation of the supporting respiratory musculature. Once these simple exercises are mastered, you are encouraged to experiment with more extended vocalises which incorporate both staccati and marcati onsets in various combinations of tempo, range, dynamic levels, and rhythmic/melodic patterns.

Exercise 6-10   NASAL CONSONANTS

Nasal consonants such as "m," "n," and "ng" are very helpful in establishing a clean vocal-fold vibration, especially when the articulators are relaxed. In addition to Exercises 8-1 and 8-2, the lip-buzz/hum is an excellent exercise for balanced phonation. Students who tend toward breathy tone will benefit from exercises that encourage more vocal-fold closure, for example, "whining," "moaning," and siren-like tonal qualities that aid efficient vocal-fold vibration. Because the voice works best as a coordinated unit, most exercises will achieve more than a single objective. Hence, an exercise using "ng" that is performed correctly will help coordinate breath, vocal-fold vibration, and resonators into a single positive response.

Phonation Assessment

Principles and Physiology.   What is your understanding of phonation? What are the primary functions of the larynx? Do you understand how the vocal folds vibrate, and can you demonstrate this by means of the two exercises mentioned at the beginning of this chapter? Do you have a fundamental understanding of the major parts of the larynx and how they function?

Vocal Tone. Can you name and demonstrate the three ways of initiating and releasing vocal tone? Are you aware of vocal onset and release as you sing? Is your tonal quality affected by the way you initiate and sustain vocal tone? What are the properties of a well-produced vocal tone? How does your voice measure up to these characteristics? Are you able to sing staccati exercises clearly and accurately?

7 CHAPTER

Connecting Voice Levels

Explanation and Description of Vocal Registers

Everyone experiences changes in voice quality when speaking or yelling at various pitch levels. This is particularly noticeable when we have laryngitis, or when we are singing from our lowest to highest vocal ranges. These high and low vocal ranges and their peculiar tonal characteristics are called **registers,** a word developed hundreds of years ago to serve the design and construction of church organs.

The smoother a voice sounds throughout its range and the more ease with which it moves through various dynamic levels, the less aware we are of vocal registers. On the other hand, the more unskilled the singer, the more likely we are to detect contrasts in registers, such as obvious voice "shifts" or "breaks" with sudden changes in tone quality and volume.

A useful analogy is to compare register changes with the gears of an automobile. The low-gear mechanism of the automobile helps negotiate slow driving speeds, while the low-voice mechanism helps negotiate low pitches. When the automobile's low gear—and the singer's low-voice mechanism—reaches its upper limits of intended use, it must give way to other mechanisms that permit extended operation. For example, the automobile's higher gears facilitate increased speed and reduce stress on mechanical parts, while the voice's higher "vocal gears" facilitate access to higher pitches with less strain on structures of the vocal mechanism.

Anyone familiar with driving motor vehicles equipped with either stick-shift or automatic transmissions has experienced differences in smoothness and comfort. While a driver's stick-shifting may be skillful, an automatic transmission is normally much smoother, especially when acceleration is moderate. It is easy to imagine the smoothness of a luxury automobile equipped with automatic transmission compared to that of a multi-geared semitrailer ("18 wheeler") as both take off from a stop light at moderate speeds. Voices are capable of behaving in similar fashions—easily and smoothly, or with difficulty and roughness.

Voice Register Theories

There are several current theories or descriptions of vocal registers, each with enthusiastic proponents. Most voice experts subscribe to one of the following three positions:

One-Register Theory

Proponents of this idealistic theory argue that when the voice is functioning correctly, there is only one seamless vocal quality throughout the vocal range. They may also argue that it is nonproductive to discuss registers with singers as it tends to confuse them—the less said, the better. Although the one-register viewpoint has merit, most students do in fact benefit from learning about the components of the voice and how they coordinate.

Two-Registers Theory

The *chest* and *head registers* theory seems to adequately explain what is evident from the average unskilled singer.

Chest register, or *heavy mechanism,* is typically the speaking and yelling voice. It is called "**chest voice**" because physical sensations (vibrations) are experienced in the chest cavity when one vocalizes in that register, usually in the lower two-thirds of one's vocal range and sometimes at louder dynamic levels. When chest voice is used in a healthy way with proper airflow and sensations of resonance in the head, it can add strength and vitality to the speaking and singing voice.

Unfortunately, chest register is overused by singers when "**belting**" or forcing high notes, a practice sometimes referred to as the "Annie syndrome." (In the original production of the musical *Annie,* the child singer blasts out the song "Tomorrow" with a very strong but overstressed voice, an unhealthy practice for a child whose voice is in the formative stage.) Belters can push chest voice up to about C_5, including operatic tenors who sing "high C" at full volume.

Head register, or *light mechanism,* is the higher and softer-voiced mechanism we use when speaking in a soft-spoken, "heady," animated conversational voice. The term *head voice* is derived from the physical sensations experienced when singing in head register, which normally encompasses the upper two-thirds of the vocal range. Contrary to what most beginning-level singers think about head voice ("it's weak," "too high in range"), this often-neglected mechanism has much dynamic vocal potential. When developed, it usually becomes quite powerful, particularly in the higher singing range.

Three-Registers Theory

The three-registers theory incorporates the chest and head registers plus an additional one called the **mixed** or **middle register** (the middle range of the voice). The mixed register is the result of blending the qualities of chest and head registers (heavy and light mechanisms) in the middle range of the voice, approximately the middle one-third of the entire singable range. Mixed registration is used mostly by female singers, while classically trained male singers use it primarily in the upper part of their pitch range. An important identifying mark of "middle voice" is that it bridges the chest and head registers without noticeable disturbances. Singers seem to experience increased head vibrations when singing in middle voice and, since the voice is not locked into a particular register, there is a greater sense of vocal security.

The three-register theory also recognizes that the entire vocal instrument is quite flexible and capable of greater or lesser adjustments of any one mechanism. For example, using more chest mechanism can create a belt-tone when carried up into the higher range. Conversely, when the head voice is carried lower, a softer, sweeter quality results—although the tone may sometimes be weaker, depending on such factors as airflow, intensity, tonal placement, and vowels. When singing in the middle register, the singer has greater possibilities of mixing registers according to dynamic and expressive objectives.

The three-registers theory helps explain how well-trained singers are able to smoothly connect chest and head registers. Supported by current research and practice, the theory appears to be the most widely used concept in teaching vocal registration.

Auxiliary Registers

In addition to the three major registers—chest, head and mixed—there are two identifiable high-voice auxiliary registers: *falsetto* and *flute/whistle,* at least one of which is common in most voices. In addition, there are two rare types of low-voice male registers which may be of interest, especially to young basses. Known as *Strohbass* (strawbass) and *Schnarrbass* (growl bass), these somewhat stressful productions, used mostly by eastern European choral basses, are not recommended for young basses.

Falsetto Register

Once believed to be produced by the false vocal folds in the larynx, the **falsetto** register is actually caused by the thin, long, stiff, and bow-shaped true vocal folds vibrating only at the marginal edges. While falsetto occurs in both sexes, it is primarily associated with male voices. Perceived as "effeminate" in character, falsetto is hooty and breathy in tone because the vocal folds do not fully resist the breath stream during phonation as they do in head voice. Inefficient vocal-fold closure means lower intensity, making it virtually impossible for a singer in falsetto register to **crescendo** (get louder) or **decrescendo** (get softer) on a sustained pitch without an obvious "break." As a technical device, falsetto may be particularly useful for helping hyperfunctional male singers gain more ease in accessing upper-middle and high notes.

Flute/Whistle Register

The **flute/whistle register** is the high-range extension of the female voice occurring approximately above the pitch C_6 (sixth C from bottom of the keyboard). This extended high register creates overtones that produce a floating, disembodied sound often well-focused, penetrating, "squeaky," or whistlelike, such as the familiar loud, high-pitched female scream. Many women feel an aversion to the flute/whistle register and often resist exploring **coloratura** potential, even though it offers opportunities for expanded range and expression.

In physiological terms, flute/whistle registration results when (1) the vocal folds vibrate at a high rate of lengthwise tension (very thin); (2) the posterior (back) portion of the folds has considerable "damping" (diminishing amplitude in successive vibrations); (3) the vibrating mass of the folds is limited; and (4) the subglottic air pressure and airflow is high (Miller, 1986, p. 148).

The Function of the Larynx in Registration

Recall from Chapter 6 that (1) larynges vary in size, shape, and other innate characteristics, and that (2) the vocal folds can be lengthened, shortened, thinned, thickened, tensed, and relaxed by the action of the intrinsic laryngeal muscles and, to a lesser degree, by the extrinsic laryngeal muscles. Individuals can therefore produce a range of pitches (frequencies of vibration) determined by the innate characteristics of their own larynges and vocal folds and by the vocal-fold muscular adjustments they can achieve. Moreover, for each individual, there is a fairly wide range of pitches that can be produced with a variety of different vocal-fold configurations, determined by a variety of coordinations of the intrinsic laryngeal muscles. It is the different degrees of contraction of the intrinsic laryngeal muscles that determine (in large part) which vocal register is being used.

Singers must learn to make smooth adjustments between chest and head registrations, and so a simple explanation of how these mechanisms work should be helpful. In the chest register, or heavy mechanism, the vocal folds are active, thickened and shortened while longitudinal tension is lessened. In the head register, or light mechanism, the folds are more passive while other muscles are more actively thinning and elongating, another example of muscular antagonism. Under the best of circumstances, these opposing muscle actions must be coordinated when singing from low to high or high to low range to achieve a unified, consistent vocal tone. However, the untrained singer will often experience an abrupt shift or audible break from one register to another. When the mixed/middle register is developed, the chances for dramatic register changes diminish.

The following experiment will demonstrate the principles by which the vocal folds and laryngeal muscles operate to produce various adjustments of pitches throughout the vocal range. The exercise requires the ability to mimic a brass instrument by using your facial lips to create a lip-buzz tone.

Exercise 7-1 PITCH AND REGISTRATION EXPERIMENT USING TRUMPET-MIMICKING

Beginning on the pitch C_5, initiate a buzzing tone with your lips very tightly closed, making sure that only the lips produce the tone, not the vocal folds. If this pitch is too high for you, start at a lower pitch. Descend the C Major Scale stepwise at a moderate speed for three octaves to C_2. As you descend pay close attention to the adjustments in your lips and the corresponding changes in tone quality and pitch. Now produce octave **portamenti** (slides) from C_5 to C_4 to C_3 to C_2 at a moderately slow tempo. You will observe that during your descent certain series of pitches are produced by specific adjustments of lip tension and breath pressure. For example, the adjustment for high pitches is characteristically very tight and for the lowest pitches very loose, primarily to facilitate the frequency of vibration. Some pitches seem to be most easily produced with a specific *embouchure* (mouth, lips, tongue adjustments) while others can be produced with a tighter (pressed) or looser (breathy) adjustment. This action is similar to the way singers create pressed or breathy vocal tones by varying vocal-fold tension and breath pressure.

Regarding the use of chest and head mechanisms according to gender and traditional vocal training, men sing primarily in chest voice, blending gradually into mixed and head voice for the upper middle and higher notes. In contrast, women, with the exception of pop-oriented vocalists, sing primarily in head voice, blending gradually into chest voice as they descend into the lower-middle to lower vocal range. This contrast in pitch is caused by the disparity between male and female larynges. Adult males have larger larynges (15–20 millimeters) than adult females (9–15 millimeters), with correspondingly longer vocal folds (Sundberg, 1977).

Negotiating Register Transitions

Register transitions occur at rather predictable points in the voice. Registration is considered *smooth* when it is coordinated, and this takes place when (1) the body and vocal tract are properly aligned, (2) all interfering tensions are eliminated (lips, jaw, tongue, soft palate, larynx, and strap muscles, etc.), and (3) adequate breath flow is provided. When transitions are rough, it is usually due to symptoms and causes of misregistration in untrained or misused/abused voices.

Most singers tend to experience register transitions when moving between low and high singing ranges or chest and head registers, depending primarily on the dynamic level and type of voice production used. One common problem is the tendency to carry excessive vocal weight too high in chest voice, as when belting, effectively prolonging the desired register change into head voice. In cases when production is overstressed, the tone will usually sound strained, perhaps even under pitch (flat), with limited upside potential.

The transition from chest register to head register, which is called the **passage zone** (*zona di passaggio*), tends to occur between D_4 and F_4 for both male and female singers. Sopranos, for example, experience this transition in their low range when moving between chest and head voice. Tenors, meanwhile, experience the same register shift in their upper-middle range, on the same pitches, when moving between head and chest registers. This octave difference between the sexes helps explain why women sing mostly in head voice while men sing mostly in chest (Titze, 1994). Moreover, among both male and female singers the passage zones will vary according to the size and weight of the individual voice, which is largely determined by physical proportions including dimensions of the larynx and resonating cavities. For instance, a heavy-voiced dramatic tenor or soprano will have a lower passage zone than a lighter-voiced lyric tenor or soprano.

While most singers will experience registration events occurring throughout the passage zone, the most troublesome transition actually encompasses an **upper pivotal zone** of only two to three pitches. For example, when the vocal technique is insecure, a lyric tenor will normally experience some difficulty at $E–F\sharp_4$ (fourth from bottom of keyboard); a lyric soprano at $F–F\sharp_5$; a lyric mezzo-soprano at $E–F_5$; and a lyric baritone at $E–E\flat_4$. Finally, it must be pointed out that the female voice must usually learn how to deal with the chest voice's **lower pivotal zone** around $E–E\flat_4$ for soprano and F_4 for mezzo-soprano. Learning how to negotiate the use of chest and head mixture—in the lower voice for all females and the upper voice for males—is a goal of all singers. For more detailed coverage of registration events, the reader is referred to Richard Miller's book *The Structure of Singing* (1986).

If the lower mechanism, or chest voice, is forced upward until an abrupt change in the voice occurs, one experiences the rigid muscular activity associated with a static adjustment of the laryngeal mechanism. Straight-tone singing is also a result of this type of adjustment. On the other hand, a dynamic adjustment facilitates responsive muscular action, which in turn encourages natural register changes, accompanied by vibrato in the tone. Normally, when approaching a register transition, an extra surge of breath energy is required, all the while maintaining high-placed facial mask sensations.

The fine tuning essential for a dynamic balance between the lower and higher mechanisms can be further explained in relation to perceived pitch, loudness, and timbre:

1. **Pitch.** Vocal pitch is determined by heavier adjustments in the lower part of the voice and lighter adjustments when ascending into the higher range.

2. **Loudness.** Tonal loudness on any given pitch is determined by a lighter vocal production (without breathiness) in softer singing and a heavier vocal production (without pressing) in louder singing.

3. **Timbre.** The tone quality produced by the heavy mechanism is a rich timbre while the lighter mechanism produces a sweeter tone.

Exercises for Coordinating Vocal Registers

One registration goal in singing is to sing an *even scale*, a scale in which registers blend, vowels match, and dynamics merge, so that the differences shade into each other with no perceptible line of demarcation: every tone from lowest to highest matches as perfectly as possible in quality and is passed smoothly from one to another—"homogenized," so to speak. The two meanings and pronunciations of the term should be noted: homogeneous (of the same or similar nature) and homogeneous (diverse elements blended into a uniform mixture). Both meanings apply in describing an even scale. Exercises 7-2, 7-3, and 7-4 are designed to help equalize registration.

Exercise 7-2   SLIDING PITCHES

One way to connect the registers smoothly is to slide from low to high pitches in the manner of a siren, using sliding pitches (**portamenti**) from low-to-high and high-to-low randomly, that is, without regard for specific pitches or keys. Use the lip-buzz hum exercise, first humming and then using random vowels, particularly the French nasal vowels [ɛ̃], [ɑ̃], and [õ] (see Fig. 9-3), which will help establish efficient vocal-fold adduction and high-placed mask sensations that promote a ringing, full tone. Imitating a sirenlike tone quality using the French vowels may be particularly helpful. The same approach can also be used when singing other intervals, such as a fifth, an octave, or random pitches. While vocalizing, be aware of extraneous tensions in the jaw, tongue, soft palate, neck, and shoulders. Stay loose but energized.

Exercise 7-2a

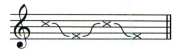

Exercise 7-2b

Exercise 7-2c

Exercise 7-3   ASCENDING/DESCENDING SCALES

Allow the voice to change by "lifting on the breath" to a lighter, headier quality when ascending in pitch. In order to experience this, it usually works best to sing lightly and easily, but firmly, on an ascending and descending scale. While singing the following exercises (Exs. 7-3a,b), hold the jaw down lightly with a finger placed horizontally in the groove between lower lip and chin. Sing each "lah" with the tongue reaching up to the upper lip and dental ridge for the articulation of the "l" and subsequently falling to the bottom lip and dental ridge to complete the "ah" vowel. These exercises help relax the articulating organs and aid in registration adjustments as the voice ascends. They may also be sung on various vowels and/or combinations of vowels at varying dynamic levels and tempi to help blend and equalize the registers.

Exercise 7-3a

Lah lah lah lah   (etc.)

Exercise 7-3b

Lah lah lah lah   (etc.)

Occasionally, some students will have difficulty with these scale exercises (Exs. 7-3a,b), especially if their tongues are "tied." The connecting membrane beneath the tongue varies considerably among individuals, resulting in diction-related tensions, particularly in high-range singing. If a professionally oriented vocal student appears to have such a problem, he or she should be referred to a medical specialist for an evaluation.

Exercise 7-4   YODELING EXERCISE

This exercise allows the freedom of moving between registers in a **yodeling** manner, allowing the voice to move quickly and smoothly between chest and head registers. It is important to allow the voice to make its own shifts at the appropriate pitches. Although your tendency might be to sing the yodeling exercise disconnected and jerkily, the goal will be to sing it smoothly and connected so that the voice sounds unified and consistent throughout. Begin by using moderate keys and tempi, eventually expanding keys, dynamic levels, tempi, and vowel/consonant combinations (such as "nyah") as your competency increases.

Exercise 7-4

Nyah _____

Exercise 7-5   CRESCENDO/DECRESCENDO

Traditionally, the technical vocal exercise favored for blending heavy and light registers on a sustained crescendo/decrescendo pitch is the **messa di voce** (soft-to-loud-to-soft). When mastered throughout the entire singing range, it indicates a well-trained singer. Since this exercise requires the utmost in mental concentration and physical control over the voice, it should first be mastered at low-to-moderate pitches before moving into upper register transition pitches. Although in most cases the "ah" vowel will be the easiest to sing, you should eventually sing the *messa di voce* on all vowels, including the French nasal vowels [ɑ̃] and [ɔ̃].

Exercise 7-5

Vocal Registration Assessment

Assessing Others.   Are you able to discern when singers are using different registers, such as head voice and chest voice? Can you tell exactly when the change occurs as they move from chest to head or from head to chest? Can you differentiate between head voice and falsetto when hearing male singers sing in the high, soft voice range? Are you aware of the flute register when it occurs in the female voice, usually above C_6? Have you ever heard a singer's voice "break"? Have you heard singers who sing smoothly throughout their vocal range with only slight modifications in their basic tonal quality? If so, what kind of vocal repertoire did they perform?

Assessing Yourself.   Are you aware of obvious changes in your voice as you sing throughout your entire vocal range? If so, on which pitches do you experience noticeable changes? How often and under what conditions do you experience these changes? Can you sense the body and head vibrations that account for the popular use of "chest" and "head" in describing these two registers? Are you able to negotiate your registration shifts smoothly or do you hear and feel such changes when they occur? Do you have difficulty in sustaining a high **tessitura,** or vocal range, for several seconds? Can you crescendo, or swell from soft to loud, a tone on a sustained pitch, in your highest transition zones and decrescendo, (diminish) from loud to soft, the same pitch without a noticeable break or glitch in the voice?

Optimizing Tone Quality

Acoustics— The Science of Sound

We experience acoustical effects every day. For instance, have you ever experimented with (1) blowing air across the top of a narrow-necked pop bottle, (2) striking glasses that contain various quantities of water with a metal utensil, (3) depressing the damper pedal after opening the top of a piano, then shouting into the piano in order to hear the response, or (4) producing and hearing echoes, reverberations of sound where the acoustical environment is responsive, such as in canyons or cathedrals? If so, you've experienced the phenomenon of resonance, the spontaneous amplification, reinforcement, or prolongation of vibration when another vibration of the same frequency is applied to it.

Singing in a shower stall is one place where exhilarating acoustical effects are often experienced by most people. Other "acoustically alive" spaces include dome-shaped buildings (capital rotunda) or cathedral naves, where vocal sounds can be easily heard, even when one is whispering. Conversely, some environments absorb or dissipate sound—an insulated automobile interior, an open field, a forest, or a room heavily upholstered with carpets, curtains, and padded furniture. All of these situations demonstrate acoustical principles, with both positive and negative effects for the singer.

A brief introduction to **acoustics**—the science of the production, propagation, and perception of sound waves—will lay the groundwork for understanding resonators, which are essential for optimizing tone quality. In scientific terms, **sound** is a disturbance of air particles or variation in air pressure that impinges on the ear. Knowledge of how sound is created, enhanced, and perceived might help improve the overall quality of your singing.

Properties and Characteristics of Sound

As mentioned earlier, all instruments, including the voice, use three essential elements in producing sound: (1) an *actuator* (air)—the source of power, (2) a *vibrator* (vocal folds)—the energy activator of sound waves, and (3) a *resonator* (nasal, mouth, and throat cavities)—a secondary vibrator that increases the intensity of the vibrator's product, thereby improving its quality.

Sound is propagated by wave action, a common natural phenomenon; for example, the ripples caused by a rock thrown into a pond or the radiating shock tremors from an earthquake's epicenter. While waves of water move primarily on the surface of the pond in a horizontal direction, **sound waves** expand outward from the sound source in *all* directions.

Air, which is composed of submicroscopic bits of matter known as *molecules*, explodes outward in all directions from the sound source when disturbed, somewhat like an expanding balloon. As sound waves move outward, molecules crowd close together, creating an area of higher pressure known as *compression*. When they return to their original position, the molecules become less dense, creating a lower pressure area known as a *rarefaction*. The continual cycling of *compression phase* and *rarefaction phase* is the sound wave, which expands outward as long as the sound source continues—a "balloon within a balloon" effect. Sound waves expand at approximately 1,130 feet (345 meters) per second, which is known as the speed of sound.

Regular, repeating sound waves create musical tone, while irregular patterns produce noise. Regular, repeating sound waves in singing are partially determined by *vowels,* while irregular patterns in speech and singing correspond to the use of *consonants* (see Chap. 9).

The four most significant properties of a musical tone are (1) *frequency* (pitch); (2) *intensity* (amplitude, loudness); (3) *timbre* (tone color), a combined product of frequency and intensity; and (4) *duration*. In addition, extraneous sound (*noise*) is also an integral property of musical sound.

Frequency   **Frequency**, the number of vibration cycles per second as measured in **Hertz (Hz)**, is perceived as **pitch**; the faster the frequency of vibration, the higher the pitch. For example, the International Standards Association concert pitch of A_4 will result in 440 vibrations or waves per second. The frequency range audible to the human ear is approximately from 20 Hz to 16,000 Hz. In speaking and singing, pitch is determined by the frequency of vocal-fold vibration, which is varied by increasing tension or changing the mass of the vibrating vocal folds.

Intensity   Although **amplitude** is the actual attribute of vibration, it is more typically measured as **intensity,** the amount of pressure generated by the vibrator (vocal folds). This vibrator-generated pressure results in sound waves moving through the air, subsequently striking the ear's tympanic membrane. The standard unit of measurement for *sound pressure level* (SPL) is the **decibel** (dB), the number of decibels roughly corresponding to what is perceived by the listener as *loudness* (not intensity).

Timbre   The audible characteristics of sound are the result of harmonic **overtones,** acoustical frequencies created by a vibrator in conjunction with its connected air cavities or resonators. In the voice, **timbre,** or tone quality (the characteristics of a particular tone), consists of the **fundamental** (tone or pitch) of the vibrator (vocal folds), plus the harmonic overtones generated in the vocal tract, a very complex and variable resonator system. When overtones are in sync with the vibrator, the tone will be perceived as being in tune and pleasant to the ear. Each music instrument produces a unique configuration of overtones that enables the human ear to distinguish one from another. In like fashion, each voice, and even each vowel, presents unique overtone configurations based on the properties of pitch, intensity, and timbre.

Duration   A sound's wave form has three durational characteristics: (1) the *attack* (onset)—the time it takes for the sound to reach its steady state, (2) the *steady state,* or relatively stable sustained quality, and (3) the *decay*—the time it takes for the sound to die away. For example, a xylophone tone has a sharp attack, no actual steady state, and an immediate decay. Conversely, when a gong is struck, the sound builds to its highest point, then gradually decays. The vocal tone also has attack and decay, known as onset and offset, and a sustained portion, which may or may not be a steady state, depending on the singer's technical facility.

Vocal Resonators

A **resonator** can be considered any object through which a sound wave can be filtered, subsequently enhancing and modifying the final sound product. Resonators are usually thought of as hollow objects with air-filled cavities that have their own natural frequency of vibration.

The three important factors in determining tone quality and pitch produced by a resonator system are size, shape and openings, and texture. The larger the resonator, the less frequent the vibrations; the smaller, the more frequent. Moreover, the larger the resonating air cavity, the lower its pitch; the smaller the cavity, the higher its pitch. Because resonator shapes and openings can determine both pitch and tone quality, a spherical cavity with a large opening will produce a high pitch. However, if a neck is added to the spherical cavity, the pitch will be lower (e.g., singers who enlarge their vocal resonators by rounding and extending their lips).

Finally, the composition and surface of resonators can affect the tonal product by either encouraging or discouraging potential overtones. For example, metal and flesh will respond differently according to their composition. In general, hard surfaces will make a tone more brilliant by reflecting high overtones, while soft surfaces will absorb the rapid, short vibrations, resulting in more mellow, sweeter tones.

We continue our discussion of vocal resonators by looking at a diagram of the human resonating system (Fig. 8-1), followed by a discussion of each area.

Chest and Subglottal Airways   Since the lungs are filled with spongy, absorbent material, they are not considered viable resonating cavities. However, singers do experience vibratory sensations in their chests, particularly when singing in low range and at full voice. Such vibratory sensations are actually the result of forced sympathetic vibrations produced within the lungs and rib

Figure 8-1
**The Human
Resonating System**

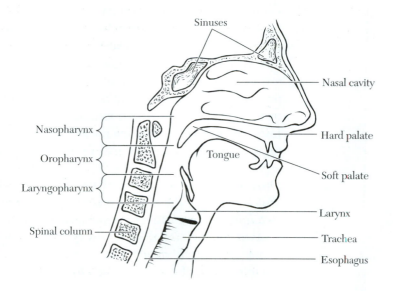

Sinuses
Nasal cavity
Nasopharynx
Oropharynx
Laryngopharynx
Spinal column
Tongue
Hard palate
Soft palate
Larynx
Trachea
Esophagus

cage. The hard surfaces of the subglottal trachea and bronchial tubes also qualify them as resonators; but the amount of resonance available to enhance the singing voice has not yet been scientifically confirmed.

Larynx   Though the laryngeal cavity is small, the larynx may be classified as a small resonator and possibly even a very important one. Sundberg (1977) has made a strong case substantiating the possibility that resonance is generated in the *laryngeal collar*, a space just above the vocal folds and below the rim of the epiglottis. Scientists speculate that this space might be the source of the typical "ring" heard in the voices of professional singers.

Pharynx and Oral Cavity   Together, the *laryngopharynx* and *oropharynx* form the largest resonating cavity and have the greatest effect on tonal quality. The laryngopharynx, extending from the base of the cricoid cartilage to the top of the epiglottis, also includes the laryngeal collar. The larger oropharynx extends from the top of the epiglottis to the soft palate. The "open throat" terminology used by many teachers refers to this combined spacious resonating cavity. In close juxtaposition to the pharynx, the mouth cavity is the most variable resonator, primarily because of constantly fluctuating tongue and jaw positions.

Nasal and Sinus Cavities   The cavity immediately above the velum (soft palate) and extending to the base of the skull is the *nasopharynx*. The opening and closing of this **nasal port** is primarily controlled by sphincter action of the velum (soft palate) and muscles connected to the velum. This action determines to a large extend the production of certain consonants as well as the tonal configuration of vowels. Although the amount and quality of resonance generated by the coupling of the nasal cavity is controversial, accomplished singers report experiencing sensations or illusions of sympathetic vibrations in the nasal cavities when they are singing well. The perceived sensations are often described in terms of *nasal resonance*, sometimes referred to as "twang," or "ring." Since the sinus cavities are small and practically inaccessible (due to their small apertures), they are thought to be unsuitable as resonators.

Finally, the coupling of all primary resonating cavities into a single, highly complex, and variable resonating system is often referred to as the *vocal tract*.

Maximizing Vocal Resonance

For maximum resonation the vocal resonators must be optimally enlarged, primarily by intrinsic and extrinsic muscular adjustments in the vocal tract that control the positioning of specific vocal organs (larynx, velum, tongue, and jaw).

Larynx

The pharynx is enlarged when the larynx is lowered in a relaxed, nondepressed manner, primarily by the action of the strap muscles. This is achieved with the assistance of the swallowing muscles which pull upward and backward toward the base of the skull and the tongue muscles which pull upward and forward toward the point of the jaw. The resonating chamber of the vocal tract can be enlarged naturally in one of three ways: (1) by chewing as when slowly eating a tasty meal with an easy, loose chewing action, which helps relax the swallowing muscles; (2) by swallowing, then feeling the relaxation of the swallowing muscles after the swallow; (3) by inhaling through the mouth, as when taking a surprise breath; and

(4) by sighing with a feeling of pleasurable contentment. The sensation felt at the beginning of a sneeze can also help accomplish a similar natural adjustment of the resonators.

Tongue

The tongue is a very large muscle that, by the nature of its strategic position and functioning, has a significant influence on the shape and size of the vocal tract. Behind the chin and under the tongue are muscles that need to be free from tension in order to produce quality tone. Massaging these muscles with your fingers during vocalization should help create a relaxed condition. The exact positioning of the tongue is determined chiefly by vowel shaping and consonant articulation. The important thought to bear in mind is that it should always be relaxed and never stiff, and the tip should be rounded and not pointed. Normally, the tongue tip is slightly touching the lower teeth and dental ridge, never curled up into the mouth or pulled back. Whether it is naturally grooved depends on your physiology. For example, on the vowel "ah" the tongue should lie relatively flat and rounded at the tip. Refer to tongue training Exercises 4-8a,b and 7-2a,b for help in developing flexible tongue control.

Pharynx

The wall of the pharynx consists of muscle tissue, including the swallowing muscles, the pharyngeal pillars, and the velum (see Fig. 8-2). When the larynx is low and the soft palate high, these muscles create the inner stretch often referred to as *open throat*. A moderate sensation of this inner stretching will suffice and can be gained by creating the sensation of singing with an "inner smile." In addition to the laryngeal collar, this firming up of the pharyngeal wall is thought to be a major source of "twang," the ringing quality heard in all highly developed voices. Figure 8-2 illustrates the natural positioning of the open mouth, including the relaxed flat tongue, the raised soft palate, and the two pairs of pharyngeal wall muscles known as the *anterior* and *posterior faucial pillars*. This positioning would most likely be suitable for a full-voiced high note sung on the vowel "ah."

Figure 8-2
Open Mouth: Pharyngeal and Tongue Positioning

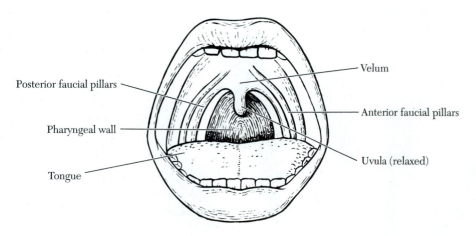

Velum

Posterior faucial pillars

Anterior faucial pillars

Pharyngeal wall

Uvula (relaxed)

Tongue

Jaw

Because the jaw is so interconnected with the tongue and other vocal tract musculature, its role in singing is crucial. Apparently we humans carry a lot of excess tension in our jaws, as indicated by such descriptions as "clenched teeth," "gritted teeth," and "tight jaw."

The correct way to completely open the mouth when singing high notes is to unhinge the jaw from the point where it intersects with the skull, slightly forward of the ears. This can be experienced by placing your fingers in this area and dropping the jaw until a slight indention is felt. The larynx then lowers and the throat feels relaxed and open. A gentle yawn will help assist this unhinging action. Although the amount of jaw drop will depend on such factors as individual anatomy, pitch levels, and vowels and consonants being articulated, one should exercise moderation, especially in the middle pitch range. Generally speaking, when the mouth is forced open beyond an approximate two-finger width, excessive muscular tension, particularly in the muscles under the jaw, is created. A helpful exercise for opening the jaw comfortably is to imagine rubber bands connecting the jaw to the skull. When dropping your jaw you should experience sensations of gentle stretching and chewing.

Another problem related to excessive manipulation is the "over-jawing" of words in order to articulate more clearly. Aggressive jaw action needs to be minimized in most vocalization, especially in the low-to-middle vocal ranges, including the speaking voice range. Only at the low and high extremes of the vocal range does the jaw need to be lowered to create an extended, yet comfortable opening. To reiterate, articulation should be flexible, loose, and precise—never tense—according to natural speechlike functioning.

[handwritten margin note: do not overextend]

Lips and Mouth

In general, lip use appears to be diminishing in the speech of most modern languages as people become more complacent in articulating consonants and shaping vowels accurately. This trend is especially noticed with North Americans, who tend to speak with lateral mouth positions and lax articulation. For example, compare the voice training and practice of the British actor Richard Burton, to that of the U.S. actor Marlon Brando, both internationally acclaimed movie celebrities. Burton's speech is recognized as being crisp and clear while Brando's mumbling is generally incomprehensible.

These thoughts are meant to encourage singers to use their lips, especially for certain vowels and consonants. Since most people rarely use their puckering muscles, it may at first seem a bit unnatural when applied to singing. With time and regular practice, however, lip flexibility will gradually improve.

The primary reason for rounding the lips is to shape "rounded vowels," such as "oo" and "oh." Acoustically, puckering to extend the oral cavity is similar to adding a neck to a resonating cavity. The result of puckering is muffling of high overtones and augmentation of low overtones. To the listener the aural perception is one of a richer, lower-pitched tone. Most singers benefit from employing a vertically stretched jaw with most vowels, particularly for the more brilliant "ee" and "ay" vowels. However, as a general approach for singing vowels, excessive puckering or rounding of the lips should be used with discretion.

In contrast to vertical mouth and lip position, infectious wide smiling does not usually provide the best configuration for the vocal tract resonator. One must learn to smile with the eyes instead of showing lots of teeth. Since there are always exceptions to every rule, one must occasionally allow some latitude with this particular issue, particularly when performing certain character, Broadway, or popular music songs.

To counteract any tendencies toward singing too laterally, that is, spread-toned or shrill, Exercise 8-1 should help establish a more relaxed vertical mouth/lip position.

Exercise 8-1   VERTICAL MOUTH/LIP SINGING POSITION

Place both hands vertically on both cheeks and the chin so that the jaw is slightly lowered and lips are relaxed and oval shaped, somewhat as when exclaiming in great surprise, "Oh, my!" While vocalizing on scales and arpeggi using all vowels, you should think of elongating more when singing into the higher range. This translates into an increased jaw drop and a more open, vertical lip and mouth position. The important objective is to strive for a natural, forward-placed tonal focus that is balanced with a relaxed, vertical position. While doing this exercise, maintain the inner-smile position to counter a tendency toward "dead-panning" or a "hung jaw."

find natural, comfortable position

Tone Placement and Focus

Without getting too technical, it is important to know that overtones are involved in the perception of focus. In the sound spectrum of any instrument there exists clusters of energy frequencies known as **formants** that produce specific tonal characteristics. For instance, specific configurations of formants make it possible for us to discern the subtle or not-so-subtle differences between various instruments, voice types, or speech phonemes. Remarkably, the well-trained human voice is identifiable by the third formant, or "singer's formant," which ranges in frequencies from 2,500–3,200 Hz. Thanks to this special formant, a singer is capable of being heard when singing with a large orchestra.

The terms *tone placement* and *focus* are frequently used by advanced singers in describing their physical sensations, which are actually sympathetic vibrations emanating from the vocal resonators. In general, tone placement is more concerned with *where* the tone is sensed, while focus is more concerned with *how* the tone is produced. In other words, **placement** describes the localization of sensations within an appropriately aligned vocal tract, usually in the facial mask, while **focus** describes an efficiently produced vocal tone that maximizes vibrational sensations, achieved by coordinating efficient vocal-fold vibration and breath flow. In vocal terms, while placing the sound in the head might result in a perceived tonal improvement, the quality might be fuzzy—unless it has focus. For this reason, most voice experts acknowledge two concepts of focus, both of which are necessary for a complete understanding of this phenomenon: (1) *phonation focus,* the result of efficient vocal-fold closure or onset that continues throughout the vocalized tone and (2) *resonance focus,* which is based on vocal tract vibrations and sensations.

Some of the more popular suggestions for establishing vocal tract alignment are to imagine and imitate (1) taking a drink of water, (2) smelling a rose or something odorous, (3) smiling inwardly (suppressed smile), (4) beginning to sneeze, (5) beginning a pleasant yawn-sigh, and (6) holding your breath while swimming underwater. All of these suggested images depict reflexive actions, and all help to align the musculature and organs of the vocal tract by subconsciously causing the soft palate to lift, the anterior-posterior faucial pillars to stretch, and the larynx to lower. The objective of these stretching actions is to achieve both a relaxed throat and a desirable vocal tract alignment. The famous singer and pedagogue Lilli Lehmann (1848–1929) compared this sensation to having a saddle over the bridge of the nose. Other singers have described the sensation as one of tension, similar to that of a drumhead being tightened over the bridge of the nose.

The imagery that the voice is actually initiated in the mask may help to alleviate excessive efforts of throat muscles and articulating organs. However, caution should be exercised in the process of intense mental concentration. One must not force, push, stick, or drive the tone into the mask. Instead, the tone should be allowed to "exist" or "hang" there, while simultaneously releasing all tensions, especially the tongue, jaw, and neck musculature.

This "height" of head-tone sensations may be said to lie approximately at the roof of the mouth, extending from the **hard palate** (at the front) to the **soft palate** (at the back), depending on the pitch or vowel vocalized. The focal area lies in the region of the eyes, but sensations might also occur at the hard palate, predominantly when singing in the low to medium-low range. The direction of focus may appear to move gradually backwards toward the soft palate as one ascends to the very top notes of the singing range. Some singers describe the sensation of singing very high pitches as coming from "out of the top of the head" or even occasionally from "back and down" (as the throat opens). Other singers report that under right conditions, the illusion is that "the tone is singing itself, out in front of the mask." As these examples of singing terminology show, there are several ways of using imagery to describe tone placement, which are mostly determined by a singer's unique physiognomy.

Usually, when tone placement is right, the vocal folds vibrate efficiently. However, this is not always so, for one can still have either a pressed or breathy phonation in tandem with a high tone placement. In some cases, it may be necessary to concentrate on achieving an efficient focus at the vocal-fold level (see Chap. 6). In addition to the yawn-sigh and the staccati and marcati exercises listed, vocal-fold closure (**adduction**) can also be achieved by humming and vocalizing on the nasal consonants "m," "n," and "ng" and the "nasty vowels" (see Chap. 9). Vocal exercises based on "moaning" and "whining" will also help induce a complete vocal-fold closure. More drastic measures can be induced by mimicking the nasal twang of a hillbilly singer, the twang of an electric guitar, or the wicked nasal laugh of the Penguin (Batman's nemesis). In all cases, one should be careful never to feel excessive muscular tensions in the soft palate, throat, tongue, and jaw.

Exercises 8-2 and 8-3 should be sung with a relaxed jaw and tongue and with a very forward, narrow (vertical) inner-smile sensation in the upper mouth area. (Again, singers should be guided in performing exercises correctly. If, for instance, the "ng" is produced with a tense tongue or a dark/backward concept, the tone will sound stressed.) The tonal concept should be that of an unpressed moan, whine, or siren. Both exercises can be sung in all the keys encompassing a comfortable vocal range. The same techniques can also be used with any number of scales and arpeggi, especially the 1-3-5-3-1 and 1-3-5-8-5-3-1 arpeggi and the nine-tone scale.

Exercise 8-2

Ng _____

Exercise 8-3

Ng _____

Resonance Assessment

Acoustics.   Are you aware of the acoustics of different kinds of spaces, as in a "live" or "dead" room? Do you have a practical understanding of the relationship between the science of sound and voice? Do you find acoustics irrelevant and boring, or interesting, stimulating, and informative? Do you think a knowledge of acoustics will make you a more informed and better singer? What are the three elements of any musical instrument? What are the properties and characteristics of sound and musical tone? Do you understand overtones and how they influence the quality of vocal tone?

Resonators.   How do shapes and sizes of resonators affect the tone quality and pitch? Do surface and composition textures affect tone quality and pitch? What are the main resonators in the human vocal mechanism? Of what significance is the resonance created in the nose, chest, throat, mouth, and sinuses? What roles do the tongue, jaw, and other articulating organs play in resonance? What are the normal positions of the larynx, tongue, pharynx, jaw, and lips in singing?

Tone Placement.   What are the two kinds of focus? Do you sense vibrations in the mask when you sing? Do these sensations change as you sing from low-to-high range and from soft-to-loud dynamics? Are you conscious of letting go of extraneous tensions in the jaw and tongue when singing? How would you describe sensations you feel when singing is difficult and when it's easy?

9

Voicing Vowels and Consonants

Communicating through Language

Visitors to foreign countries quickly discover to what extent communication is hindered without rudimentary language skills. Language greatly influences how people relate to one another and to the world at large. As the early twentieth-century Viennese philosopher Ludwig Wittgenstein so succinctly said: "The limits of my language stand for the limits of my world." On the singing journey, the singer whose artistic intent is to stir people's emotions learns that the value of being well-grounded in all aspects of language opens up a more extensive, colorful palette of expressive means.

We have said that every musical instrument has three elements in common. The violin, for example, has (1) an actuator (bow), (2) a vibrator (strings), and (3) a resonator (soundboard). In addition to these three elements as found in human voice production (breath, vocal folds, and resonating cavities), the fourth, an articulator, includes all movements and adjustments of the speech organs for shaping and producing an infinite variety of sounds. It is this particular function that makes the human voice unique compared to other musical instruments.

[handwritten margin note: try to use front of tongue, less back of tongue "la" "bee-dee" – looser tip of tongue]

Linguistic Terminology

When discussing effective speech and language communication, the terms *articulation, enunciation, pronunciation*, and *diction* are sometimes used interchangeably, often without attention to precise technical denotation. As the following definitions demonstrate, however, each term represents a specific aspect of expressive linguistic communication.

1. **Articulation** refers to the mechanics of producing speech sounds. Specifically, articulation includes the movements and adjustments of speech organs (lips, tongue, jaw, velum, cheeks, larynx) in pronouncing a particular speech sound, called a **phoneme,** in its entirety. For example, the sound "ng" requires the lowering of the soft palate (velum), which directs the sound into the nasal passages, and the raising of the body of the tongue to the velum, effectively closing the passage into the mouth. More generally, articulation also includes connecting phonemes (*vowels* and *consonants*) to form words in the fluent and cohesive manner dictated by the language being spoken or sung.

2. **Enunciation,** a less frequently used term, refers to the act or manner of pronouncing syllables, words, or sentences in an articulate manner. Enunciation is also associated with definite statements, declarations, or proclamations.

3. **Pronunciation** is the act or result of uttering phonemes, syllables, words, and phrases in a particular manner according to accepted standards. In American English, for example, though the word "poor" is generally pronounced as "oo" throughout most of the United States, in certain regions it is pronounced "oh," as in "pore." In singing practice, the former ("oo") is accepted as standard pronunciation, although exceptions are found in folk and pop music where regional dialects are more common.

4. **Diction** refers to the prevailing standards of word usage and pronunciation in a comprehensible manner and style. For example, a singer is said to have excellent diction when a listener hears and understands every word and phrase of a song text expressively presented.

How words are uttered and expressed is largely determined by a particular language's general characteristics. Each language has its own peculiar sounds, expressions, and inflections that comprise its identity. A language is often recognized by its unique pronunciations (generally referred to as "accent"). When speaking a foreign language, for instance, most people normally have difficulty disguising their "foreign accent," because of a lack of genuine, native pronunciation, word treatment, and expression.

Primary Singing Languages

Singing experts concur that the four languages in which American classical singers are expected to be proficient are English, Italian, German, and French. These four languages are considered the most vital because of the vast vocal repertoire composed over the past 300 years in the United States, Britain, Italy, Germany, and France. Some brief observations for the student follow.

Native Language (English)   Assuming one has good speech habits, the beginning student's native language usually affords the greatest ease and facility. Thus, the North American student is more comfortable singing in "American English," a general North American dialect similar to that used by the typical national TV or radio newscaster. Except for occasions when a certain style and character of vocal dialect is required for authenticity, singers normally avoid such regional vocal mannerisms as southern drawl, eastern Brooklynese, and midwestern twang.

Italian and Latin   Novice singers usually begin foreign language singing with Italian or Latin because of its simplicity and ease of execution. Since Italian contains a minimum of vowel and consonant phonemes and makes generous use of pure vowels, its relative simplicity encourages efficient vocalism. Latin, the classic language from which contemporary Italian evolved, is used primarily in sacred texts, with either Italian or German pronunciations. Spanish is also quite similar to Italian and Latin in basic pronunciation. Using these languages can challenge the student with fresh, uncomplicated concepts about phoneme formation, a practice that can circumvent incorrect habits in one's native language.

German   Though English is somewhat more complex than German (mostly because of multilanguage derivations), both languages employ a variety of consonants. The German *umlaut* vowels—[ø], [œ], [y], and [ʏ]—add color and warmth to the voice. German is stereotypically thought of as a guttural, harsh language, but this is not the case when it is spoken in a cultured, expressive manner.

French   The French language is noted for its fluidity, which results from the merging of vowels and consonants, flowing together to create legato singing style. The plentiful use of the French nasal vowels—[ɛ̃], [ɑ̃], [õ], and [œ̃]—help in adding nasal resonance to the voice. As in German, the "mixed vowels"—[ø], [œ], [y], and [ʏ]—also provide extra colors in the overall tonal spectrum.

Most European languages share the same basic vowels and consonants, with some notable exceptions. For example, the [ɪ] vowel—as in the English word "lip"—is never used in Italian and Spanish, occasionally used in German, and rarely used in French. Also, some consonants are treated differently, such as [p] and [t] which are more imploded (less air) in Italian and French, but more exploded (more air) in English and German. Becoming aware of the differences in these languages will help a singer gain greater sophistication in foreign language diction.

Introduction to Vowels

Up to this point all vowels and consonants have been presented in their standard usage format ("ee," "ah," "oo," etc.). This chapter introduces the International Phonetic Alphabet (IPA), a worldwide standardized system for transliterating all speech sounds into phonetic symbols that can be read and translated back into uniform sounds of speech. Since IPA symbols are merely close approximate representations of phonemes, users need to be aware that, among the world's many languages, there are subtle differences of pronouncing certain phonemes. Though an initial exposure to the IPA might seem bewildering, most people find the system easy to learn and easy to apply in vocal study.

Figures used in this chapter will illustrate all of the IPA vowels and consonants used in English, Italian (I), French (F), and German (G). In all *word* IPA figures, the phoneme illustrated is italicized; for example, "ee" is illustrated as "s*ea*t." In the text IPA symbols are enclosed in brackets; for example, "ee" is symbolized as [i]. Figure 9-1 contains all the basic vowel symbols used in the primary singing languages.

Vowels may be thought of as the different tonal colors or timbres that can be produced with no constrictions in the vocal tract. Most scientists concur that effective vowel resonation is dependent upon tuning the vocal tract cavities, either separately or as a single unit. Since each vowel is recognized by the human ear as having specific acoustical properties—created by a unique configuration of the vocal tract—slight adjustments within this delicately balanced tonal system produce the entire spectrum of vowels used in all languages. Since most singing occurs on vowels, vocal study usually begins with the student practicing accurate vowel formation, which provides a firm foundation for producing efficient vocal tone.

Vowel formation is a complex activity involving shaping of the resonators by the articulators (jaw, tongue, lips, teeth, etc.), which in turn produces certain overtone structures characteristic of specific vowel sounds. Factors that determine the subtle differences in vowel formation are: (1) individual vowel characteristics, (2) individual differences in articulating organs, (3) gender differences, (4) range of vocalization, (5) peculiar dialects or accents, (6) intended emotional effects, and (7) dynamic levels. Given all the above factors, singers must strive to produce the most efficient vowels possible.

Vowels can be better understood by looking at such characteristics as pitch, timbre, and action of the articulating mechanism (tongue, jaw, and larynx). All of the following characteristics can be experienced by singing the suggested vowel sequence slowly on a single, sustained, comfortable pitch.

Figure 9-1. Basic English and Foreign Language Vowels

Basic Phonemes	IPA Symbol	English	Italian	German	French
ee	[i]	seat	si	sie	hiver
ih	[ɪ]	sit		immer	
ay	[e]	day	vero	leben	été
eh	[ɛ]	get	belle	denn	clair
	[æ]	back			
ah	[a]				parle
	[ɑ]	father	casa	Mann	ras
aw	[ɔ]	crawl	gloria	kommt	folie
uh	[ʌ]	shut			
oh	[o]	tone	dove	so	hôtel
	[ʊ]	look		und	
oo	[u]	soothe	sua	zu	boule

Pitch Perception and Timbre

While singing a sequence of vowels from [i] to [u] on a single pitch, one perceives the higher frequencies of the [i] vowel's second formant as a brighter timbre, while subsequent vowels gradually appear lower as one sings through [e], [ɑ], [o], and finally [u], which sounds the lowest because lower formants predominate. The vowel sequence can be reversed, beginning with [u], a darker, lower-pitched timbre, and ending with [i], a brighter, higher-pitched timbre. Exercises 9-1 and 9-2 will help illustrate the phenomena of pitch perception and timbre.

Exercise 9-1   STAGE WHISPERING AND CHEEK THUMPING

In order to better understand the effects of formant frequencies in the absence of vocal-fold vibration, use a stage whisper to produce the vowel sequence [i-e-ɑ-o-u]. Next, whisper from [i] to [u] back and forth at various speeds to observe the changes in pitch. You can also experience this acoustical phenomenon by thumping on your cheeks with your index finger while shaping the articulators for each vowel, again using the [i-e-ɑ-o-u] sequence. Then try it from [i] to [u] back and forth, and notice the pitch change. What interval do you hear? Find the pitch on a keyboard instrument.

Exercise 9-2   ADJUSTING VOWELS MANUALLY AND WITH LIP ROUNDING

You can experience how vowels can affect timbre by adjusting the degree of your mouth opening while singing a particular vowel to manipulate formant structure. For example, while vocalizing a sustained [ɑ] vowel, cover half of your mouth opening with closed fingers. You will observe that the vowel quality becomes richer and, in fact, modifies toward [ɔ]. Next, try it with other vowels, noticing the change in vowel color. You can also accomplish similar results by rounding or slightly puckering your lips. Using sustained pitches on single vowels, begin the vowel without lip rounding, and change to rounded lips a second or so after you start. Does the resultant quality sound richer? Does the pitch also seem lower as a result of the lip rounding?

Tongue Positioning

The tongue is the most important factor in varying the size of the vocal-tract resonator for vowel formation, which occurs principally through high-low and front-back adjustments. For instance, the tongue moves through the vowel sequence from a high frontal position on [i], to a middle position on [ɑ], and finally to a high back position on [u]. Other vowels are shaped by graduated tongue adjustments between the [i] to [u] positions.

Exercise 9-3 helps explain how tongue positioning affects vowel formation. This exercise is most effective when using a mirror to closely observe your mouth and tongue action.

Exercise 9-3   VOWEL TONGUE POSITIONS ON [i-e-ɑ-o-u]

Place a clean finger on the central portion of the tongue and sing through the [i-e-ɑ-o-u] vowel sequence. As you experiment with singing this sequence of vowels on a sustained, comfortable pitch, you will notice that the tongue is frontally arched for [i] and gradually lowers and moves slightly backward as you sing toward [u]. You can also reverse the sequence, from [u] to [i]. Next, try other vowels, including those found in Figure 9-1. Be careful not to exaggerate lip or jaw movements.

Larynx Position

The larynx is in its highest frontal position on [i] and gradually moves through the vowel sequence to its lowest position on [u]. Under ideal singing conditions, laryngeal movement should be very slight, with the larynx remaining comfortably low throughout the vocal range.

Laryngeal positioning in vowel production is affected by activity of the articulators, namely the jaw, lips, and tongue. Sundberg (1977) reports several studies of singers showing that the larynx is lowered with rising phonation frequency, which coincides with increased jaw opening on ascending pitches. He also claims that lip rounding tends to lower the larynx, while lip spreading tends to raise it. Furthermore, depressing or relaxing the tongue (and jaw), especially when singing the darker vowels [ɑ], [o], and [u], will effectively lower the larynx; raising the tongue, especially when singing the brighter vowels [i] and [e], will raise it.

By experimenting with the cat's familiar "meow" (Ex. 9-4), you can experience all of the above vowel characteristics—subtle pitch and timbre changes and corresponding jaw, tongue, and laryngeal adjustments—as the vowel sequence migrates from the frontal vowel [i] to the back vowel [u].

Exercise 9-4   THE CAT'S "MEOW"

Simply mimic the sound of a cat by slowly voicing "meow" [m-i-ɪ-e-ɛ-æ-a-ɑ-ɔ-o-ʊ-u], first on a sustained pitch level and then using inflected pitch levels. You will observe that almost all standard English vowel sounds appear to be incorporated in this exercise.

Voicing Vowels and Consonants

Tense/Closed and Lax/Open Vowels

Since the basic vowels [i], [e], [a], [o], and [u] require a more active involvement of the tongue for shaping them, these are often described as either "tense" or "closed" vowels. Their counterparts [ɪ], [ɛ], [ɑ], [ɔ], and [ʊ] are termed "lax" or "open" because their formations require less tongue elevation. Figure 9-2 presents a comparison of the primary tense/closed and lax/open vowels.

Nasal and "Nasty" Vowels

The four French *nasal vowels*—[ɛ̃], [ɑ̃], [ɔ̃], and [œ̃]—are vocalized by allowing the velum (soft palate) to relax and the nasal port to remain slightly open, thereby allowing the tone to resonate more in the nasal cavity. Refer to Figure 9-3.

The less nasal vowel [æ], often referred to as the unpleasant "nasty" vowel (as in the word "nasty"), is used rather frequently in the English language, the American version being more nasal than the British. Actually the American [æ] is a close cousin to the French nasal [ɛ̃]. Both can be used in vocalises to develop more twang and ring in the voice, especially singers who evidence such vocal deficiencies as breathiness, weakness, darkness, or throatiness. Since it is sometimes difficult for students to initially vocalize the [æ] correctly, a competent teacher's guidance is needed. Some singers have a tendency to press or tighten pharyngeal and laryngeal muscles in an effort to create the [æ] sound, when sensations should be experienced more in the upper pharyngeal and facial mask areas. Singers can

Figure 9-2. Tense/Closed and Lax/Open Vowels

Tense/Closed			Lax/Open		
[i]		seat	[ɪ]		sit
[e]		gate	[ɛ]		get
[a]		crop	[ɑ]		father
[o]		mole	[ɔ]		mawl
[u]		shoot	[ʊ]		shook
[y]	(G,F)	Hüte (G)	[ʏ]	(G,F)	Hütte (G)
[ø]	(G,F)	Goethe (G)	[œ]	(G,F)	Götter (G)

Figure 9-3. Vowels Peculiar to German and French

IPA Symbol	Type	German Word	French Word
[ə]	schwa	Erde	je
[ɛ̃]	nasal		sainte
[ɑ̃]	nasal		blanc
[ɔ̃]	nasal		bon
[œ̃]	nasal		un
[y]	umlaut/mixed (F)	über	sur
[ʏ]	umlaut	Hütte	
[ø]	umlaut/mixed	schön	deux
[œ]	umlaut/mixed	Götter	fleur

gain strength, brilliance, and projection by vocalizing both [æ] or [ɛ̃], followed by [a] or [ɑ], and returning to [æ] or [ɛ̃], as illustrated in Exercise 9-5.

Exercise 9-5

IPA: [ɲæ ‿ ɑ __   ɲæ ‿ ɑ __   ɲæ]
      [ɲɛ̃ ‿ ɑ __   ɲɛ̃ ‿ ɑ __   ɲɛ̃]

Umlaut (Mixed) Vowels

The umlaut vowels may be thought of as a mixture of two vowels. For example: [y] is produced by shaping the mouth and lips for [u] and singing [i]; [ʏ] is produced by shaping for [ʊ] and singing [ɪ]; [ø] is produced by shaping for [o] and singing [e]; and [œ] is produced by shaping for [o] and singing [ɛ]. If this is confusing, be patient. It is normal for beginning singers to experience some difficulty in producing these mixed vowels (see Fig. 9-3). However, by listening carefully to native speech and singing, and practicing (with feedback from a teacher or tape recorder), foreign phonemes will eventually sound more authentic.

Neutral Vowels

The vowels that occur at the ends of words, plus many monosyllabic single words, are often thought of as neutral sounds, basically because they do not require prolonged vocalization. Such vowels present problems in singing, sometimes requiring a more Italianate [ɑ] vowel in lieu of the neutral vowels, especially on higher, sustained pitches. The [ə] vowel, sometimes referred to as "schwa vowel"—a Hebraic/German derivative—is frequently found in German (liebe), and French (je), while the "dull" neutral vowel [ʌ] is primarily found in English (e.g., "the").

Semivowels (Glides)

Semivowels or **glides** are a combination of at least two vowels that effectively merge to become one sound. Six examples are illustrated in Figure 9-4.

Diphthongs and Triphthongs

Diphthongs are double vowels, sounded together as a single unit with a primary emphasis on the first of the two vowels, which is especially emphasized when singing. Similarly, **triphthongs** are triple vowels sounded together as a single unit. Because French does not use either diphthongs or triphthongs, it is conspicuously absent from the chart below. Although there are approximately twenty-nine possible diphthongs and eight triphthongs, some of the more commonly used ones are illustrated in Figure 9-5.

One problem common to untrained singers is the tendency to give premature attention to the second vowel in a diphthong. In almost all instances the

Figure 9-4. **Semivowels (Glides)**

IPA		English	Italian	German	French
[hw]		*which*			
[w]		*suave*	*quando*		*oui*
[j]		*you*	*ieri*	*jahr*	*hier*
[ɥ]					*puis*
[ɝ]	(silent r)	*word*			
[ɚ]	(silent r)	*per*			

Figure 9-5. **Diphthongs and Triphthongs**

	IPA	English Word	Italian	German
Diphthongs	[ɪə]	*ear*		
	[ɛɪ]	*day*		
	[ɛi]		*sei*	
	[ɛə]	*air*		
	[ɑɪ]	*sigh*		*Mai*
	[ɑu]	*now*	*aura*	
	[ɑʊ]			*Haus*
	[oə]	*ore (oar)*		
	[ɔɪ]	*boy*		
	[ɔi]		*vuoi*	
	[ɔʏ]			*Häuser*
	[ou]	*no*		
	[uə]	*sure*		
Triphthongs	[ɑɪə]	*fire*		
	[ɑʊə]	*our*		

first vowel in a diphthong should be lengthened and the second vowel minimized, as illustrated in Exercise 9-6.

One diphthong syllable combination that American singers have problems with is the [uɚ], as found in the words *your* or *sure*. The tendency in some regions of the United States is to pronounce these words as "yore" or "shore." The English and general American accents require a [u] in lieu of [o] and only a hint of an [r], if any at all. Ideally the words are pronounced [juɚ] and [ʃuɚ]. Refer to Figure 9-7 for consonant phonemes.

Exercise 9-6

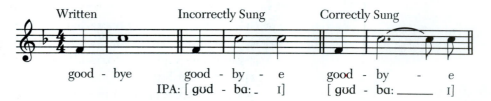

Vowel Modification and Efficiency

The laws of acoustics require that vowels be modified by slight physical adjustments, particularly when one is singing from low-to-high range. Although there is some controversy within the vocal profession regarding the concept of **vowel modification,** scientific and empirical evidence tends to support the concept. Vowel modification partly explains what happens when the voice is dynamically balanced throughout the vocal range—creating a tone characterized by both bright and dark qualities. Vowel modification is especially appropriate when used to counteract vocal tones that are strident, spread, or piercing in timbre.

Since singers spend most of their time singing vowels, it is desirable to produce the vowels as efficiently as possible, making the best use of all the factors that combine to produce the sound that reaches the ears of listeners. As discussed briefly in Chapter 8, singers try to align their vocal-tract formants with the overtones of the fundamental frequency of the vibrating vocal folds. Although singers must sing the pitch intended by the composer, they can manipulate their own vocal tract to a certain degree, trying to coincide the formants of the vocal tract with the overtones, a process known as *formant tracking* or *formant tuning.*

However, singers are also at the mercy of the composer or lyricist, who dictates which vowels are to be sung on given pitches. Therefore, singers' vocal tracts must conform to shapes that produce sounds recognizable as specific vowels. Tongue and jaw adjustments are limited to those that will produce the intended vowels, or whatever vowel modification the singer is willing to accept, which is especially problematic in the case of female singers singing at very high pitches. For acoustical reasons too complex to explain at this time, sopranos have difficulty singing recognizable vowels in their upper range.

Vowel modification occurs when negotiating the transition zones between registers (for example, between chest and head), reaching a crucial peak at the pivotal register transition point. The typical lyric tenor, for instance, will experience a major register event around $F\sharp_4$, at which time the vowel must be adjusted acoustically. The important point to bear in mind is that vowel modification will occur naturally when the singer maintains (1) a properly aligned body and vocal tract, (2) sensations of forward mask (head) placement, (3) a natural involvement of the articulating organs, and (4) sufficient breath management. When approaching the higher register transition zones, most singers, especially females, might find it more helpful to modify vowels toward more open, relaxed articulatory adjustments in conjunction with increased jaw dropping. On the other hand, male singers might benefit from closing the vowels as they sing through their upper passage zone. In all cases, however, singers should be cautioned against using manipulative tactics to superficially "cover" or darken the tone in negotiating register transitions.

Associated with vowel modification is the concept of the *pure vowel,* a term used by some teachers to indicate a vowel that is lean and unencumbered. Related to the pure vowel is the concept of *closed vocal timbre,* which is the opposite of open or spread timbre. One effective approach to achieving a closed voice timbre is to *think* of singing vowels in their most efficient formations—formations nearer to tense/closed vowel positions than lax/open ones (see Fig. 9-6). Some singers tend to pronounce vowels with a spread, "mouthy" position, which is contrary to the desirable high-placed head position advocated throughout this text. It becomes more possible for the closed vowel to be experienced by concentrating on closed vowels throughout the singing range—all the while maintaining a sensation of frontal resonance at the level of the mask (eyes, nose), hard palate, and alveolar ridge. Successful ventriloquists, by way of illustration, are masters at employing the minimal vowel to project a variety of voice types.

A good example of vowel clarity is the oftentimes problematic [e] vowel, which is usually pronounced as a diphthong in English in such words as "day" and "same." If one vocalizes "say" with the closed [e] used in German and French, it will be experienced in a higher mouth position. The same holds true for other vowels. This does not imply that the so-called open or relaxed vowels should be avoided, for one should have no problem making distinctions in subtle vowel colorings after establishing a correct concept of the "vowel-placement tract."

Singing vowels throughout your entire vocal range with consistent tone quality requires first a mental commitment to producing the intended vowel in its most natural yet sophisticated form. For example, an [ɑ] will resemble the bright/dark (balanced) qualities of Italian tonal preferences, and therefore will not sound like the darker [ɔ]. In general, more interior (mouth and throat) space and airflow are needed in singing high pitches, and each vowel needs more resonating space as one ascends in pitch. This action is accomplished by gradually allowing the jaw to drop or open depending on the vowel space required for each pitch. Throughout this process, the tongue is relaxed, the jaw is comfortably dropped, the pharyngeal wall is stretched vertically and laterally, and the larynx remains in a free-floating but relatively low position. Be aware that if too much tension-produced space is created for any given pitch, the result can be an overly dark, "weighted" tone. Of course the solution to problems caused by unnecessary jaw influence is to maintain a consistent high-placed head focus, effectively creating conditions for a freely produced tone.

Exercise 9-7 will help you experience the principle of vowel modification when singing from low to high and back to low range. Please note that this exercise is primarily descriptive of what appears to happen naturally, and not necessarily prescriptive of what a singer should do to achieve a balanced vocal tone with accurate vowel formation.

Exercise 9-7

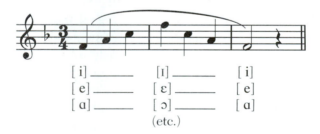

Vowels are also used to develop a legato vocal style. **Legato** literally means "bound," and in singing it means singing in a smooth, connected manner. Legato singing technique is based on the practice of sustaining pure vowel sounds by avoiding the prolongation of consonants (keeping them crisply energized), and postponing the final vowel of a diphthong by giving primary attention to the first vowel. Although it may take time to develop these skills, one way to achieve this "vocal line" is to practice singing all vocal literature on the textual vowel sounds minus the consonants. A phrase excerpted from "Amazing Grace" demonstrates how a singer can apply this technique to any song (Ex. 9-8).

Exercise 9-8

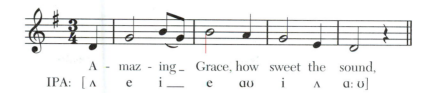

A - maz - ing _ Grace, how sweet the sound,
IPA: [ʌ   e   i __   e   ɑʊ   i   ʌ   ɑː ʊ]

Introduction to Consonants

Consonants are phonemes—other than vowels—produced by (1) closing—as with [p, b, t, d, k, g], (2) diverting—as with [m, n], or (3) constricting—as with [f, v, s, z] the air from the lungs by means of the speech articulating organs: lips, teeth, alveolar ridge, hard and soft palates, tongue, cheeks, and jaw. Consonants carry more "information" than do vowels since they clarify and reveal the meaning and expressive power of languages. Consonants also aid in voice projection by generating positive noise in the acoustic spectrum. The power of consonants to add meaning can be quickly demonstrated by speaking a sentence or singing a phrase of a song text using only vowels (see Ex. 9-8).

By voicing consonants in a greatly exaggerated stage whisper, followed by louder dynamic levels of speaking and singing, one can experience the expressive power of consonant articulation (see Exs. 9-9 through 9-12). Beginning students are very much encouraged to strongly energize and exaggerate consonant articulation, to the extent that listeners report distinctly hearing every consonant and word. This exercise is often very strange to novice singers, who are understandably shy and unaccustomed to exaggerated speech. The results, however, are almost always an improvement in both overall vocal tone and expression of text and well worth taking the risk.

Although consonants can be classified in several ways, the most logical way is according to "place" of articulation, that is, positions of articulating organs (lips, tongue, soft palate, cheeks, and jaw) in relationship to the stationary mouth parts (teeth, dental ridges, and hard palate). The other two major ways of classifying consonants are based on "manner" of articulation and **voiced** and **unvoiced** characteristics. These three categories are summarized below.

1. **Place of Articulation**

   Bilabials   Both lips working in coordination produce the consonants [p], [b], and [w].

   Labiodentals   The lower lip working in contact with the upper teeth produces [f] and [v]. Loosely closed lips are used for [m].

   Lingua-dentals   The tongue tip in contact with the upper teeth produces the voiceless "th" [θ] and voiced "th" [ð].

   Lingua-alveolars   The tongue tip in contact with the upper dental ridge produces [d], [t], [l], and [n]; also, the flipped [ɾ] as in "very" ("veddy").

   Lingua-velars   The tongue body in contact with the velum produces "ng" [ŋ].

   Lingua-palato/alveolar   The tongue blade in contact with the back of the alveolar ridge and hard palate produces "sh" [ʃ]; also the glide [j], as in "you."

   Lingua-palatals   The tongue blade in contact with the hard palate produces [k] and [g].

2. Manner of Articulation

Stops and Plosives   Consonants halted abruptly include [d], [k], [p], and [t]. Stops are at ends, **plosives** at beginnings, and stop-plosives in middles of words.

Continuants   Consonants with prolonged sound (voiced and unvoiced) include [f], [l], [m], [n], [s], [v], and [z].

3. Voiced and Unvoiced

Voiced   Examples of consonants produced by vocal-fold vibration are [b], [d], [l], [m], [n], [z], [v], and [g].

Unvoiced   Examples of consonants produced without vocal-fold vibration are [h], [f], [p], [s], [t], and [k].

Cognates   **Cognates** are consonants produced with the same place and manner of articulation, differing only by unvoiced or voiced characteristics. Some examples:

Unvoiced	*Voiced*
[p]	[b]
[t]	[d]
[f]	[v]
[k]	[g]
[tʃ]	[dʒ]
[θ]	[ð]

Chart of Consonants   The following International Phonetic Alphabet chart (Fig. 9-7) lists most of the consonants used in speech and singing, in their classification according to the three categories mentioned above. A key to the chart (Fig. 9-6) is supplied to familiarize you with the examples and symbols used in each of the six columns.

Figure 9-6. **Key to the IPA Chart of Consonants**

Column	*Key to Chart of Consonants*	
1. Consonants	IPA: International Phonetic Alphabet Symbol	
2. Word Example	**I** = Italian **G** = German **F** = French	
3. Place	**l** = lip	**l (2)** = both lips
	tt = tongue tip	**tb** = tongue body
	ar = alveolar ridge	**hp** = hard palate
	sp = soft palate	**te** = teeth
	ute = upper teeth	**lte** = lower teeth
4. Voiced/Unvoiced	**+v** = voiced	**−v** = unvoiced
5. Manner	**s** = stop	**c** = continuant
6. Other	**glides** (semivowels) = brief sound moving to another	

Figure 9-7. IPA Chart of Consonants

1. IPA Consonant	2. Word Example	3. Position	4. Voiced/ Unvoiced	5. Duration	6. Other
[b]	be	1 (2)	+v	s	
[ç]	hue, ich (G)	tb, hp	−v	c	glide
[tʃ]	church	tb, hp	−v	s	
[ts]	its	tt, ar, te (closed)	−v	s	
[d]	do	tt, ar	+v	s	
[dʒ]	gym	ar, te, tb, hp	+v	s, c	
[f]	fast	l (lower), ue	−v	c	
[g]	go	tb, hp	+v	s	
[h]	hot	glottal	−v	c	
[hw]	when	glottal, l (2)	−v	c	glide
[x]	Bach (G)	tb, sp	−v	c	
[j]	yes, iato (I)	tb, hp	+v	c	glide
[k]	kitten, cat	tb, hp	−v	s	
[kw]	quick, quando (I)	tb, hp	−v	s	glide
[l]	love	tt, ar	+v	c	
[ʎ]	foglia (I)	tb, ar	+v	c	
[m]	me	1 (2)	+v	c	
[n]	now	tt, ar	+v	c	
[ɲ]	onion, ogni (I) ligne (F)	tb, ar, hp	+v	c	
[ŋ]	sing, angola (I)	tb, hp/sp	+v	c	
[p]	pet	l (2)	+v	c	
[r]	rare	tb, hp (retroflex)	+v	c	
[ɾ]	caro (I)	tt, ar (flipped)	+v	c	
[r̃]	rapido (I)	tt, ar (rolled)	+v	c	
[s]	see	tt, ar, (te)	−v	c	
[ʃ]	she	tb, hp, te	−v	c	
[t]	to	tt, ar	−v	s	
[θ]	thin	tt, te	−v	c	
[ð]	this	tt, te	+v	c	
[v]	vine	l (lower), te	+v	c	
[w]	we, oui (F)	l (2)	+v	c	glide
[z]	zeal	tb, hp (te)	+v	c	
[ʒ]	azure	tb, hp, te	+v	c	

Sounding Consonants

All consonants can be problematic for certain individuals, especially in cases of speech impediments due to missing teeth, malocclusion ("buck teeth" or "over-jet"), cleft palates, TMD (temporomandibular disorder, also known as TMJ), and neurological ailments. However, there are a few consonants that seem to be especially difficult for many people to articulate correctly, notably "r's," "l's," and most consonants that end words. IPA symbols and word examples of all problematic consonants are found in Figure 9-7.

Typical Problematic Consonants

The "r" is classified as a semivowel and can be used in several ways depending on language peculiarities. For example, the rolled or trilled [r̃] is accomplished by air flowing over the top of the tongue as it touches the alveolar ridge, causing the tongue to flutter. It is used extensively in Italian, less so in German, French, and British English, and very infrequently in American English, except for dramatic effects. An example in British English would be the word *break* which sounds "br-r-r-eak."

The flipped [ɾ] is a single flutter that sounds somewhat like the substitution of a [d] for an "r" as in "veddy" for "very." Though rarely used in American English, the flipped [ɾ] is frequently used in most languages, especially when occurring between two vowels (as in the Italian word "amo*r*e" meaning "love").

The uvular [ʀ] sound, in which the velum is fluttered against the back of the tongue, is typically used in spoken French and by French cabaret singers. It is almost never used in singing classical song repertoire or in refined dramatic speech. This throaty consonant is related to the uvular "ch" [x] that occurs at the end of the German word "ach" [ɑx].

Finally, the retroflex [ɝ] or [ɚ] sound which is characteristically midwestern American, can sound rather unpleasantly twangy when prolonged; for example, the word *are* becomes "ar——," which is called *rhotacizing* in linguistic circles. One can improve its quality by minimizing it or quieting it down, perhaps even thinking more toward a neutral vowel such as [ɜ] as in "word." It should be noted, however, that, as unpleasant as this sound is in producing standard diction, it has its merits as a tone-building device. For instance, when the articulators are relaxed and ample resonating space is provided, the retroflex "r" can help develop the desirable high-placed, frontal mask sensations discussed earlier.

The "l" is a particularly obvious problem for certain regional Americans who tend to "swallow and wallow" in it. The movie actor Jimmy Stewart has typified this problematic consonant in a rather endearing way. In contrast, the European [l] is produced with the tongue tip placed forward on the upper dental (**alveolar**) ridge rather than on the front of the hard palate. The tongue and jaw exercises (Exs. 7-2a,b) use the "lah-lah-lah" technique to help achieve a high, forward-placed tongue in articulating a proper [l]. Even when singing English, the singer is encouraged to use the more European pronunciation in lieu of the backward-placed American version.

Most singers exhibit some minor difficulties articulating all consonants clearly, regardless of when or where they occur. Typically, however, there seems to be a preponderance of slip-ups when sounding final consonants. For example, [d] is often weakly voiced or eliminated altogether, and when voiced, is often voiced as [t]. This practice changes the word God [gɔd]) into [gɔt] which is correctly pronounced only if one is singing in German. (The American pronunciation of *God* is usually more toward an [ɑ] vowel instead of the more acceptable [ɔ] vowel.) Another final-consonant problem can occur when ending strongly by adding an extra syllable. For example, "soun*d*" becomes [sɔundʌ] and "mine" becomes [mɑːinʌ]. It takes practice to articulate precisely without adding a pronounced extra syllable.

Some singers, particularly in the U.S. Midwest, tend to omit the final "ng" [ŋ] in such words as "sing*ing*" by substituting "een" [in] for the final syllable.

Like many other diction problems, these habits take awareness of the specific problem and lots of practice to rectify.

Voice-Building Consonants

The value of consonants in assisting and enhancing correct voice functioning has been discussed previously in this book, particularly the use of the nasal consonants [m], [n], [ŋ], and [ɲ] (Chap. 8) for inducing nasal resonance or head placement; [j], [l], and [r̃] for developing a flexible tongue and jaw (Chap. 4); and [h] for achieving a healthy, relaxed, nonpressed vocal onset (Chap. 6). Other consonants helpful in freeing the articulators and causing the natural voice to emerge are [bl] as in "blah" and [fl] as in "flah." The voiced consonants [ð] "th," [z], and [v] are useful in inducing both sufficient airflow and mask sensations, and [g] and [k] are particularly good for exercising soft palate and tongue coordination. In addition, there is a difference in the acoustic energy of consonants. For example, the relative acoustic power of the consonant [r̃] is 200 times as intense as [θ], which is the weakest.

All of the above consonants can be coupled with the primary vowels in vocalises based on the musical scales and arpeggi listed earlier throughout this book, for instance: 5-4-3-2-1; 1-5-4-3-2-1; 1-2-3-4-5-4-3-2-1; 1-3-5-3-1; 1-3-5-8-5-3-1; 1-2-3-4-5-6-7-8-9-8-7-6-5-4-3-2-1. All exercises can be sung in various tempi (slow, moderate, and fast), dynamics (soft, moderately loud, and loud), and styles (legato, staccato, and marcato).

Though the possible combinations of vocalises are extensive, it is best to limit most vocalizing to a few simple scales and arpeggi for warming up the voice. Then, to continue giving attention to specific technical objectives, one can treat suitable song repertoire as vocalises by singing the vocal line with various vowel and consonant combinations. For example, if your major problem is related to jaw and tongue tension, it might help to sing the entire song on "blah" or [bl] in conjunction with the primary vowels [i], [e], [ɑ], [o], and [u]. Or, if tonal placement is too dark and in the throat, it might work best to sing the song using various combinations of nasal consonants in conjunction with vowels (e.g., "nyahm" [njɑm] or "ming" [miŋ]). Although most singers will benefit from traditional generic vocalises, one should invent or tailor vocalises for unique, individual problems.

Suggestions for Improving Diction

How does one set about developing good singing diction? In general, overall diction will improve as you learn to release unnecessary tensions in the articulating organs. This muscular freedom is only a starting point, however, for you must make a concerted effort to master all of the elements of dynamic expression discussed thus far.

First, you must imprint an "aural image" of expressive diction. This can be accomplished by listening to vocal artists who exemplify the best singing diction in all languages being studied. Then, in a large space, use an exaggerated diction level while repeatedly practicing and perfecting all vowels and consonants until every phoneme is easily intelligible. But diction is effective only when you master the subtle points of expression, including dynamics, word stress, and meaning. The following exercises should help you become a more dynamic communicator.

Exercise 9-9   STAGE WHISPER

Whisper the consonants of a song text in an exaggerated manner, slowing down the tempo and prolonging the consonants.

Exercise 9-10   DRAMATIC READING

Read a selected song text aloud in a dramatic, oratorical manner with a fully supported voice. Concentrate on articulation, pronunciation, word emphasis, and interpretation. Next, chant the text on a single pitch and in the rhythm of the song.

Exercise 9-11   TEXTS WITH ALLITERATION

Practice speaking complex texts that employ alliteration to emphasize specific consonants. For example, use the familiar "Peter Piper picked a peck of pickled peppers" and "Sister Sue sells sea shells down by the seashore." Some excellent examples can be found in David Blair McCloskey's book, *Your Voice at Its Best* (1972).

Exercise 9-12   "PATTER" SONGS

Study a song with a text that requires rapid articulation, for example, Gilbert and Sullivan operetta songs. Prior to singing, recite the text aloud using suggestions in Exercise 11-6.

Exercise 9-13   MINIMIZING "JAWING"

To avoid overusing the jaw when working toward effective diction skills, try to minimize jaw movement by adjusting the jaw drop to suit the demands of dynamics and range. You can work on this by placing the top of one hand horizontally under your jaw to sense the amount of jaw movement; or even better, observe your jaw movements in a mirror. The important objective is to keep the jaw loose and floppy, never tensed or overworked.

Diction Assessment

Vowels.   Do you understand vowel characteristics as based on pitch perception, timbre, and tongue position? Are you aware of the subtleties of tongue and jaw positions on all vowel sounds as you speak or sing them? Do you allow the vowel sounds to be natural, without undue shaping of the mouth and lips? Do you understand the differences between open and closed vowels? Have you experimented with the cat's "meow"? Are you aware of singing diphthongs correctly when they occur on sustained pitches, for example, "*night*" or "*by*"? Are you aware of vowels being modified as you sing from low to high pitch range? Are you able to sing a song comfortably using *only* the vowel sounds of the words and not the consonants?

Consonants.   Are you aware of all the articulating parts of the vocal mechanism? Do you understand voiced and unvoiced consonants? Do you have any problems articulating specific consonants? Can you demonstrate how to use all the forms of the [r], particularly the rolled and flipped versions? Are you able to recite a song text without leaving out any consonants, especially the final "d's" and "t's"? Can you articulate an [l] with your tongue tip on the upper dental ridge?

General Diction. Do you have facility in languages other than English? If so, are you aware of both the differences and the similarities with English, notably how vowels and consonants are sounded? Which language do you most enjoy singing? Why? Do you understand the differences between the uses of articulation, pronunciation, and diction? Do you understand the difference between jawing and floppy jaw? When learning a song, do you make it a practice to read the text in a dramatic, expressive manner?

CHAPTER

Integrating the Vocal Process

Coordination in singing refers to the effective interrelationship and unity of all components of the vocal process—cognition, respiration, phonation, registration, resonation, and articulation—for the sake of expressive communication. Since each component is influenced by the functioning of the others, all must be considered and understood as parts of a whole, united in a single act or response. The miracle of this complex coordinated activity is that it occurs instantaneously, usually within seconds. The coordinated processes and their characteristic actions are summarized below.

1. **Volition.** The brain (thought or will) and body interactively transmit instructions throughout the body, resulting in an instantaneous chain reaction of neuromuscular responses.

2. **Respiration.** Air is inhaled and momentarily suspended in the lungs.

3. **Phonation.** Airflow, released by passive forces of exhalation in combination with action of the abdominal wall muscles, meets resistance by the vocal folds.

4. **Resonation.** The vibrating vocal folds excite the air column in the vocal tract (laryngopharynx, oropharynx, and nasopharynx).

5. **Articulation.** Finely tuned movements of the articulating organs produce vocal sounds that take shape as words.

6. **Communication.** Ideas, moods, and actions are expressed.

Only when the voice is well coordinated is a singer capable of dynamic performance in a wide range of musical styles suitable for his or her specific voice type. Hence, a balanced, flexible coordination, or complete "hook-up," is the ultimate objective of all aspiring singers.

Elements of Dynamic Vocalism

Though some aspects of a coordinated voice have been previously covered, we will now consider these additional characteristics: intonation, vibrato, agility, sostenuto, and dynamic flexibility.

Intonation

A singer who is "out of tune" is said to have poor intonation. **Intonation**—the ability to sing "in tune," or reproduce accurate pitches—depends on a well-tuned "musical ear." Vennard (1967) reminds us that intonation is highly affected by the ability of singers to tune their resonators with their fundamental frequencies, which helps explain why singers with good musical ears but poor technique can sing "off key." Concerning the so-called tone deaf person, there is mounting evidence that it may be possible for anyone to achieve a respectable level of in-tune singing, with patient, nurturing training, regular practice, and physical maturation.

Although out-of-tune singing is frequently attributed to faulty hearing, the reality is that a tendency to sing either flat or sharp in pitch is usually the result of one or more malfunctioning components of the vocal process (i.e., respiration, phonation, registration, resonation, and articulation) and is often difficult to diagnose. For example, "flat singing" is commonly caused by a lack of energy (airflow) or proper vocal-fold adjustment, but it can also be the result of "oversinging," as when using a heavy, dark vocal production. On the other hand, "sharp singing" can result from forcing too much air through the folds, another form of stressful vocalism. Such singing might also seem strident and "spread-toned." When the tone is properly coordinated, intonation is accurately perceived as being "on pitch," or "in tune."

Vibrato

Vibrato may be defined as the audible, regular pulsation, oscillation, or fluctuation of a single pitch that varies no more than a semitone or a third of a whole tone. Such a variation in pitch is normally perceived by the ear as a quality characteristic of the tone rather than a pitch deviation.

Vibrato occurs when the nerves supply impulses to the laryngeal muscles as an alternating current, creating movements alternating between muscles, one relaxing (**agonist**) and the other contracting (**antagonist**). This is combined with the activity of the breathing muscles and diaphragm, resonating cavities, and laryngeal cricothyroid muscles. As a result, vibrato is integrally related to pitch, timbre, airflow, and intensity (nerve energy).

Normally the frequency of vibrato pulsations is between 5.5 to 7.5 times per second. Any frequency pattern faster than 7.5 per second results in a **tremolo** or **bleat**, which is usually caused by a hyperactive manipulation of laryngeal muscles. A vibratory pattern slower than 5.5 is known as a **wobble** and is usually caused by overloading the voice or creating a "false vibrato" by pulsing the abdominal muscles. Irregularity in the vibrato pattern usually indicates some form of malfunctioning in the vocal process, such as hyperfunctional or hypofunctional muscular activity, emotional imbalance, physical and vocal fatigue, nervous system disorders, or vocal-fold injury.

Voices lacking a vibrato are usually described as breathy, dull, straight, spread, or yell-like. One explanation of vibratoless (straight) tone is that intrinsic laryngeal muscular tension causes the mechanism to be rigid or static instead of the relaxed and flexible condition necessary for proper vibrato functioning. This might suggest a good reason to avoid excessive use of straight-tone singing techniques often associated with pop music styles and some choral music.

Finally, one must be cautioned against manipulating vibrato patterns to satisfy personal tastes. According to principles of efficient vocal production, the natural vibrato pattern occurs only when appropriate conditions result in a well-coordinated voice.

Agility

Agility in singing is based on the singer's ability to negotiate musical challenges nimbly and quickly, including wide pitch intervals, coloratura (fast-note) scales and passages, and dynamic variations. A sensation of elasticity and suppleness must ever be present in the singer's technique to safeguard against potentially negative muscular tensions and to counterbalance the technical requirements of sostenuto singing.

One characteristic of agility is illustrated by the singer's technical ability to produce a **trill** (which can be thought of as an exaggerated vibrato), produced by rapidly alternating between two notes, usually at an interval of a major (whole-step pitch) or minor (half-step pitch) second (see Chap. 11). One way to understand a trill is to think of it as an exaggerated vibrato. Trilling is primarily an involuntary action, with the exception of the beginning and ending which are controlled. Trills should be practiced if for no other reason than to encourage agility in the vocal mechanism.

Exercises 10-1 and 10-2 are designed to help develop a trill. Both may be sung on all vowels, beginning with [ɑ] at middle-range pitches, then moving higher as one becomes comfortable.

Exercise 10-1

[ɑ]

Exercise 10-2

[ɑ]_ [ɑ]_   [ɑ]_ [ɑ]_ [ɑ]_ [ɑ]_   [ɑ]_

The ability to sing each note of a rapid scale (coloratura phrase) with agility and precise intonation requires total freedom of the singing mechanism. When sung at slower tempi, rapid scale work is normally felt as originating from the abdominal musculature. In contrast, fast-scale singing is associated with continuous steady breath pressure and a vocal articulation that seems to occur in the larynx as an almost involuntary flutter, somewhat similar to giggling. Ideally, one only has to think vowel and pitch when applying a steady breath pressure to the larynx in order to achieve an accurate execution of a fast moving scale. Although the practice of articulating an [h] on every note of a fast scale may be a helpful technique for the beginning singer, the advanced student is cautioned against it, except perhaps in extremely fast passages where the *aspirato* (using h's to articulate fast notes) technique can be particularly helpful.

Vocal exercises for agility include scale work plus fast tempi musical phrases from the vocal literature of such composers as Purcell, Handel, and Bach. The following vocal exercises (Exs. 10-3 and 10-4) illustrate types of scales useful in developing agility. Use [ɑ] and other vowels throughout both exercises.

Exercise 10-3

Exercise 10-4

Sostenuto

Sostenuto refers to the sustaining capabilities of the voice and depends on coordination of respiration, phonation, resonance, and articulation. Primarily because of the pervasive "beat" commonly experienced in popular music forms, especially rock, most beginning voice students are extremely challenged by energetic sustained singing. The long, sustained phrases in certain vocal compositions of such composers as Handel, Mozart, Verdi, and Brahms, for instance, demand high energy and skillful execution.

One of the main objectives of sostenuto singing is to find the delicate balance between using energy and remaining free of negative tensions. For example, when singing ascending vocal lines directed toward dramatic high notes, one is often tempted to over-sing. Conversely, when descending from high-note peaks, the opposite tendency of over-relaxing frequently occurs, resulting in a fizzling-out tone toward the end of phrases. Thus, the goal of every singer should be to sing or sustain the entire musical phrase with an eye toward the final note, never flagging in thought and physical energy.

The following sostenuto exercise (Ex. 10-5) may be sung on either a single vowel such as [ɑ] or a combination of vowels. Begin with comfortable medium keys and work up and down in various keys to exercise and stretch the voice throughout the entire singing range. The tempi might begin moderately fast and gradually slow down as greater muscular and vocal control is gained.

Exercise 10-5

The basis of sostenuto is *legato*, the vocal result of binding or connecting one phoneme and note to the next. When delivering a song text in legato style, for instance, singers are usually instructed to lengthen vowels and crisply articulate consonants in a smooth, flowing manner. However, vocal authorities are not in complete agreement as to how legato singing style is best accomplished. While some experts suggest that singers focus on vocal sound to shape and move a phrase, others concentrate on interpretive details. Both approaches are valid, but beginning singers are well-advised to concentrate primarily on achieving sostenuto with a secure vocal technique.

Dynamic Flexibility

Controlling dynamic levels is a prerequisite for artistic, expressive singing. Ultimately, the singer must be able to sing easily and effectively in all musical styles: **legato** (smooth and connected), **marcato** (strongly accented), **staccato** (crisp and detached), and ***aspirato*** (using h's to articulate fast notes). Again, the best way to achieve dynamic flexibility is through the performance of appropriate vocal literature. Moreover, exercises can be designed to incorporate all dynamic levels and styles, including sustained, arpeggiated and coloratura passages, as Exercise 10-6 illustrates.

Exercise 10-6

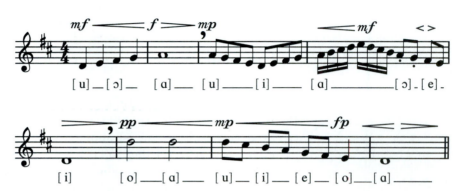

One of the traditional devices for mastering a wide range of dynamic variations is the ***messa di voce,*** which is soft-to-loud-to-soft singing on a sustained pitch while maintaining uniform timbre (see Ex. 7-4). The technique can be compared to what happens when a radio volume control knob is turned up and down, slowly and gradually, from soft to loud, then back to soft.

A singer's control over soft-to-loud-to-soft dynamics is determined principally by the ability to balance inspiratory and expiratory musculature. While maintaining the "gesture of inhalation," concentrate on frontal mask focus, coordinated vocal-fold onset, release of articulator tensions, and increased air pressure to sing louder. The trick is to start the tone with clarity and intensity at a low dynamic level, without pressing or forcing, and allow the tone to expand as it swells to the louder dynamic level. Diminishing a sustained tone requires even more concentration and coordination of inspiratory and expiratory muscles, with very little decrease in focused tone during the process. As adequate technique develops, you will discover that the mind will control vocal dynamics according to expressive considerations.

Young singers must be forewarned not to be overly zealous in practicing the *messa di voce* exercise on high pitches, especially in register transition zones at loud dynamic levels. Since the laryngeal cartilages are not secure until the singer is in his or her mid-twenties, loud singing should not be the primary objective. With time and coordination of the vocal process, the voice will continue to grow in strength and quality.

Range Extension

Although well-trained singers may be able to vocalize a three-octave range, it does not necessarily follow that their effective singing range will encompass such wide parameters of pitch. In fact, most singers manage to sing most of the vocal repertoire for their voice types by performing in a range that lies within a range of one-and-a-half octaves, occasionally stretching to two octaves for more demanding repertoire, such as coloratura soprano arias and contemporary vocal music encompassing extended techniques. The truth is that most singers are evaluated in terms of their tonal quality, not their singing range. Nevertheless, as a precautionary safety net, it helps if a singer can vocalize beyond the normal singing range, both high and low.

In general, the voice will extend itself when inhibiting tensions are relieved and vocal efficiency is established. In practice, the use of the high mechanism (head voice) will aid in extending the upper range while the low mechanism (chest) will help in extending the lower range. Below are some exercises for assisting range extension, all of which should be explained and monitored by a voice teacher. Singing the cardinal vowels [i, e, ɑ, o, u] on octave arpeggi (1-3-5-8-5-3-1) in various vowel combinations using low-to-high keys is recommended for most of these exercises.

Exercise 10-7 PITCH CONCEPTS

Since pitch is actually the frequency of vibrations per second, singers should be cautioned against thinking of pitches as being high or low. Yet, the concept of high and low pitches might be put to good use in stabilizing the vocal range. Suggestions: When singing high, think low; when singing low, think high. Visualize pitch on a horizontal plane, with the lower pitches near you and higher pitches out and away from you. Use your hand to depict this imagery by singing an octave scale ascending and then descending. Move your hand and forearm smoothly in (low pitches) and out (high pitches) in synchronization to the rising and falling pitches.

Exercise 10-8 JAW POSITIONING

When singing an ascending scale, the jaw should gradually drop, effectively enlarging the resonating cavity. This action is reversed on the descending scale until reaching the lower range, when, again, the jaw drop might be more necessary in order to allow the singing mechanism to function freely. The main thought should always be to let go of any tensions in the jaw by allowing it to drop and unhinge without force and tension.

Exercise 10-9 HIGH-LOW BODY CONNECTION

Concentrate on a high/low feeling when singing. This sensation of stretching incorporates the qualities described earlier in discussions of the bright-dark tone known as **chiaroscuro.** In terms of imagery, the "high sensation" is a tonal placement in the top of the head, as though there were an open dome for resonance, while the "low sensation" is an anchoring of tone to the supporting musculature of the lower abdominal area, primarily below the waist. Using this imagery, you will become more aware that "the body sings the tone." The octave arpeggio can be used in progressively higher keys.

Exercise 10-10 TONAL FOCUS

The changing direction of tone-focus as you sing up and down the scale has been discussed (see Chap. 8). Tonal sensations should be experienced in the mask area. It might help to be aware that the tone-focus for low notes is directed more toward the hard palate and gradually moves backward along the roof of the mouth (toward the soft palate) as you ascend into the top range. Rather than sticking or forcing the sound into any specific place, simply *allow* the tone to be sensed in the mask. Use the octave arpeggio in low-to-high keys while observing these tone-focus sensations.

Exercise 10-11   HEAD/CHEST REGISTRATION

In ascending a scale, concentrate on lightening the voice by using more head-voice registration. This process might need to be reversed for singers who tend to employ too much of the lower mechanism. In such cases, lighten the voice and refrain from pressing when descending.

Exercise 10-12   HIGH/LOUD PITCHES

When singing louder, particularly in the upper vocal range, increase breath flow, remain free of nonproductive tensions, and trust the vocal mechanism and ear to execute pitches accurately. Higher singing normally requires a relatively louder dynamic level, hence more breath flow.

Exercise 10-13   POSITION OF LARYNX

Although the larynx should remain relatively low and neutralized throughout the vocal range, there will be a slight lifting (caused by the upward pull of the cricoid cartilage in response to cricothyroid contraction) when ascending into higher-pitch range. The larynx should be allowed to float freely, and it should never be forced or depressed beyond its comfortable range of motion.

Classification of the Singing Voice

Do you know what type of voice you have? Because of potential difficulties associated with accurate voice classification, this delicate subject has been saved for inclusion at this time. According to all preceding information, accurate voice classifications can only be made when the singing voice is coordinated, which means functioning efficiently. Physical maturation will also determine when to classify the voice and what type of voice you may have. In fact, most voices continue to change throughout the aging process, which means singers must be receptive to possible reclassification.

The four primary factors that help determine voice type are (1) **timbre,** the color or tone quality characteristics, (2) **vocal range,** the comfortable extent of the singing range, low and high, (3) *tessitura,* the comfortable pitch level a singer can sustain for a prolonged period without obvious strain, and (4) **register** changes, the points of transitions or passages (pitches in the scale) where the voice changes when in correct function.

As considered from the highest to lowest voice types, most young singers usually fit the solo classifications of **coloratura-soprano, soprano, mezzo-soprano (alto), tenor, baritone,** and **bass.** Since most young singers tend to have mid-ranged voices (at least at the outset of study), the rarest types are coloratura-soprano (highest) and bass (lowest). Of course there are several other voice classifications reserved for mature, professional opera singers, presently beyond the scope of this text. As you continue your studies, you will become more familiar with these interesting types of singers, most of which are rather large-sounding voices.

Reconciliation of Opposites

Italian singing technique has traditionally been concerned with establishing efficient coordinated vocal function based on natural principles. The Italian masters coined the term **appoggio** (literally "to lean") to describe the sensations one experiences when the vocal mechanism, with its many parts and processes, is in dynamic equilibrium. Although most written sources refer to the importance of breath management as a central coordinating function, scant information is available about the literal meaning, "to lean." The concept of leaning into the sound probably derives from (1) the psycho-physical acts of concentrating the sound "forward" into the mask, lips, teeth, and hard palate, (2) lifting the chest and expanding the rib cage "outward," and (3) imaging the tone materializing "out there" beyond the singer's body. *Appoggio* represents the epitome of the reconciliation of opposites concept because precise mind-body functioning requires interdependence and synergy. In the words of G. B. Lamperti: "The singing voice in reality is born of the clash of opposing principles, the tension of conflicting forces, brought to an equilibrium" (Brown, 1973, p. 63).

Vocal Coordination Skills Assessment

Intonation.   Are you aware when singers are out of tune? Are you able to tell when and if you have pitch problems? Does it bother you to hear faulty intonation? What do you think causes it?

Vibrato and Trill.   Are you aware of your vibrato when you sing? When singing on a sustained pitch at various levels (low, medium, and high) and dynamic levels (soft, moderately loud, and loud), how many pulses do you count per second? Are you aware of vibrato when listening to others sing? Do you think it enhances the overall effect of the voice or does it detract? Can you tell the difference between a tremolo (bleat), a wobble, and a healthy vibrato? Using the two listed exercises (Exs. 10-1 and 10-2), are you able to sing a trill?

Agility, Sostenuto, Flexibility, and Dynamics.   Does your voice move easily when singing "runs" or fast-note passages, or do you find it difficult? What technique do you use when singing runs? How does it feel and how do you *think* you do it? Are you able to sustain a single pitch or musical phrase with a steady, flowing tone? Can you sing the *messa di voce* exercise on a single pitch with a change in dynamics and consistent tone? Are you able to change dynamic levels without changing your vocal production, or do you have to make obvious adjustments to do so? Can you sing Exercise 10-3 according to the suggested dynamic markings?

Vocal Classification.   Do you have an idea of what type of voice you have? Has some vocal expert suggested a voice-type classification with which you either agree or disagree? What criteria should you use in determining voice classification? Do you understand the difference between choral and solo voice designations? What voice types have you heard, and which ones are unfamiliar?

Vocal Coordination.   Do you understand the *appoggio* concept? What do you think of Lamperti's explanation of coordination? Based on what you experience when you sing, do these explanations make sense, or does the coordination process remain elusive?

C H A P T E R

Learning a Song

Basic Musicianship

To develop full vocal potential, the singer needs a solid foundation in the fundamentals of music. Ideally speaking, one should have basic musical training *before* undertaking voice study; but if you happen to lack music skills, you can learn as you proceed, provided you have the interest, patience, and discipline to stick with it.

Practical musicianship includes a working knowledge of five fundamental areas of music: (1) rhythm, (2) pitch, (3) harmony, (4) form, and (5) dynamics, phrasing, and articulation. If you are already proficient in music reading skills, you might prefer to skip this section.

Music Notation

Notation is a system of symbols used for writing, reading, and performing (playing) music. Using Figure 11-1 as a reference, you can associate terms discussed below with their corresponding line and space letters.

Figure 11-1
Treble and Bass Staves with Pitch Letterings

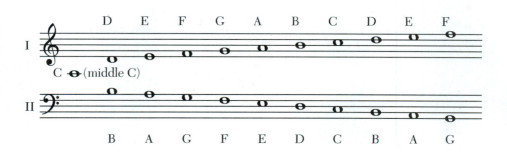

Music is written on a *staff* consisting of five lines and four spaces. Two staves (plural) appear in Figure 11-1, a *treble staff* (I) above, and a *bass staff* (II) below. You will notice that the two staves use different letters for the same lines and spaces. Since mnemonic devices facilitate learning and memorization, the letter names (representing pitches) of lines and spaces on both staves are presented. The following words should be read from the bottom lines and spaces upwards:

Treble clef lines:	Every Good Boy Does Fine.
Treble clef spaces:	F-A-C-E
Bass clef lines:	Good Boys Do Fine Always.
Bass clef spaces:	All Cows Eat Grass.

Rhythm

Rhythm is the whole feeling of movement in music in relation to time. Time values are signified by symbols (notation) that indicate length of beats occurring within a given tempo (speed). Figure 11-2 lists the most common note values used to depict both sounded values and their corresponding silent value (rests).

Bar lines are the regularly recurring vertical lines on a staff. They signify units of time measurement; hence, the spaces between these lines are known as *measures*.

Figure 11-2
Note Values: Sounded and Silent

Note Value Name	Sounded	Silent (rest)	No. of beats
Whole Note	o		4
Half Note	♩ or ρ		2
Quarter Note	♩ or ρ		1
Eighth Note	♪ or ♭		1/2
Sixteenth Note	♬ or ♭		1/4

Meters are used to indicate regular rhythmic **pulses** or **beats** occurring within measures. The meter designation is usually placed only at the beginning of a song, or at any measure when the meter changes. The top (first) number indicates the number of beats in each measure, and the bottom (second) number indicates the type of note that receives the beat. For example, in $\frac{4}{4}$ meter there are four beats to the measure, and the beat lasts a quarter note in duration (four quarter notes to the measure). The same procedure is used for $\frac{2}{2}$, $\frac{3}{4}$, and $\frac{6}{8}$, some of the standard meters found in music.

All of the above mentioned terms (bar lines, measures, and meters) are illustrated in Figure 11-3.

Figure 11-3
Bar Lines, Measures, and Meters

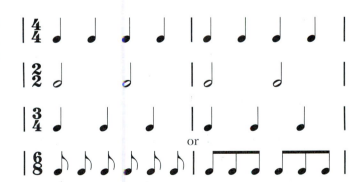

Learning a Song

Tempo (singular), or tempi (plural), is an indication of speed, slow or fast. Traditionally, Italian terms are frequently used to designate tempo, for example, **largo** (slow), **moderato** (moderate), **allegro** (fast), and **presto** (very fast). A tempo marking is usually given at the beginning of a piece, placed above the time signature.

Pitch

Pitch refers to the location of a musical sound in the tonal scale. The tonal scale, or arrangement of pitches upon which music is constructed, is notated with *key signatures*. These signatures appear in the first measure of each staff and are notated by means of *sharps* (♯) and *flats* (♭). Sharps are used to raise pitches by a half step, and flats, to lower pitches by a half step.

Thus, for example, if one flat is indicated in the key signature, it will be located on the middle or third line of the treble clef, which is the pitch B. This indicates the key of F Major (Fig. 11-4), which contains only one flat in its **scale** (a stepwise organization of rising pitches) that begins on F at the bottom, and continues through G, A, B♭, C, D, E, concluding with F on the top. This means that every B sounded within the key of F Major will be B♭ (the black note between A and B on the keyboard).

Figure 11-4
F Major Scale

F G A B♭ C D E F

Sometimes, particularly in the harmonic (chordal) structure, sharp and flat pitches are altered by means of lowering sharp pitches or raising flat pitches by a half step. The notation used in such cases is a *natural sign* (♮). A natural sign appears before the note and cancels the sharp or flat, thus returning the note to its original pitch.

Major scales and keys are represented by a series of pitches that include *half steps* and *whole steps*. The scale of F Major, for example, is constructed on whole steps (F–G, G–A, B♭–C, and C–D) with the exception of pitches A–B♭ and E–F which are half steps. This same configuration applies to all twelve major keys and scales; that is, all major scales have half steps between pitches 3–4 and 7–8. In Figure 11-5, a keyboard segment illustrates all eight pitches that comprise an **octave,** with the half steps indicated in brackets. Observe that the black key notes may be labeled either sharp or flat, depending on the key of the scale used.

Some of the more frequently encountered major scales in the Song Anthology are C, G, D, F, and B♭ (Fig. 11-6).

A minor key (scale) is often described as sounding somewhat sad. A good example is the English folk song "Greensleeves" (see the Song Anthology). **Minor scales** are distinguished by an organization of pitches that include a half step between pitches 2–3 (instead of 3–4 as in the major scale). The 6th and 7th pitches of the scale are flexible, capable of being raised or lowered, depending on the wishes of the composer.

Figure 11-5
Octave Keyboard
Indicating Whole
and Half Steps

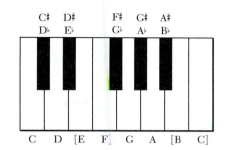

Figure 11-6
Common Key Signatures

C   G   D   F   B♭

An **interval** indicates the distance between two pitches. Since two notes of the same pitch are not recognized as an interval, they are commonly referred to being in **unison.** This term is often used to describe the practice of all instruments or voices sounding the same pitch simultaneously. For example, when a group of people sing the melody of a song together, they are singing in unison. Figure 11-7 depicts all pitch intervals, beginning with the interval of a second, and ending with an octave.

Figure 11-7
Pitch Intervals

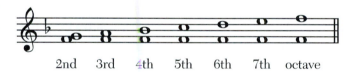

2nd   3rd   4th   5th   6th   7th   octave

Harmony

Harmony is the vertical or chordal structure of music that plays a crucial role in creating the overall effect of any composition. Harmony is constructed upon **chords,** which result from the simultaneous sounding of three pitches (*triad*) or more. Though there are numerous chordal configurations based on each note of a scale, the chord constructed on the first note of a scale is the most common. For example, Figure 11-8 illustrates a chord formed on the first note of the F Major scale.

Figure 11-8
Chord (Triad) Constructed
on the First Note of an F
Major Scale

Root
position

Harmonic progression is the rhythmic movement and chordal changes (strong and weak) that occur throughout a music composition. The most common chord progression here is the I–IV–V–I pattern (Fig. 11-9) consisting of *tonic* (first scale note chordal construction), *subdominant* (fourth scale note), *dominant* (fifth scale note), and return to tonic. Variations of this progression are frequently heard, especially in performances of **folk songs** and **hymns.**

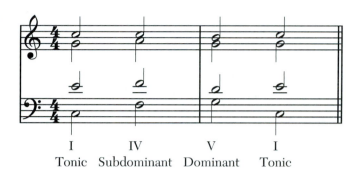

Figure 11-9
I–IV–V–I Harmonic Progression

I   IV   V   I
Tonic Subdominant Dominant Tonic

Form

Form exists in nature and in art. It is especially observable in architecture, notably in classical style. For example, most of the state capitol buildings throughout the United States reflect the classical ABA form. The middle section, consisting of the columned entryway topped with a dome, represents the B section, while the flanking and usually identically matching (balanced) wings represent the A sections. A similar kind of ABA structure is found in songs, for example, "Simple Gifts" (in the Song Anthology), which is discussed later in this chapter in the section related to song study.

There are several kinds of **song form,** the most common being the following:

Strophic   all stanzas of a text set to the same music, as with folk songs and hymns.

Two Part (Binary or AB)   two principal, contrasting but mutually dependent, sections that form a complete musical idea, both of which may be repeated.

Three Part (Ternary or ABA)   three principal sections, the first (A) and third (A prime) essentially the same musical idea but often modified. The **da capo** aria may also be considered a three-part form.

Through-Composed   new music for each stanza throughout the composition.

Dynamics, Phrasing, and Musical Articulation

When learning the basics of musicianship, you should give serious attention to some of the finer points of musical performance, including dynamics, phrasing, and musical articulation.

   Dynamics refers to degrees of loudness [(e.g., soft = **piano** (**p**); moderately loud = **mezzo forte** (**mf**); and very loud = **fortissimo** (**ff**)]. One related aspect of volume is that of **accent,** the amount of emphasis or stress treatment placed on specific pitches. Two symbols connoting variations of emphasis are **marcato** (>), which is heavily stressed and **staccato** (•), which is detached and crisp.

   Phrasing refers to the separation of melody into its constituent parts (**phrases**). It also refers to performing music intelligently with meaning, somewhat comparable to an expressive poetic reading. Musical **articulation** (which is different from linguistic articulation) normally refers to the subdivision of a melodic phrase into smaller units. Figure 11-10 presents a 3-measure phrase, with phrasing (a) indicated by an arching line over the entire three measures and the articulation (b) indicated by the shorter slur marks that connect the descending pairs of quarter notes in the second measure.

Figure 11-10
Phrasing and Musical Articulation

Once the ABCs of music are learned, the whole world of vocal music (like the world of literature for the person who learns to read) opens up to everyone who has a desire to sing. If you lack musical skills and wish to continue improving, you might consider enrolling in a music fundamentals course and/or a piano class. Should you immediately need additional materials and assistance, consult your teacher. One highly recommended music fundamentals text is *Understanding Music Fundamentals* by Phyllis Gelineau (Prentice-Hall, 2nd ed., 1992), a user-friendly publication which can serve as a self-study instructional guide.

Song Study and Preparation

Most professional singers approach song learning in a systematic way, with a definite strategy. In this section we will look at a systematic method which should be very helpful for the novice who is learning a song in a step-by-step manner.

First, any song you undertake to learn should be both musically and textually worthy. It should also suit your particular vocal and musical abilities, which usually means that the song should not be too difficult nor too demanding to learn. On the other hand, you may occasionally be ready for repertoire that will challenge and stretch you. Consult with your teacher for appropriate literature recommendations.

The most efficient way to learn a song is to study each component separately until it is mastered independently. This is in contrast to rote repetition, which is suggested for the final stages of memorization. A logical order of study might include the following steps.

Introduction

Begin by listening to the entire song, by either attending a live performance or listening to a recording—or perhaps in a read-through session with a competent pianist. In group instruction, it is beneficial to hear the song sung by the whole group in unison. As noted previously, you will have a better understanding of the song if you learn what you can about the composer and the textual source. A little research will reveal information concerning creative and historical aspects of the song, a practice that will increase your appreciation, interest, and enthusiasm for songs.

Component Study

Component study involves detailed examination of (1) text, (2) rhythm, meter, and tempo, (3) melody, (4) form, (5) voice, (6) harmony, and (7) dynamics, phrasing, and musical articulation.

Text   Begin by reading the text through silently for pronunciation, inflection, articulation, phrasing, and meaning. When you're satisfied that you understand the text, read it aloud, first in a normal poetic reading and then in a dramatic manner with attention to word emphasis and expression. Numerous repetitions will make you comfortable and secure with the text *before* voicing it to the rhythm of the song.

Rhythm, Meter, and Tempo   After checking the time signature ($\frac{6}{8}$, $\frac{4}{4}$, $\frac{2}{4}$, etc.), count aloud the number of pulses per measure ("*one*, two, three," etc.) with slight emphasis on the downbeat, or first beat of each measure. Now clap or tap the rhythm of each musical phrase until you have mastered the entire song. In the beginning, clap in a slow tempo. When you feel secure with the song's rhythm, clap it in the correct tempo. The important thing is accuracy, not speed.

Melody   After determining the key signature (treble and/or bass clefs), check the notated pitches either by playing them on a piano or by sight-reading them. Since you want to avoid unnecessary, careless singing, learn the melody by singing it mentally before vocalizing aloud.

Form   Examine the song for its underlying song structure: strophic, AB, ABA, or through-composed forms. Look for major musical sections, themes, and repetitions of musical material. Knowing the form of a song will help you to "frame" it mentally for learning purposes. For example, the arrangement of the folk song "Simple Gifts" reveals an ABA song structure. The A (first part) section begins with the piano introduction in measure 1 (m. 1) and ends with "love and delight" (m. 10). The B (second part) section commences with "When true simplicity" (m. 11) and ends with "comes 'round right" (m. 18). The return to the A section begins in measure 19 and continues to the end (**coda**).

Voice   Now you can focus on trying to achieve efficient vocal production with a fully resonated, physically supported vocal tone. First, sing through the song on a single vowel or a combination of vowels. Next, sing on the vowels of the words. This procedure will help you gradually build up to full-voiced singing, including the use of dynamic levels. At this stage it is not necessary to use an accompanying musical instrument.

Harmony   If your piano skills are limited, have an accomplished pianist record the accompaniment for you so you can hear and imprint the harmonic sounds into your memory. This will greatly accelerate your overall learning pace. Be aware of changes in harmony and tonality, and also of the nature and relationship of particular chords to the text.

Dynamics and Musical Articulation   Some dynamic levels will have been worked out throughout the process of studying, especially textual dynamics. Now is the time to give more thought to fine-tuning the dynamics and articulations as indicated by the composer's and/or editor's markings in the musical score.

Component Synthesis and Memorization

When all components have been mastered, you are probably ready to integrate them by singing the whole song with **accompaniment.** At this point you can use either a taped accompaniment or, better yet, a competent accompanist ("artist collaborator").

Although rote repetition is an acceptable way to memorize a song, three techniques are particularly helpful for enhancing recall. One is to select and memorize key words in each phrase to help trigger memory. Even more effective is to dramatize the song aloud in an exaggerated, melodramatic manner. Finally, you also can stage the song, complete with props and all imagined trappings (scenery, locale, supporting cast, etc.), in the manner of an opera aria. These "acting-out" techniques will aid you in creating a matrix of visual, auditory, and kinesthetic sensations, greatly facilitating recall.

Musicianship and Learning Assessment

Basic Musicianship.   Are you able to read music at sight? Do you have a grounding in music fundamentals, or is music like a foreign language to you? What general rating would you give your musicianship upon starting this course (excellent, good, fair, or poor)? After studying this chapter, do you have a better grasp of how music is notated and how to apply your newfound knowledge to reading and learning music? Do you appreciate the ability to read music in order to truly enjoy the substance of music and music making? What are your future plans for continuing to improve your musical skills?

Song Study.   Are you able to learn your songs after hearing the vocal lines several times, or do you have difficulty in learning them? Does the piano accompaniment "throw" you when you try to sing with it, or do you adjust quickly with practice? What musical experiences (instrumental study, band, chorus, etc.) have you had that have helped you with song learning? Do you systematically study your songs according to the musical components of melody, rhythm, meter, harmony, form, and dynamics? Have you tried using key words and staging (acting-out) techniques to facilitate memorization?

CHAPTER 12

Performing a Song

Style in Vocal Performance

At the highest level of proficiency in any art form (poetry, dance, painting, or architecture) we speak in terms of *style,* a characteristic manner or mode of expression. In vocal music it is helpful to distinguish between two kinds of style: style in composition and style in performance. Generally, one's performance style must follow the composition style. One's individual imprint is always there, but always in a proportion that allows the music and text to predominate. In the words of voice pedagogue Van Christy (1966), "The singer fits the style of the song, not the song the style of the singer."

There are many styles in vocal music. In vocal literature each particular style bears characteristic manners and modes of expression. For example, some popular musical styles familiar to contemporary singers are soft rock, hard rock, rap, easy listening, jazz, country-western, gospel, and musical theater.

Most of the vocal music performed today in the Western world was written in the last 600 years. These six centuries are usually divided (approximate dates) into at least five historical periods: (1) **Renaissance** (1425–1600), (2) **Baroque** (1600–1750), (3) **Classical** (1750–1825), (4) **Romantic** (1825–1875), and (5) Modern/Contemporary (1875–present). Because each of these periods exhibit uniquely distinct, musical stylistic features, the period of origin of an unfamiliar song can often be identified on the basis of its general musical characteristics.

In the notes preceding the Song Anthology (see the section "Information About the Art Songs and Arias"), some of the most prominent historic, national, and generic styles of vocal music in Western civilization are discussed briefly. Please consult the Bibliography for more thorough treatments and examples.

Expressive Use of Body and Voice

A performer is concerned not only with "what" is communicated but "how" it is communicated. How a singer communicates the inner feeling of a song brings us to a second vital skill in addition to musicianship: the ability to portray a song's poetic and dramatic content.

When performing, the singer is understandably preoccupied with producing beautiful vocal tones. But singing also involves language, and the primary literary genre of vocal literature is *poetry*—the language of imagination and intense perception. A thorough understanding of poetry (including denotation and connotation, imagery, figurative language, allusion, meter, tone, and pattern) can help the singer understand and express not only the sound, but also the meaning of songs.

Beyond poetic insight and feeling, singing calls on the ability to physically portray and communicate the inner drama of a song. It is not possible within the scope of this book to cover the field of acting as thoroughly as its importance to singing would justify. Therefore, three increasingly advanced level books by H. Wesley Balk are recommended for further reading: *The Complete Singing Actor* (1977), *Performing Power* (1985), and *The Radiant Performer* (1989), all published by the University of Minnesota Press.

Song Performance

Vocal performance can be divided into three stages: (1) preparation, (2) performance, and (3) postperformance.

Preparation

There is no substitute for thorough preparation of music to be performed in public. Whatever anxiety or *stage fright* you may feel prior to and occasionally during a performance, painstaking preparation is the best antidote. When dealing with stage fright, it is best to accept the normalcy of the affliction and to use the rush of adrenaline to your advantage. Peak performance preparation involves several factors associated with mind and body health. The following techniques will help you with "performance jitters."

General Health Stay healthy by eating and sleeping well and by avoiding overstressing the mind and body in advance of the performance. You need energy to perform well. Avoid depressants (alcohol) and stimulants (caffeine) as they will only aggravate nervous symptoms.

Positive Thinking Avoid negative thoughts ("I can't," "I'm scared," "They won't like me") by focusing on your desire to perform, the value of the performing experience to you personally, the aesthetic and expressive content of the song or songs, and the needs of your audience. Program your thinking with positive affirmations and with repeated visualizations of yourself performing well. See your audience enjoying the performance and giving you an enthusiastic ovation.

Relaxation Concentrate on your breathing by relaxing physically and taking slow, deep breaths while focusing on your "center," located 2 inches below the navel. By releasing physical tensions and slowing your breathing, your anxiety should dissipate gradually.

Performance

In Place Offstage Assuming all musical preparations have been made and physical conditions arranged (piano, piano bench, lights, and so forth), you are now offstage and standing ready to go on. Take a few moments at this point to concentrate on your entrance and to set the proper mood. Relax, take a slow, deep breath, straighten your posture, and tell yourself: "This is the moment I've prepared for with eager anticipation, and I'm really looking forward to it."

Stage Entrance As you enter the performance area slightly ahead of your accompanist, your bearing should be one of confidence and purpose. Walk enthusiastically and briskly to the crook in the piano. Bow graciously as if to say "Thank you for your welcoming applause. I appreciate your coming to hear me."

If there are no programs listing musical selections and performers' names, introduce yourself, your accompanist, and your selections in a firm, moderately paced, audible voice. Wait a few moments for the pianist to make preparations and the audience to become quiet. Concentrate on the mood of the first song and its message. When you're ready to begin, look up and out with an expression of anticipation toward communicating the song's intent.

Presentation   The song actually begins just prior to the accompaniment, with the mood having been set by your personal and physical demeanor. Since it is very amateurish to treat the piano introduction as simply "marking time" until you sing, you will want to be in character during every moment of the song, not only when you're singing. During the performance you need only to honestly portray what you feel the song is about. You don't have to *do* something. It's enough to let the song flow through you as though you are nothing more than a vessel, containing and then releasing the song's contents. In doing this, it will help if you are able to project your visualization and inner experience of the song. This will give you something upon which to concentrate so that your eyes will not wander aimlessly. What you see, the audience also will see. Or at least the audience will be aware you are personally experiencing something, whether it be an idea, event, emotion, or mood. As the song ends, maintain your concentration to the very end, carefully observing the amount of time you need to release the final mood. With a serious song, the release will be slower than with a fast, upbeat song. At the right moment, recognize the audience's applause by bowing graciously, saying under your breath, "Thank you very much." Recognize your accompanist and share a duet bow.

Stage Exit   After the solo and duet bows, exit briskly ahead of the accompanist to offstage. Should the audience continue applauding, briskly enter again with your accompanist to take another duet bow at center stage. The number of bows is normally a matter of sensing the audience's response. Extra bows are normally expected only when presenting an extended program.

Postperformance

Depending on the scope, nature, and outcome of your performance, you probably will breathe a sigh of relief for having survived the experience relatively unscathed. Your feelings at this point very likely will reflect your satisfaction or dissatisfaction with part or all of your performance. You also will review your performance based on the audience's general reaction and the comments made by individuals thoughtful enough to offer them. Although most people welcome constructive criticism in the right place and at the right time, the period immediately following a performance is normally reserved for well-wishers with their congratulations. The exception to this would be educational situations where immediate critical feedback is expected.

It is important that you maintain a confident attitude regarding your performance even though you may think it was not up to par. Though every minor mistake might have been painfully apparent to you, the chances are the audience didn't notice anything amiss. The point is to avoid volunteering nonconstructive critical comments about your performance and to accept congratulations graciously. Keep reminding yourself that now is the time to celebrate your courage, determination, and success in performing publicly. Celebrate the occasion by going out with relatives or friends for fellowship and refreshments. Give yourself a well-deserved reward.

When you are ready to be objective about your performance (the time will vary with each person), take a few minutes to honestly evaluate what happened. Ideally, you will have access to an audio or video recording of your performance, which is an invaluable way to study your performance from the audience's perspective. If you have a knowledgeable friend or teacher, someone whose opinion you respect, consult with them regarding your performance. Try not to take any criticism personally. Instead, look at your performance objectively with the eyes and ears of an interested observer. Ask yourself what went well and what needs improvement. Break your evaluation down into the areas discussed in this text: (1) *musicianship*—accuracy in pitch, rhythm, tempo, dynamics, and phrasing; (2) *vocal technique*—breath management, tone quality, and coordination; (3) *diction*—pronunciation and articulation; (4) *stage presence*—posture, poise, and specific body language; and (5) *music/dramatic presentation*—interpretation, style, and expression.

Don't be too hard on yourself in your self-evaluation. Be realistic in considering your present level of development and in forgiving your shortcomings. It takes a lot of productive time and energy to learn all the skills used in vocal performance. In short, you need to be patient yet persistent.

Continuing Your Vocal Study

Now that you've completed this course of study, you may be wondering, "what's the next step?" Depending upon your level of commitment, there are three avenues (levels of participation) you can take as a singer: (1) avocational, (2) semiprofessional, and (3) professional. Each of these categories offers opportunities for you to continue pursuing your love of singing.

1. **Avocational.** This category includes the majority of singers, comprising anyone who sings in community, religious, and educational musical/dramatic organizations on a volunteer basis. A "hobby singer" can be just as capable as any professional, provided he or she has the requisite talent and skills and is willing to devote the necessary time and effort. If this is your chosen level of participation, you will have lots of good company and loads of respect from all who enjoy listening to music.

2. **Semiprofessional.** There are many well-trained, experienced singers who have found a compromise situation between the avocational and professional categories that suits them well. These singers normally have part-time or even full-time nonmusic jobs that allow opportunities for evening and weekend professional singing engagements (e.g., church soloists, choristers, music/opera theater, and supper clubs). Such people may be highly trained professionals and, for whatever reasons, have intentionally chosen this semiprofessional status. For example, many vocal music teachers are included in this category.

3. **Professional.** A professional singer is one who pursues a full-time singing career that provides remuneration to cover all living necessities. Because of such factors as marketplace supply and demand, heavy financial burden, lengthy study and apprenticeship periods, enormous competition, and lifestyle, the professional should enter upon such a challenging career armed with an unwavering dedication and commitment to succeed. If you are interested in investigating this matter more

thoroughly, you should begin by seeking the evaluations and advice of several respected professionals.

Regardless of which of these three paths you decide to take, if you are interested in continuing to explore and improve your singing, you will need someone to guide and counsel you. Begin by consulting your current teacher for suggestions, securing a list of voice teachers in your area who are members of the National Association of Teachers of Singing, and inquiring among respected area singers for recommendations. Once you have narrowed your prospects down to two or three teachers, spend some time observing their students in action. Perhaps you can get permission from both the student and teacher to observe a lesson or two. What's important is your confidence in the teacher's professional expertise, personal qualities, and concern for your personal growth.

As stated earlier in this book, anyone can learn to sing, and since singing is one of the best disciplines for overall self-improvement, everyone can benefit from vocal study. If *Adventures in Singing* has aided you in the exploration, discovery, and development of your vocal talent, then the original goal of the book has been met. There is no greater satisfaction for a teacher than to guide others on paths leading to increased self-understanding and self-expression.

In the words of an anonymous sage: "Develop the wisdom to know yourself, and the courage to be yourself." Such advice certainly applies to the study of voice. May your unique voice adventure continue to be one of opening up to new possibilities in personal growth and fulfillment through a love of singing.

Performance Skills Assessment

Stylistic Skills. Do you have a clear understanding of what style is, and how it applies to performance? Do you have a unique, personal performing style? Do you try to present each song's style in performance? Can you differentiate among the various styles associated with musical periods and nationalities and between popular and classical vocal music styles?

Dramatic Skills. Are you an outgoing, expressive person, one who uses gestures and vocal dynamics when communicating, or are you reserved and quiet-spoken? Are you adept at pretending or mimicking the actions and voices of others, or do you find it difficult to "be someone else"? What stage experiences have you had with public performance? Are you willing to make a fool of yourself in the process of becoming a more expressive person? What kind of persona do you portray to the public, to your friends and relatives, and to yourself when alone? Do you study your songs with the objective of "acting out" the song's textual content in a staged practice presentation?

Performance Skills. When performing, are you able to concentrate on technical objectives and the communication of the song's meaning, or do you find yourself thinking about unrelated, distracting matters? Are you able to suspend self-judgment and self-criticism during performance situations, or do you constantly chastise and berate yourself for real and even imagined mistakes? Do you really *enjoy* the act of performing or is it just something you *have* to do? Do you maintain your concentration from the very beginning of each song to its ultimate conclusion, or does your focus tend to wander? Do you always remember to acknowledge your accompanist at the appropriate moment? Following the performance, do you accept compliments graciously, or do you offer excuses and apologies for your performance?

Future Study and Performance. Are you enthusiastic or disheartened about your vocal studies to date? Have you been encouraged or discouraged in any way during your studies? Based on what you have learned about yourself, what are your assets and liabilities as a singer? Do you have plans to continue your vocal studies? If so, at which level will you be content to function: avocational, semiprofessional, or professional? Have you sought professional guidance regarding your singing interests and talents? Do you have a plan of action for exploring your future as a singer?

Song Anthology

GENERAL INFORMATION

This Song Anthology has been assembled according to several specific guidelines, all of which have been adhered to as closely as possible. These guidelines are discussed below and include information that should help clarify how one can best make use of this Anthology.

Texts

In almost all instances songs may be sung by either female or male voice. In a few cases, for example, "Greensleeves," adjustments in wording allow for a broader gender reference ("lover" can be substituted for "lady"). The textual content is varied in subject matter and for the most part is high-quality literary material, representing such renowned authors as Shakespeare, Goethe, Heine, William Blake, George Herbert, and Ben Jonson. Where English translations have been made of foreign texts, an attempt has been made to be faithful as possible to the original language's word meaning, and at the same time to produce an English text that is singable—not an altogether easy task. The selection of a majority of texts in English, German, French, and Italian has been dictated primarily by the volume and type of vocal repertoire used by the North American singer trained in the classical vocal tradition. International Phonetic Alphabet transcriptions are offered in the last section of the Anthology.

Song Sources

Selection of songs by composers of English, American, German, French, and Italian heritage is necessitated by the expectations and demands for training singers in the European tradition of vocal education (which has greatly influenced the vocal music curriculum in the United States). The songs in this volume are representative of typical standard song repertoire, having proven with the test of time their pedagogical, musical, and literary value. There is a balance of musical styles from folk and art song to musical theater, and a variety of composers and arrangers are represented.

Vocal Objectives

Perhaps the most important guideline has been that of selecting songs that will assist with educational objectives, particularly in the development of appropriate technical skills. Careful attention has been given to selecting songs that allow for an easy to moderate level of vocal difficulty, essentially choosing lower to middle range voicings. The range of most songs is limited to approximately an octave or slightly more, and tessitura levels are comfortably challenging. Though keys of most songs are suitable for the majority of mid-ranged singers, there are some songs in keys for lower voices. In addition, a few songs are presented in both high and low keys. Since it is impossible to provide the ideal key for every song and voice, a sufficient number of songs have been included in the Anthology to provide some options for all students. Although an attempt has been made to select songs with a variety of tempi, dynamics, and melodic line configurations (scales, arpeggi), there is an intentional preponderance of songs with moderate demands. In most cases, phrases are of short to moderate length with breathing places indicated as either an optional breath [(,)] or required breath [,].

Musical Objectives

The inclusion of a variety of solo vocal musical styles representative of outstanding composers of the sixteenth through the twentieth centuries was the major guideline in selecting repertoire for this Anthology. Because individual instructional time is limited in voice class, most songs are brief and packed with musical substance. The piano accompaniment is usually supportive of the voice line, often duplicating it, and the harmonies are generally uncomplicated. An attempt has been made to keep the piano part simple enough for the average accompanist to master yet musically challenging enough to maintain artistic interest. The basic elements of music—song form, dynamics, tempi, meter, harmony—are provided in a variety of combinations to enhance both learning and performing experience.

Support Materials

To aid the student in becoming a more knowledgeable vocal artist, information has been provided about each song: (1) background data on textual and musical sources, (2) performance suggestions, (3) word-by-word translations, and (4) figures simplifying IPA transcriptions for all foreign texts. Cassette tapes and CDs containing piano accompaniments are provided as learning devices for study and practice.

other than European derivations are encouraged to share their traditional songs with the class, perhaps as the first solo vocal performance assignment. This is an opportunity to become familiar with each person's unique sociocultural background while broadening the musical horizons of all class members. Especially in situations where the class composition of ethnic backgrounds is widely mixed, this procedure is highly recommended.

INFORMATION ABOUT THE GROUP SONGS

As people have been increasingly lured into passive spectator participation in such fields as sports and music, group singing has declined as a social activity. Although at one time family members occasionally gathered around the parlor piano to engage in group singing, one rarely hears of such events today. Moreover, school music programs are being reduced or eliminated for economic reasons, resulting in less exposure to traditional group singing.

The question may well be asked, "What are the advantages of using group songs in a voice class situation?" First of all, group songs—especially **rounds**—are very easy to learn. This enables students to begin singing sooner, possibly during the first class. In addition to building group spirit, sharing the singing experience takes the pressure off individuals to perform solo in unfamiliar circumstances. The ease of learning and singing a very simple song gives the individual a sense of immediate accomplishment. It also allows the teacher and others in the class the opportunity to hear all class members as soon as possible, without undue pressure caused by musical and vocal concerns.

After warming up with vocal and physical exercises, and prior to singing individual solo songs, group songs can be useful as an intermediate level warm-up exercise. And, because of the short duration of a group song, it can provide an opportunity for everyone to sing during every class session. One useful approach is for individuals to sing group songs as solos. For example, three to four singers might perform a simple round such as "Row, Row, Row Your Boat" (also listed herein as "Sing, Sing, Sing a Song"), each one singing the melody three or four times. As skill and confidence grow, more vocal independence can be developed by using more advanced songs, such as the "Orchestra Song" and "Vive L'Amour" (especially the latter, which has some simple four-part harmony). An approach that works well with this selection is to have individuals solo on the verses and the rest of the class join in on the **chorus.** It's a great rouser and spirit builder, too.

In addition to the songs contained in this collection, there are innumerable high-quality group songs from all over the world. Class members with ethnic backgrounds

INFORMATION ABOUT THE FOLK SONGS AND HYMNS

Traditional songs form an historical musical continuity in all world cultures and civilizations. Many of the world's great composers have acknowledged the folk music of their respective countries or geographical regions as the inspirational source of their musical creativity, either directly or indirectly. There's ample evidence that the popular music traditions of the United States, particularly country, blues, gospel, and folk ballads, are outgrowths of folk music origins.

As part of the oral tradition of a people, the origins of folk song are hard to pinpoint. In most cases folk songs are notated only after many years of evolving through essentially primitive forms, gradually becoming more and more refined. Eventually, some popular folk songs are discovered by classical music composers, and subsequently, updated arrangements are written that may or may not enhance the original folklike qualities. The folk songs and **hymns** in this collection have been treated simply, but with an awareness of modern performing standards. According to the nature of the folk song, there is no "right" or "perfect" version. Thus, the arrangers and editors of this edition have taken minor liberties to enhance and adapt these folk songs for current performance practice.

All through the Night, page 146. The authorship of both the words and music are unknown. The first known printing of the melody was in 1784 with Welsh words and English translation, in Edward Jones' *Musical and Poetical Relicks for the Welsh Bards* (London, 1784). The song appears under the title "Ar Hyd Y Nos" and the English translation by Jones does not mention the phrase "all through the night." The first verse begins with words typical of a lullaby. However, the second verse reveals that it is actually a love song—for it is not a child, but one's beloved who is being watched over while asleep. The attitude should be one of tenderness and sincere attention to the task of keeping a nightly vigil. Be careful to pronounce the word "hover" to rhyme with "lover," not "over." A feeling of two beats to the measure will help smooth out the phrasing and make it flow more easily.

Amazing Grace, page 143. Although this well-known hymn is commonly thought of as American in origin, it is actually the composition of the Englishman, John Newton (1725–1807). As a youthful godless sailor in the Royal Navy, he deserted, was recaptured, severely punished, and degraded. He spent several years of service in the slave trade and for some time as a captain of a slave ship. Some near misses with death at sea and his subsequent religious studies in Liverpool led to his conversion and eventual ordination as a priest in the Church of England. He became known as a great evangelical preacher and writer of several well-known hymns. The tune is of unknown origin, appearing for the first time in the "Virginia Harmony" (1831), compiled by J. P. Carrell and D. S. Clayton. In performing this particular version of the hymn, one should refrain from tendencies to embellish the basic melody, thereby maintaining the simple traditional nature of the hymn. The spirit of performance must be that of deep religious conviction, sung with quiet fervor. The meaning of the word *grace* in theological terms can be thought of as the freely given and unmerited love of God, the spirit of God working in persons, and the favor of God. The hymn begins with quiet wonder and amazement at God's love for one so unworthy, focuses on the conversion experience in the second verse, and ends triumphantly and victoriously with the final verse.

Balm in Gilead, page 148. The actual derivation of this hymn is unknown but it is widely accepted as having origins as an African American spiritual. Versions of it are included in such sources as *Folksingers Wordbook* (Irwin and Fred Silver) and *American Negro Songs and Spirituals* (John Work). The text is based on Jeremiah 8:22 and 46:11 with references such as: "Is there no medicine in Gilead? Is there no physician there: Why doesn't God do something? Why doesn't he help?"; and "Go up to Gilead for medicine, O virgin daughter of Egypt! Yet there is no cure for your wounds. Though you have used many medicines, there is no healing for you." Gilead is the ancient name of a country now designated as the area east of the river Jordan, extending from the Dead Sea to the Sea of Galilee. The term *balm* refers to healing medicine, which means that the singer should aim for a soothingly smooth vocal line in the first (A) section (mm. 2–11). The second (B) section (mm. 12–20) can be sung with more energy to suit the textual intent. *Gilead* should be pronounced without an abrasive sounding last syllable ("ad"), preferably with a more relaxed rounding of the vowel, but not an "ahd." A slight, graceful **portamento** (delayed slide) from the lower to upper pitch on the word *whole* is encouraged—but not a slow scoop.

Con qué la lavaré (Oh, What Can Wash Away), page 170. The origins of this plaintive Spanish song are loosely associated with the term *villancicos,* a reference to a poetical and music form that has undergone many modifications over the past few centuries. At least two arrangements are available in folk-song collections of sixteenth-century composers: Eduardo M. Toner's *Marváez* and Juan Vazques's *Coleccion de Vihuelistas Españoles del Siglio XVI.* Joaquin Rodrigo, a twentieth-century Spanish composer, also includes the song in his four-song set for voice and chamber orchestra entitled, *Cuatro Madrigales Amatorious.* The mood set by the song's languid melodic and harmonic treatment reflects the quasi-religious nature of the text, an expression of anguish and penitence, possibly for committing some transgression which requires a self-imposed ritual of cleansing. The song should be sung legato, with deep feeling. (See Fig. 1, p. 125.)

Da unten im Tale (Below in the Valley), page 150. Recognized as one of the major nineteenth-century Viennese composers, Johannes Brahms (1833–1897) had a strong attraction to folk song, especially those of German and Slavic origins. Many of his lieder have folk-song characteristics, particularly in terms of melodic influences, and a large portion of them are folk-song arrangements. This Swabian (southwestern Germany) dialect folk song is from *49 Deutsche Volkslieder,* No. 6 (1894). In its original form it is a dialogue between two lovers, one of whom has been unfaithful. The female sings verses one and three, and the male sings two and four. Brahms' version is a bit slower and is intended as a solo. However, as an educational experiment, it should work very well to have a male and female sing it as a "lovers' parting" dialogue. (See Fig. 2, p. 126.)

Down in the Valley, page 152. Commonly thought to be an authentic "hillbilly tune," this popular American folk song stems from the Kentucky mountain region. The work first appeared in 1917 in G. L. Kittredge's "Ballads and Songs" in the *Journal of American Folklore,* Lancaster, Pennsylvania. It has subsequently been published in many versions and under various titles, such as "Bird In a Cage," "Birmingham Jail," and "Down On the Levee." Kurt Weill and Arnold Sundgaard based a one-act folk opera on the song in 1948. This song should be sung nostalgically and with great longing, as though writing a love letter filled with one's deepest feelings. In addition to the three verses included in this version, the verses that were omitted would give a more complete picture. For example, "write me a letter, send it by mail, send it in care of Birmingham jail," gives the impression the writer might not have long to live. Because of the strophic construction and repetitiveness, try to sing each verse with a different point of view, using varying dynamics to suit the meaning of the words.

Drink to Me Only with Thine Eyes, page 154. This well-known poem by Ben Jonson (1573–1637) was first published in a collection of poems entitled "The Forest" (1616), included in *The Works of Benjamin Jonson.* The original tune was entitled "Song to Celia." Beginning around 1750, the poem was used in several other musical settings, but all of these have been forgotten. The present version of the tune was published in 1780 in a number of editions, several of which were set as *glees*, eighteenth-century genres of unaccompanied English choral music for three or more parts of solo men's voices. Although the composer is unknown, some speculation has been offered that a possible contender is J. W. Callcott, who included the song in a publication of his in which he claimed authorship. Because of the sophistication of the poem, this love song requires a delicate, sophisticated interpretation. The vocal line must be very smooth and the words well-articulated, especially the numerous voiced and voiceless "th's." To maintain a sustained, legato flow, feel main pulses as two to the measure instead of six.

Greensleeves, page 156. One of the most cherished English folk tunes, "Greensleeves" is equally well-known as the Christmas carol/hymn "What Child Is This?" One of the earliest references to this tune is found in Shakespeare, with Falstaff's cry, "Let the sky . . . thunder to the tune of 'Greensleeves'." This accounting supports the evidence that the tune was originally a lively dance tune. The text was first published in 1580 as a separate ballad by Richard Jones, entitled "Lady Greensleeves," and the melody's first printing was its inclusion (without words) in 1652 in *A Booke of New Lessons for the Cithern and Gittern*, under the title "Greensleeves." Because of its probable dance derivation, this version connects the last two pitches at the end of most measures. Consequently, the pickup word is sung on two pitches instead of only the last one, resulting in a snappy lilting effect. One should still try to sing the song in legato style, reflecting the tender emotional content of the text. The word *adieu* is pronounced "adyou" [adju] to rhyme with "true."

Long Time Ago, page 158. This lyrical ballad was first mentioned in 1837 as an anonymous, original tune adapted by George Pope Morris (words) and Charles Edward Horn (music). It is also included in the *Harris Collection*. The song has become more known by its inclusion in Aaron Copland's collection of *Old American Songs*. The singer can sing this nostalgic song from either a personal or narrative point of view. The descriptively quaint text paints a clear picture of the almost primitive natural surroundings in which the lovers knew one another. A suggested image: a small log cabin situated by a lake with a stream flowing into it, in a valley surrounded by mountains. A *billow* is a wave of water, caused by a rock being tossed into the lake, resulting in a sunlit white cap "brighter than snow."

Niño precioso (Precious Child), page 160. Although its origins are difficult to ascertain, this Nicaraguan folk song is a product of traditions related to both Spanish

Catholic religious rites and Native Central-American Indian customs. The original two-part musical form and melodic characteristics substantiate its kinship with songs from the western European tradition. According to the text, the "God of love" is possibly a reference to the Christ child, indicating it could also be sung as a Christmas carol. The reference of the child being compared to precious ermine acknowledges the particularly luxurious fur common in Central America. The person singing must assume the role of one keeping peaceful, loving watch over a sleeping child. Artistic license has been exercised with the decision to have the song end with the return to the A section of the first verse, which effectively changes the form to ABA. (See Fig. 3, p. 127.)

O Shenandoah, page 162. Perhaps one of the most memorable of all sea chanteys in English, "Shenandoah" has been presented in many versions and in many forms over the years, several of which exist as choral arrangements. Discrepancies over its origins create a bit of mystery surrounding the song. According to one theory (James F. Leisy, *The Folk Song Abecedary*), the name *Shenandoah* is an adaptation of the name used by the Iroquois Indians for the mountains surrounding the Shenandoah valley in Virginia, meaning "land of big mountains." It was a popular tune among the voyageurs on the rivers west of the Mississippi, probably accounting for one version entitled "Across the Wide Missouri." It became a capstan chantey known as "Shanandore" on American ships following the Civil War and later a favorite song of the U.S. Calvary during the Indian wars in the West. In keeping with some of the free rhythmic traditions associated with the song, this version alternates between duple and triple meter to follow the textual inflections. Setting it to a consistent rhythmic pulse can restrain the natural suppleness of the melodic line, so a certain amount of freedom, or *rubato*, is acceptable. The loneliness of one who has been away from home for an extended period (seven years) is felt throughout the song. One can easily imagine singing casually with companions prior to retiring after a full day of travel and experiencing the homesickness this song conveys.

Over the Meadows, page 173. This cheerful up-tempo song is listed in several community song books as a Czechoslovakian folk song, but its exact origins are somewhat obscured by the scarcity of Czech editions. The musical and textual characteristics are similar to songs sung throughout the mountain areas of central and southern Europe where there are plenteous blooming meadows in springtime, nourished by the melting of winter snows. Based on available English edition translations, the song was originally sung by field workers as they hiked to and from mountainside fields at the beginning and close of spring days. It is also likely that, over the years, this song has been adopted by hikers (this author and his wife enjoy singing it on mountain treks). Employing a vigorous, marchlike tempo, the song stimulates a great-to-be-alive, "can-do" attitude. It may be sung in various ways using piano accompaniment: (1) as a solo, (2) with alternate soloists, (3) with soloist(s) and group, or (4) group only, in unison or in improvised two-part harmony. As with other folk songs, it may also be sung *a cappella* or with guitar accompaniment.

Simple Gifts, page 164. From the period 1837–1847, this song was a favorite of the Shakers, a celibate, communitarian religious sect located primarily in New York and New England at the end of the seventeenth century, who later established settlements in Ohio, Kentucky, and Indiana. The Shakers were known for neat, well-planned, peaceful villages, pure architecture and fine craftsmanship, progressive agricultural practices, concern for social betterment, and distinctive songs, dances, and rituals. Because of these peculiar Shaker characteristics, it is easy to understand the simplicity of this lovely song, popularized through several contemporary musical versions, including Aaron Copland's version in his *Old American Songs* for voice and orchestra (also piano). The basic message is that striving for true humility is "to come down where we ought to be," resulting in freedom from worldly cares and concerns, and eventually reaching "the valley of love and delight." The use of *turning* might mean to keep trying for human perfection until "you come round right," or it might simply be a literal dance movement response reflecting the music and text.

Sometimes I Feel like a Motherless Child, page 166. The first account of this African American spiritual was in William E. Barton's *Old Plantation Hymns* (1899). Like all folk songs, the song has had many modifications over the centuries, yet its basic characteristics have remained intact. Several versions by contemporary composers have been arranged, including John Carter's unique rendition in his song cycle *Cantata,* based on four spirituals with a very challenging piano accompaniment. The simple text of mournful longing depicts the extreme feeling of separation from one's roots, interpreted as family, homeland, or even heaven. To be a "motherless child" is to say "I don't feel as though I exist . . . I'm completely useless . . . a nobody." Because so many slave children were sold off and separated from their families, it is easy to imagine their feelings of desolation and dejection as they strove to adjust to a harsh, strange, and often degrading existence. Hence, there is no single interpretation; the final choice is up to the singer. Because of the difficulty of effecting the appropriate authentic dialect, use your natural singing diction but with a slight relaxation of the diphthong vowels, such as [ɑɪ], on such words as "times" and "like." Also, there must be no hint of an "r" in the word "mother*less*."

The Water Is Wide, page 168. Known also as "O Waly, Waly," this plaintive love song originated in the southwest section of England known as Somerset. The eigh-

teenth-century Austrian composer Josef Haydn produced one charming arrangement of this lovely anonymous folk song. *Waly* (also *wally* or *walie*) is an obscure word that has a cognate with *woe,* meaning an exclamation of sorrow. Although various verses have been used, the general theme of this beautiful song is essentially a story of young love and its sad dissolution. The first verse is hopeful. Although a gulf separates them, perhaps they could make things work if only they could find the means. The second verse reveals that one lover turned out to be unfaithful, and the third verse summarizes, philosophically, that even though love is sweet when new, nothing lasts forever. Communicating the changing moods of each verse is the major challenge. Sing the second verse more impassioned when expressing the trusty tree's bending and breaking.

INFORMATION ABOUT THE ART SONGS AND ARIAS

An **art song** is a composition of high artistic intent, the entirety of which is written by a musically sophisticated composer. With the exception of the textual source, all musical invention is the composer's responsibility. This is in contrast to a folk song arrangement where only the accompaniment part is invented. However, many folk songs (tunes and texts) have been arranged or incorporated into art songs at the hands of skillful composers. An art song in German is called a "**lied,**" and in French "*mélodie.*" One of the distinguishing characteristics of an art song is the integration of harmony (accompaniment), melody (voice), and text into a cohesive art form. The characteristic art song as we know it today came into existence in the early nineteenth century through such composers as Beethoven and Schubert. This means that some earlier songs—such as the *lute songs* composed by Dowland and Morley—are not generally classified as art songs.

An **aria** is a solo vocal composition, usually from a major work (such as opera, cantata, or oratorio), with instrumental accompaniment. It is generally distinguished from the art song by greater length, expanded song form, and more emphasis on musical design and expression, often at the expense of the text. Five of the selections in this Anthology may be classified as arias, including all Handel selections and "Nel cor più non mi sento." It is standard practice to perform such works with piano accompaniment in lieu of orchestra, especially sixteenth and seventeenth-century Italian songs and arias which are widely used by beginning voice students. In some cases, a harpsichord and continuo instrument (cello on the bass line) are used as accompaniment.

The Renaissance Era

Most solo songs of the late fifteenth century, and throughout the sixteenth century, were created for courtly entertainment.

With the growing popularity of the lute (a precursor to the modern guitar), composers began writing songs for voice with lute and bass viol accompaniment. Due to a lack of accomplished lute and viol players, these songs are commonly performed with either piano or guitar (and sometimes cello) accompaniments in modern-day performances.

One of the outstanding composers in Renaissance England, Thomas Morley established a strong reputation as organist at St. Giles, Cripplegate, and subsequently at St. Paul's Cathedral in London. In 1598, he joined the Chapel Royal and obtained the monopoly of music printing. His secular works are more important than his church compositions, and his *Plaine and Easie Introduction to Practicall Musick* (1597) is valuable to the music historian. Following are two songs by Morley.

It Was a Lover and His Lass, page 176. Composed by Morley for the play *As You Like It* by William Shakespeare (1564–1616), this song is unique as one of the surviving original songs created specifically for the great bard's plays. The song was first published by Morley in *First Book of Ayres* (1600). It occurs near the end of the play and is performed by two page boys as entertainment for a clown and his intended bride. Keeping this comic scene in mind should help maintain a lively, brisk tempo and mood. Some words needing clarification are: *corn-field* meaning "wheat field"; *ring-time* meaning "wedding season"; *fools* meaning "folks"; and *prime* meaning "springtime." This song may be sung by several solo singers as an opportunity for more students to learn it, each taking a verse.

Now Is the Month of Maying, page 178. Set by Morley to an anonymous text and published originally as a five-part madrigal in the composer's *First Book of Ballets to Five Voices* (1595), this song has also been adapted in several versions for solo voice. In the same category as "It Was a Lover and His Lass," this selection is also very spirited and is about lovers frolicking in the springtime. It too may be effectively used as a group-singing activity, perhaps as a vocal warm-up. Individuals may be assigned a solo verse with the group joining on the "fa la la" refrains. Some words requiring clarification are *nymphs,* a reference to beautiful, graceful young women, and *barley-break,* which refers to a group game of "catch" played by both sexes in a cornfield (wheat field). The *break* is a reference to when everyone separates to get away from the "catcher."

Come Again, Sweet Love, page 180. Recognized as one of England's outstanding composers and lutenists, John Dowland (1563–1626), spent much of his career outside of England (Paris, Florence, and Denmark) before accepting patronage by Charles I. His primary contributions to music literature are his songs for voice and lute. His "Come

Again, Sweet Love" is perhaps the most well-known song of this genre. On the surface this song appears, quite innocuously, as a typical sweet love song. However, as is often the case with lyrics of this period (and also with some of the rock music today) there is an underlying meaning that reveals a more passionate subtext. Understanding both levels should provide a reason to sing this song with more than the customary straightforward approach. Almost any reasonable interpretation is acceptable when sung with substantiated conviction.

The Baroque Era

Around the turn of the seventeenth century, some major changes and developments in every field of human endeavor paralleled the creation of a new musical language. When opera began in Italy with Jacopo Peri's *Euridice* (1600), singing moved from an intimate art form to one of larger proportions. At first the aesthetic vocal ideal was to support and express the text with musical means, but as the century progressed the equation between text and music evolved, eventually swinging more toward elaborate vocal display. Throughout the seventeenth century, and up to the middle of the eighteenth century, a predominant form of musical writing was the **continuo** (also *basso continuo* or through bass), characterized by the important interplay of melodic and bass lines with inner musical parts serving a chord-filling function. The chief instruments used in realizing the harmony were the harpsichord and organ, while the viola da gamba or cello doubled on the bass line. The standard method of music notation was a form of shorthand with melodic and bass lines filled in and inner parts indicated by numbers representing specific chord structures. All performers were expected to know how to fulfill the composer's intentions, and particularly, opera singers were expected to embellish the vocal line at appropriate places in an improvisatory manner. The peak of Baroque composition was reached with the two masters, J. S. Bach and G. F. Handel.

Star vicino (To Be Close), page 182. Formerly attributed to the Italian poet-painter, Salvator Rosa (1615– 1673), the authorship of this lovely song is currently in question. The English author-historian Dr. Charles Burney procured some handwritten songs, including some set to Rosa's poems. Assuming all works had been produced by Rosa, he subsequently included some excerpts from the collection in his book, *A General History of Music.* For the past four decades research begun by Frank Walker, an English musicologist, has raised serious doubts regarding Rosa's authorship, instead attributing some of the songs to Alessandro Scarlatti, Antonio Cesti, and Giovanni Bononcini. Regardless of the true authorship, the anonymous composer has left a vocal gem for singers to perform. The version included here is patterned after several existing performing editions, utilizing what may be considered interpolated material from measure 20 to the end. The message is the familiar theme of one longing to be with one's beloved, presumably because of a long separation. The first verse is purportedly by Rosa, while the second verse may have been written by Count Pepoli of Bologna. (See Fig. 4, p. 127.)

Toglietemi la vita ancor (Oh, Take Away My Breath, My Life), p. 186. Alessandro Scarlatti (1660–1725) produced numerous operas, including *Pompeo* (1683), from which this aria is extracted. At the time, he was 22 years old and serving as music director to Queen Christina of Sweden, who was in exile from her native Lutheran country because of her conversion to Catholicism. The opera story, which was originally written by Nicolò Minato but revised by an anonymous librettist, is set in Rome during the first century B.C., when the Roman general Pompey has defeated Pontus. Since Pompey has taken the queen of Pontus to Rome as captive, Mitridate, the King of Pontus enters Rome in disguise, searching for his wife. Not finding her, he despairingly states his emotions in this aria, fearing he will never see her again. When performing this aria, the rhythmic pulse must remain vigorous and steady, with slight ritards only at cadences. (See Fig. 5, p. 128.)

Considered by most musicologists as England's greatest composer, Purcell (1659–1695) had an uncanny natural gift for writing vocal music. Though some of the texts he set to music are a bit antiquated for modern ears, his songs are considered standards in the modern singer's repertoire. In addition to positions as organist at Westminster Abbey and the Chapel Royal, he had a distinguished career in service to Charles II as principal composer and keeper of the king's instruments. Following are two songs by Purcell.

I Attempt from Love's Sickness to Fly, page 190. Written for the masque *Indian Queen* to a text by dramatist John Dryden (1631–1700), this song is sung by Queen Zempoalla. It was later published as a separate song in the collection *Orpheus Britannicus*. Purcell's baroque affinity for "word painting" is illustrated with the word *fly*, accompanied by a fleeting, florid passage. The word *mien* refers to one's bearing or aspect. The meaning of the song is obvious: One is feverishly coping with lovesickness and would like to break away but can't quite find the courage to act. Performing this song requires a delicate balance between expressive delivery and clear delineation of the musical line.

If Music Be the Food of Love, page 184. This is the first of three versions (1692–1695) Purcell set to this text. The text is attributed to H. Heveningham (dates unknown). The song was published in a collection called *Orpheus Britannicus* (London). Only one of two verses is used in this version. As a vocal exercise, this song contains scale work in both descending and ascending patterns at a moderate pace, the only difficulty being a lack of breathing opportunities. To handle this problem, the singer and accompanist must slightly stretch phrases at points where quick breaths are needed. The intoxicated mood is a sensuous and joyous expression of music's ability to create amorous feelings.

Bist du bei mir (If You Are Near), page 193. Although this song is traditionally attributed to Johann Sebastian Bach (1685–1750), there is some speculation that it is possibly by Gottfried Heinrich Stölzel, one of Bach's contemporaries. To be ascribed authorship of this charming song would be an honor for any composer. It is listed as No. 25 in the *Notebook for Anna Magdelena Bach* (BWV 508) as the second of "Drei Arien" (Three Airs). According to most historical accounts, if Bach did write this song for his second wife, Anna Magdelena, it is the only known love song he ever wrote. Because the anonymous text in English translation is a bit obscure— the meaning could refer to both one's beloved as well as God's—this song has been effectively used in funeral services. However, the textual "giveaway" is the familiar use of the German word *du*, which is used only on a personal level of familiarity. A keyboard introduction has been added prior to the entrance of the vocal line. (See Fig 6, p. 128.)

Known internationally as the composer of *Messiah*, Handel (1685–1759) is unquestionably one of the world's most prolific and celebrated composers. Soon after his appointment as Kapellmeister to the Elector of Hannover in 1710, he visited London to produce his opera *Rinaldo* (1711). Having achieved great success in England, he settled there for a lifelong stay, eventually serving his former Hannoverian employer who ascended the English throne as George II. During the remainder of his career, he composed numerous operas for the King's Theater. As opera fell increasingly out of public favor, he turned to producing oratorios, which were essentially operas minus stage trappings. Since Handel displayed a remarkable affinity for vocal composition, he is often referred to as a "singer's composer." According to standard performing practice, singers who have other than the voice types for whom arias were originally written may sing the arias in this Anthology. Following are three arias by Handel.

Lascia ch'io pianga (Let Me in Weeping) [O Lord, I Pray Thee], page 196. Set to a libretto by Giacomo Rossi, this beautiful aria from *Rinaldo* (Act II, scene 4), is sung by Almirena, (daughter of Godfrey of Bouillon, leader of the First Crusade), who is in love with Rinaldo (brave knight of the Templars). Under the spell of the sorceress Armida, Almirena sings this song of pathos and longing for freedom. In the style of the period, embellishments have been added to the vocal line, beginning with the B section and continuing throughout the recapitulation of the A section (***da capo***). The singer is free to eliminate these embellishments or otherwise create new ones to enhance textual and vocal expression. An optional religious text is provided for church performance. (See Fig. 7, p. 129.)

Non lo dirò col labbro (At Evening), page 200.
From Handel's opera pastiche *Tolomeo* (1778), with libretto by Nicola Haym (1679–1730), this simple composition bears more resemblance to a song than an aria. It has become better known to the public as "Silent Worship," a version popularized by the English composer Arthur Somervell (1863–1937). Written in a similar mode of adapting an existing tune to new words—a standard Baroque practice—the English text "At Evening" provides a new tranquil setting extolling the beauty of evening's refreshing rest in preparation for a new day. A literal translation of the original Italian is provided with the IPA transcription. Anyone desiring and willing to create an interesting English text based on the original Italian text is encouraged to give it a try. The idea being expressed is: "I don't dare say what I feel for you, but when I look at you the flames in my eyes reveal my burning passion." (See Fig. 8, p. 129.)

Oh, Sleep, Why Dost Thou Leave Me? page 203.
In the oratorio *Semele* (1744), libretto by W. Congreve, this aria is sung by Semele, a princess of Thebes who longs to be reunited with her beloved. The loss of sleep deprives her of dreams and hopes of being restored to her "wandering love." The statement "O sleep! again deceive me" is a plea that she may at least "dream" of reunification. A religious text ("O Lord, Hear My Prayer") has been added for use in church. Both versions require an ability to sustain a vibrant vocal tone when singing at lower dynamic levels, as with the opening unaccompanied line.

The Classical Era

As the tendency for extensive musical elaboration reached its extremes in the mid-eighteenth century, such philosophical ideals as formal elegance, clarity, dignity, order, and correctness of style became moderating influences. Beginning with the famous sons of J. S. Bach, and continuing with composers of the Viennese classic school, such as Franz Josef Haydn, Wolfgang Amadeus Mozart, and Ludwig van Beethoven, the newly emerging piano became the main instrument for song accompaniment.

Preach Not Me Your Musty Rules, page 210. In the genre of eighteenth-century solo vocal music, Dr. Arne (1710–1778) deserves a place at the front echelon of minor composers. His career consisted of producing several major works for the stage, among them an ambitious

opera entitled *Artaxerxes*. The composer's music possesses distinct charm and grace, expertly crafted according to the conventional mode of his day, which was predominantly influenced by such dance forms as the minuet and gavotte. Based on John Milton's *Comus* with libretto fashioned by stage director John Dalton, Arne composed his opera *Comus* in 1738. Excerpted from that work, this spirited song is set to a lively dance rhythm and humorous text. The gist of the text is simply "not to worry, follow your heart and senses, be happy and live life to its fullest." A *drone* is a male, nonworker bee; an idler. This song may be sung directly to the audience, even to the point of making eye contact with individuals.

Flocks Are Sporting, page 206. Henry Carey (1689–1743) is recognized for his versatility as an English dramatist, poet, and composer. He began his career as a writer and, in his late 20s, became more interested in composition. His first well-known song, "Sally in Our Alley," written for a staged production, was accomplished with the assistance of a professional composer. Carey's genuine talent for inventing fresh-sounding, pleasant melodies resulted in numerous ballad-style songs, a few of which are performed today. "Flocks Are Sporting" is a popular favorite for young sopranos in particular. This version also offers a religious text which may be used for Easter celebrations. The tune may also be adapted to a Christmas carol text (e.g., "Angels Singing") should anyone be interested in inventing an appropriate text. When singing the original Carey text, the mood should be carefree and gay. In contrast, the Easter text needs a more triumphant, celebratory approach, which implies the elimination of all grace notes.

My Lovely Celia, page 208. In contrast to the facile, florid songs of the period, George Monro (1680–1731), a minor English composer, wrote a number of very charming simple songs which were published in the *Musical Miscellany* (1731). "My Lovely Celia" is imbued with a reserved English sentiment that is also full of warmth and affection. With its short phrases, gracefully moving tempo, and well-contoured melodic line, the song is a fine vocalise for developing legato vocal technique. Though the song is usually performed by young tenors, it may also be sung by other voice types, including sopranos and mezzo-sopranos. If preferred, the optional words "O, my beloved" may be substituted for "My lovely Celia" at the opening of the song. Sing with a gentle, impassioned ardor throughout, allowing for contrasts in dynamics.

Nel cor più non mi sento (My Heart Has Lost Its Feeling), page 216. In his time Giovanni Paisiello (1740–1816) was very popular as a comic opera composer. In addition to his *Il Barbieri di Seviglia* (eventually eclipsed by Rossini's opera of the same title), he wrote more than a hundred operas, including *L'Amor contrastato*

("The Hard-Won Love") from which this aria is taken. In the opera, Rachelina, a wealthy mill owner near Naples sings this aria about the confusion love causes when one is being pursued by three lovers. At other points in the opera the melody is also sung by both tenor and baritone suitors, becoming a duet at the end of each solo. This version is a variation of editions currently being used. It is most important to convey a genuine feeling of confused, fluctuating emotions. There's plenty of opportunity to contrast these emotions with subtle facial and body language, and to have fun doing it! (See Fig. 9, p. 129.)

Ridente la calma (May Calm Joy Awaken), p. 218. Recent scholarship (Paton 1992) proposed that Wolfgang Amadeus Mozart (1719–1787) composed this version of "Ridente la calma" based on an original composition by his old friend Josef Mysliveček (1737–1781), a successful Czech opera composer. For unknown reasons, around 1773–1775 Mozart undertook a revision of the aria that included a new text, a new second part, and a shortened postlude. The combined result is an exquisite Italianate song of arialike characteristics. Since the eighteenth-century compositional style presents some minor interpretative problems for novice singers, this edition features some unique "user-friendly" solutions. First, the original $\frac{3}{8}$ time has been converted to $\frac{3}{4}$ time, primarily for easier viewing and studying without impinging on the original artistic intent. Second, all typical embellishments (appoggiaturas, turns, and cadenza) have been written-in (indicated with the use of small notes). Third, notes have been added to clarify how certain syllables of the Italian text should be rhythmically voiced using a very fluid connection (see measures 12, 20, 24, 37, 39, 41, et al). Perform the song with a happy, serene attitude throughout. (See Fig. 10, p. 130.)

Ich liebe dich (I Love You Dear), page 213. The musical giant Ludwig van Beethoven (1770–1827) is recognized more for his instrumental compositions than for his vocal works. His rebellious, freedom-loving nature caused him to write music that expanded the limits of eighteenth-century classicism, opening the door for the romantic movement of the nineteenth century. As a song writer of sixty-eight lieder, he was innovative in his use of the piano and helped set the stage for Schubert and Schumann, and those who followed. Often his opera and oratorio writing for the voice is uncomplimentary in its vocal demands, especially in terms of tessitura. However, he wrote many songs capable of being performed well by students, including "Ich liebe dich." Set to a text by Karl Friedrich Herrosee, this gentle, tender song is an expression pledging enduring love through life's ups and downs. In contrast to the typical popular wedding song heard today, this song offers a high-quality option, especially when using the English text. (See Fig. 11, p. 130.)

The Romantic Era

Social unrest in Europe became increasingly exacerbated during the eighteenth century, reaching a peak with the Napoleonic Wars at the beginning of the nineteenth century. The fall of established monarchies, the advent of the industrial revolution, and the rising prosperity of the common person—juxtaposed with the extreme poverty of others—were some characteristics of an era churning with emotional social issues. In the search for individual freedom of expression, artists in all fields sought to explore and expand the parameters of their art. In music, on one end of the continuum, there was a growth of large-scale musical works, such as massive symphonies and operas. On the other end, there was the growth of intimate musical forms such as the art song, primarily intended to be performed for friends and colleagues in intimate home gatherings. The advent of public performances by world-class artists, such as pianist/composer Franz Liszt and singer Jenny Lind, led to the evolution of the soloist concertizing from the parlor to the stage. The predominant art song during the nineteenth century was the German *lied* (represented herein by three prominent composers: Schubert, Schumann, and Brahms). The French *mélodie* is represented by the two selections "Le Charme," by Chausson, and "Romance," by Debussy.

Vaga luna (Lovely Moon), page 222. Not all of the music written in the nineteenth century was innovative in creating a new musical language. For instance, in the first half of the century notable Italian opera composers, such as Gioacchino Rossini (1792–1868), Gaetano Donizetti (1797–1848), and Vincenzo Bellini (1801–1835), were particularly predisposed to advancing the eighteenth-century **bel canto** style. Primarily an opera composer, Bellini wrote arietti, songs similar in style and substance to opera arias, but on a reduced scale. Though he loved poetry, he focused chiefly on the ecstasy of sound created by a curving, flowing melodic line. Composed after 1825, "Vaga luna" is No. 26 in *Aurora d'Italia e di Germania arietta* (Vienna). The version contained here is based on an edition by the famous singer/teacher Pauline Viardot-Garcia in the *'Echos i'Italie*, Vol. 1 (Paris, 1860s). The text expresses amorous wishes that the all-seeing moon convey one's thoughts of love to the distant beloved. (See Fig. 12, p. 131.)

With over 600 songs to his credit, Franz Schubert (1797–1828) is justifiably recognized as the most prolific genius of art song composition. His Viennese lifestyle represents the epitome of the nineteenth-century intellectual artist, avidly pursuing his love of music while living in a state of virtual poverty. His greatest contribution to the growth and development of the lied is the integration of text, piano part, and vocal line (melody) into a synthesized whole. Though many of his songs reflect the simple strophic construction of earlier composers, he succeeds in giving the piano accompaniment a major role—other than merely filling out supportive harmonies for the melody. Following are three songs by Schubert.

An die Musik (To Music), page 225. Schubert's close friend Franz von Schober (1796–1882) wrote the words to this particularly well-known song, which the composer set to music in 1817. Because of the song's great beauty and textual meaning, the National Association of Teachers of Singing traditionally opens every convention with the entire membership singing it in unison. The poem may be thought of as a hymn of thanksgiving to music, extolling its virtuous influences on human existence. Since performing this song requires solemn dignity and finesse, one should strive to maintain a secure, flowing vocal tone and give careful attention to subtleties in textual meaning. (See Fig. 13, p. 132.)

Heidenröslein (The Hedgerose), page 238. A simple strophic setting of a charming text by the great German poet Johann Wolfgang von Goethe (1749–1832), this little gem is one of those songs that can be performed on two levels: (1) as a straightforward accounting of a hedgerose that has an unpleasant encounter with a mischievous little boy; and (2) with a more symbolic interpretation of a young, astute maiden being taken advantage of by a rascally young lad. Either way the song will work very effectively. Vocally and dramatically, you ideally should strive to create the roles of narrator, rosebud, and boy with variations in characterization and vocal tone. It is a story-telling opportunity, with all the necessary ingredients to make it interesting. (See Fig. 14, p. 133.)

Seligkeit (Bliss), p. 228. Schubert set "Seligkeit" in 1816 to a poem by Ludwig Heinrich Christoph Hölty (1748–1776), a gifted poet who died prematurely at age 28. Written simply in strophic form, the lighthearted melodies of the vocal part and the piano accompaniment pass back and forth in a joyful interplay. Although this simple lied has been performed by numerous singers, perhaps the most memorable renditions, both live concerts and recordings, can be attributed to the great German soprano, Elizabeth Schumann. While this upbeat song needs to be performed straightforwardly, subtle variations of each verse are needed to create dramatic contrast and interest. The piano introduction/interlude provides an opportunity to create and maintain dramatic interest when not singing, so resist any tendency to merely "bide time." (See Fig. 15, p. 134.)

Du bist wie eine Blume (You Are So Like a Flower), page 232. Though not quite as prolific as Schubert, Robert Schumann (1810–1856) is often cited as the most representative romantic composer of lieder. As a writer he was widely known for cofounding the *Neue Zeitschrift für Musik,* a journal devoted to promoting the cause of new music. Many of Schumann's songs were inspired by his love for Clara Wieck, daughter of his piano teacher Herr Wieck, who initially vehemently opposed their relationship. This poem by the highly respected Heinrich Heine (1797–1856), is one of his most frequently set poems. Because of its compact construction with interweaving of piano and voice (plus text), this perfect gem is one of Schumann's most frequently performed works. The performing attitude should be one of absolute devotion and adoration of one's beloved. (See Fig. 16, p. 135.)

Le Charme (The Charm), page 234. Though Ernest Chausson (1855–1899) cannot be considered a major composer, his contributions to the French mélodie repertoire are highly respected among art song enthusiasts. As an administrator, he did much to further the cause of French music in his influential position as secretary of the Société de Nationale de Musique. Since most of his later songs are somewhat musically and interpretatively difficult, "Le Charme" (1879), a song from the composer's early period set to a poem from *Chanson des heures* by Armand Silvestre, gives the singer an opportunity to sample the composer's highly individual use of harmonies and rhythms in a moderately easy format. This song must be sung smoothly and with suppleness according to clear indications of dynamics and tempo in the score. The basic story is recalling the first encounter with one's sweetheart, when it was "instant love." (See Fig. 17, p. 135.)

Romance (Romance), page 236. The compositional style of Claude Debussy (1862–1918) is closely associated with *impressionism,* an artistic movement prevalent in France circa 1890–1910 that favored softly focused, somewhat "blurred" images in describing a scene or expressing emotions. In addition to visual art influences, his musical characteristics were also shaped by French poets, notably the mysticism and sensuality of symbolist poet Paul Verlaine. "Romance" (1891), composed to a poem by Paul Bourget, a minor French poet, is representative of Debussy's early style of impressionistic writing. The song is characterized by graceful declamatory musical phrasing that contours the textual rhythms, and the harmonic treatment enhances the overall impressionistic mood of the text. The sensitive nature of the song calls for a supple vocal line, with a slight rubato throughout, and variable dynamics according to the specific markings in the score. (See Fig. 18, p. 136.)

The Modern Era

At the turn of the twentieth century, advancing technologies affected every aspect of human existence, including music. Between the two world wars the radical concepts of atonality and irregular meter were incorporated into musical composition, effectively creating a large chasm in the music world between conservative and radical forces. Though radical experimentation abated during the 40s and 50s, the increasing impact of electronic technologies on composers and audiences caused experimentation to accelerate in the 1960s. The two prominent art song trends of this century stem from the traditional branches of neoclassicism and neo-romanticism, or combinations of the two. Since most singers and audiences are generally conservative in musical preferences, most frequently performed songs exhibit appealing melodic, textual, rhythmic, and harmonic components. The contemporary British and American songs in this Anthology share these fundamental characteristics.

The Call, page 244. The foremost British composer of the first half of the twentieth century, Ralph Vaughan Williams (1872–1958) is recognized for his extensive use of British folk-song melodic and rhythmic patterns. As this setting of a poem by clergyman poet George Herbert (1593–1633) aptly illustrates, he set the English language to music in an impeccable manner. "The Call," from *Five Mystical Songs*, was originally conceived for baritone and piano, but may be used by any voice type capable of singing it in the key presented. *Way, Truth,* and *Life; Light, Feast,* and *Strength;* and *Joy, Love,* and *Heart* are all symbolic references to the deity (Christ or God) as one fervently prays for divine guidance. As you sing the song, be aware of the fluctuating meters, and sustain a very legato tone.

Roger Quilter (1877–1953), known for his refined, conservative compositional style, is one of the most beloved British art song composers. Several of his 112 well-crafted songs are considered standard repertoire for singers, from avocational to professional levels. Many were written for his favorite singer, Gervase Elwes, who also premiered them. Two of Quilter's more popular compositions, "Dream Valley" and "Weep You No More Sad Fountains," represent his characteristic writing style, which is exemplified by flowing melodic lines set to texts of high quality, and rich harmonic colorations in the piano accompaniment. Both songs are discussed below.

Dream Valley, page 246. Quilter's exquisite setting of William Blake's melancholy poem creates an appropriate dreamlike atmosphere, achieved by his simple harmonic treatment, relaxed tempi, and gently flowing melodies. The second stanza, which begins at measure 13, is a freely improvised treatment of the first stanza. One possible interpretation of the poem may be that day dreams are the result of conscious fantasies, while night dreams are influenced more by subconscious fears and urges. Although low dynamic levels and a peaceful mood are suggested, the singer should maintain an energized, vibrant tone throughout.

Weep You No More, Sad Fountains, page 241. This tender song is No. 1 of *Seven Elizabethan Lyrics*, Opus 12 (1908), set to an anonymous text taken from John Dowland's *Third Book of Ayres*. Intended as a lover's profound expression, attention is focused on one's beloved who is sleeping. The word *fountains* refers to the eyes of the beloved. In a soothing, comforting manner, the singer should convey a tranquil mood for restful sleep and restoration.

The Singer, page 250. English composer Michael Head (1900–1976) switched from mechanical engineering to pursue musical training in singing and piano at the Royal Academy of Music where he later taught as a professor of piano. Recognized chiefly as a vocal composer who wrote in a conservative, eclectic style, Head produced 122 art songs, many of which he performed on promotional recital tours. "The Singer" provides independent performers a unique opportunity in experimenting with various keys and musicodramatic nuances. (An optional piano accompaniment is provided in the original score.) In order to create the appropriate storytelling effect, one should practice reading the text aloud in an exaggerated manner, giving attention to clear diction, specific gestures, facial expressions, variable tempi, dynamic levels, and vocal color. This same approach should then be applied when singing the song. Although careful attention should be given to the composer's indications, certain liberties may be taken, especially at the song's end on the cascading "la" phrase, which is difficult to sing accurately.

A Memory, page 252. Rudolph Ganz (1877–1972) was a well-known Swiss American pianist, conductor, composer, and pedagogue. He spent his musical career as a concert pianist, conductor of the St. Louis Symphony Orchestra, teacher/administrator of Chicago Musical College (later Roosevelt University), and composer. His adeptness at song composition was undoubtedly inspired and nourished by his sequential marriages to two singers. Since information concerning Minnie K. Breid is limited, it is assumed she was a minor poet. "A Memory" (1919) uses through-composed form with simple harmonic techniques. Originally written in the key of G Major, the Song Anthology presents the song in F Major. The mood of the song is wistful, a longing for someone whose presence is intensely experienced, but only in the keen imagination of memory.

The Pasture, page 258. The American pianist and composer Charles Naginski (1909–1940) attended the Juilliard School to study and teach composition. Because of his untimely death from drowning at age 31, his compositional output is limited to a few symphonic works, two string quartets, and several songs. "The Pasture" (1940) was written for Paula Frisch, a well-known Danish American soprano who championed modern international song literature. Much of the success of the song is due to the charming poem by Robert Frost (1874–1963), one of America's most gifted poets. Frost's poetic language is based on a combination of humor and seriousness that was common to the folk of rural New England, where he lived for most of his adult life. The musical material is straightforward in its support of the cheerful nature of the text. The playful piano accompaniment moves along in a skipping mood, pausing only when reference is made to "fetch the little calf." Cleaning the pasture spring to keep it clear of debris is a regular farm chore to guarantee clean drinking water. The person singing can be portrayed as either a young person speaking to a friend or sibling, or a young parent speaking to a child.

The Daisies, page 254. One of America's most outstanding composers, Samuel Barber (1910–1981) has bequeathed a treasured body of song repertoire representative of the very best in art song composition. He was the recipient of numerous honors and awards, including the prestigious Pulitzer Prize. Set to the poem "The Daisies" by the Irish author James Stephens (1882–1950), this brief, exquisite song is folklike in its simplicity. Since the text is self-explanatory, the only performance suggestions are for the singer to keep it moving along lightly and gracefully with no noticeable awkward meter changes. For female singers, it should be perfectly acceptable to substitute *he* for *she* in measure 21.

Heavenly Grass, page 261. Paul Bowles (b. 1910) is known as a folk music specialist and writer of incidental stage music. His other career is that of novelist, and his most successful publication is *The Sheltering Sky* (1949). "Heavenly Grass" is from *Blue Mountains Ballads,* a collection of folk-style songs set to texts by Tennessee Williams (1911–1983). The meaning of the poem is somewhat obscure and free to interpretation. A rather obvious interpretation can be based on the religious belief that we come from God (heaven), live on earth, and long to eventually return home to God. In other words, we are all angels who spend some time on earth as a way of experiencing the human condition. One can almost imagine the ethereal world of clouds and light in the placid opening section, the almost abrupt, dramatic change (m. 14) when coming down to earth, and the longing "itch" to return "home" in the last seven measures.

It's All I Bring Today, page 264. Ernst Bacon (1898–1990) enjoyed a long and versatile professional career in his native United States—as concert pianist, conductor, administrator, artist/teacher, writer, and composer. After completing his musical studies at the University of Chicago and Northwestern University, he served as assistant conductor of the Rochester Opera and taught piano at Eastman. Later on he served as dean and professor of piano at the University of South Carolina–Spartanburg, followed by a directorship at Syracuse School of Music. His deep interest in song composition was strongly influenced by American writers, notably nineteenth-century poets Walt Whitman and Emily Dickinson, the latter whose eloquent poem inspired this lovely song. Written in a traditional neo-romantic style, Bacon sets Dickinson's poem

simply and sensitively. Presented from either a male or female perspective, the poem seems to express sincere love and devotion, a total surrender to one's beloved in a pastoral setting on a peaceful, pleasant day. This delicate song should be performed as smoothly and tenderly as possible, with special attention given to the high opening pitches (measures 1 and 15) at the beginning of the descending phrases. Initiate both high notes gracefully, avoiding strong, loud accents.

Infant Joy, page 266. David Evan Thomas (b. 1958) holds degrees from Northwestern University, the Eastman School, and the University of Minnesota, where he earned a doctorate in theory/composition under the tutelage of composer Dominick Argento. His work has been honored by the American Academy and Institute of Arts and Letters, The American Guild of Organists, and the McKnight Foundation. Because his interest in writing for voice has resulted in steady commissions and requests from vocalists eager to perform his music, his production of solo voice repertoire is steadily growing. Set to a familiar poem from the illuminated manuscript *Songs of Innocence* by the English poet/artist William Blake (1757–1827), "Infant Joy" was written in 1989 for the baptism of Jennifer Anne Fitzwater, the composer's godchild. In Blake's illuminated manuscript, one of the illuminations depicts the infant held in the bud of a flower. This charming song's nature is pure innocence and joyful wonder and should be sung delicately and with simplicity.

INFORMATION ABOUT THE MUSICAL THEATER SONGS

The popularity of American and British musical theater has become a love affair with the general public in these two countries and has gradually spread all over the world, especially throughout continental Europe. In many of the provincial German opera houses it has become standard practice to include at least one musical in the performing repertoire of the annual ten-month season. And in the United States, many regional companies regularly produce *musicals,* though sometimes only in the summer. In addition to professional activity, numerous performances are produced under the auspices of educational institutions and community groups. In almost every community (or at least within a reasonable commuting distance) the average American has an opportunity to attend a musical show at least occasionally.

Current musical comedy is directly descended from the burlesque, extravaganza, and comic opera prominent in London during the 1890s. These works were characterized by having a loose plot combining comic and romantic interests and a musical score of catchy songs, ensembles, and dances. In general, both **operetta** and musical comedy are still characterized as lighthearted musical theater pieces based on entertaining stories, appealingly accessible music, and spoken dialogue. A prime example of early operetta is discussed below.

Tipsy Song, page 268. Jacques Offenbach (1819–1880), a French composer of German heritage, is celebrated as one of the most outstanding late-nineteenth century composers of popular music, especially operetta. Among his numerous stage works is *La Périchole* (1868), set to a libretto by the renowned Ludovic Halévy (1834–1908). Set in eighteenth-century Peru, the story is centered around Périchole and Piquillo, street singers/lovers struggling to earn a living in Lima, which is ruled by the eccentric viceroy, Don Andres de Ribera. Much smitten by Périchole, the roving viceroy takes advantage of her destitute condition by offering her a position in the palace as a lady-in-waiting to his nonexistent wife. However, since only married women are allowed to live in the palace, the viceroy arranges a "marriage of convenience" between Périchole and the wretched Piquillo. Following the official wedding, the married couple (unrecognized by one another) enjoy an unaccustomed feast of much food and drink. Both become inebriated, prompting Périchole to sing about her tipsy condition in this simple aria. (*Note:* This selection is provided in the Anthology because it offers singers an opportunity to "loosen up" and "let go" of performing inhibitions; it is *not* an endorsement of *drunkenness*, nor is it intended to make fun of those who have a drinking problem.) The appropriate attitude for this aria is one of being pleasantly *tipsy*, or slightly off-balance, not falling-down drunk. (See Fig. 19, p. 137.)

During the 1920s and 1930s, a plethora of shows by such composers as George Gershwin, Jerome Kern, and Vincent Youmans solidified the pattern for success for the musical plays that were extremely popular on and off Broadway. From the 1940s through the 1960s, the "golden age" of musical theater, there was an enormous output of first-class shows by such acclaimed composer/lyricist teams as Richard Rodgers and Oscar Hammerstein II, and Frederick Loewe and Alan Jay Lerner. In more recent times some outstanding musicals have been created, notably by such popular composers as Andrew Lloyd Webber and Stephen Sondheim.

The reason for emphasizing shows produced during the 1940s through the 1960s in this Anthology is based on the vocal, musical, and artistic challenges inherent in these works. Although these musicals provide some opportunities for character voices, a majority of the songs require a high level of vocal skills. The songs in this Anthology are selected for their educational potential in the development of vocal, musical, and dramatic skills. According to standard performing practice, any voice type may perform these songs, regardless of the original role designation in the musicals. The only criterion should be whether or not the song is suitable for an individual singer's composite capabilities.

Oh, What a Beautiful Morning, page 272. Composer Rodgers (1902–1979) and lyricist Hammerstein (1895–1960) were the most prolific and successful musical comedy duo team during the 1940s and 1950s. From a total of nine musicals, five are still considered monuments of the American musical theater: *Oklahoma!, Carousel, South Pacific, The King and I,* and *The Sound of Music.* The musical *Oklahoma!* (1943) was the first collaborative effort of Rodgers and Hammerstein, and it was a highly successful one. The rural setting and the down-home story struck a familiar chord in the hearts of Americans. The song is sung at the beginning of the show by the young man, Curly, as he arrives to court Laurey at her farm home. He's a positive, outgoing type and is happy over his prospects of seeing her again. As is the case with most musical show songs, there's nothing wrong with a Laurey singing the song either. This song is a delight for anyone to sing and is a great way to start a new day.

Almost Like Being in Love, page 278. Frederick Loewe (1904–1988) was an accomplished piano virtuoso from Berlin who became an aficionado of American music when he began playing in nightclubs in New York City as a young man. When he teamed up with Alan Jay Lerner (1918–1986), a talented scriptwriter with a wealthy background (Lerner Shops), the alliance produced several hit musicals, including *Brigadoon* in 1947. The success of this endearingly sentimental show was a combination of the enchanting story and the fetching music. Tommy, on a hunting trip from New York City to Scotland, sings "Almost Like Being In Love" after meeting the village lass Fiona for the first time. The song became an instant hit and secured the reputations of Loewe and Lerner. The song should be sung with exuberance and ecstasy, as though falling in love for the first time.

On a Clear Day, page 275. In the musical *On a Clear Day You Can See Forever,* lyricist Alan Jay Lerner joined up with composer Burton Lane (b. 1912) to produce a story set in New York City. The song is sung by Daisy Gambel, a highly susceptible and somewhat "kooky" young woman who claims she is also Melinda, an eighteenth-century wench. An affair gradually develops with her psychiatrist/hypnotist Dr. Mark Bruckner, who falls in love with her. In performing the song, imagine a clear day in the city, when the smog has dissipated, viewing the blue skies and smelling the fresh air. Then, too, there's a parallel meaning relating to how your mental and emotional life affects the way things appear and ultimately influence you. ". . . When completely lucid and happy, you can see forever." This is a happy song, full of encouragement and hope.

Put On a Happy Face, page 298.   Charles Strouse (b. 1928), classically trained composer and jazz pianist, teamed up with Lee Adams (b. 1924) to produce *Bye, Bye, Birdie* (1961), a musical based loosely on the emerging popularity of rock-and-roller Elvis Presley. Another successful collaboration was "Those Were the Days," the theme song for *All In the Family,* the best-known sitcom in television history. In the musical, Albert Peters is the enthusiastic agent ("music business bum") of Conrad Birdie, rock star. He sings this "toe-tapping" song early in the show to reinforce his confidence that his promotional schemes will ultimately bear fruit. The only suggestion is to sing it straight with solid vocal technique, avoiding any temptation to create a "character voice."

'S Wonderful, page 282.   Born of Russian Jewish immigrant parents, George Gershwin (1898–1937) and his brother Ira Gershwin (1896–1983) collaborated on the production of several musicals, including *Of Thee I Sing,* for which they received the Pulitzer Prize, and *Funny Face,* for which this clever song was written. Fred and Adele Astaire portrayed the roles of the lovers, Peter Thurston and Frankie, respectively. The lyrics play upon typical American speech colloquialisms, such as slurring and contracting words. For example, the very proper "It is wonderful" can be partially shortened to "It's wonderful" and finally can be fully abbreviated to "'S wonderful." Intended to be sung in a carefree, playful manner, the song may be sung either as a solo or with a "he" and a "she" singing to one another as indicated in the score. For persons who have difficulty with subtleties in American English, certain words may present some interpretative difficulties, such as *fash* meaning "fashion"; *pash* meaning "passion"; *emosh* meaning "emotion"; and *devosh* meaning "devotion." *Four leaf clover time* means "good luck time." Enjoy!

Till There Was You, page 286.   Serving the dual capacities of lyricist and composer, Meredith Willson (1902– 1984) established his musical reputation with the big hit *The Music Man* (1957), a traditional musical evoking the life of a small American town at the turn of the century. The story presents Harold Hill, an evangelistic music salesman who arrives in town to hawk musical instruments and ends up falling in love with the prudish and lovely Marian (the librarian). They each sing this charming old-fashioned love song at different times in the show as an expression of their true feelings about one another. Strive for simplicity and sincerity when singing this song, and maintain a flowing musical line, avoiding any tendency toward "crooning." Since the one verse may be repeated, it will need a slightly different treatment to make it interesting. It would also work to have a "he" and "she" sing the song, each taking a turn, beginning with the woman. At the pickup to measure 33

and lasting to the end, the two singers might harmonize a closing duet, effectively dramatizing the romantic angle.

Try to Remember, page 290.   Composer Harvey Schmidt (b. 1929), and lyricist Tom Jones (b. 1928), met while attending the University of Texas. Their first collaboration was a college show entitled *Hipsy-Boo,* and their first professional venture was a one-act version of *Fantasticks* for Bernard College's summer theater program. In 1960 a two-act version debuted on off-Broadway, eventually gaining sufficient positive acclaim to be awarded the Vernon Rice Prize for outstanding off-Broadway production. "Try to Remember," the opening song sung by the narrator, El Gallo, became a hit tune. Sung from the perspective of a mature person (one over 30), the song asks you to try to remember how it felt to be young and in love for the first time. The bittersweet, nostalgic mood should remind you of a sweetly remembered past, of times gone by but fondly remembered. The challenge with singing the same music three times is to make each verse slightly different to suit the subtle changes of the text.

Any Dream Will Do, page 294.   Sir Andrew Lloyd Webber (b. 1948) has been called by some the "Sir Arthur Sullivan of the Rock Age" a testament to his popularity as a composer of popular music with a classical twist. His many notable stage works are revered worldwide, for example, the highly celebrated musical, *The Phantom of the Opera.* Webber received his musical training at the Royal College of Music where he studied piano, violin, and french horn. In collaboration with Tim Rice, a law student and lyricist, the duo created their first musical, *Joseph and the Amazing Technicolor Dreamcoat,* a liberal adaptation that combined Biblical scripture with country music and French chanson. Written in 1968 for a student performance at a London school, *Joseph* soon was moved to the West End Theater where it had a successful professional run, including a record album and national television in 1972. Joseph, the protagonist, sings "Any Dream Will Do" at the conclusion of the show, when reunited with his brothers. From the Bible we learn that Joseph, the highly favored eleventh son of Jacob and Rachel, is given a many colored coat. Joseph's envious brothers sell him into Egyptian slavery, reporting to their parents that he has been murdered. As an interpreter of dreams, Joseph rises from slavery to serve wisely and successfully as the Pharaoh's prime minister. When his brothers are sent to Egypt to buy corn, Joseph recognizes them, conceals his identity, and sends them back with money hidden in their bags. When they next return, he reveals himself to them, treats them kindly, and offers them a home in Egypt. The text of the song speaks of Joseph's dreams, with references to his mournful parents, prized coat, descent into slavery, and desire to experience his original dreams.

FOREIGN LANGUAGE SONG TEXTS: IPA AND LITERAL TRANSLATIONS

There is perhaps no more controversial subject in voice study than that of correct diction. Although experts generally agree on most fundamental vowel and consonant sounds, some particular phonemes are open to question. Such factors as a singer's vocal technique, regional speech differences within a single country, a composer's unique textual setting, and contradictory authoritative information (language dictionaries) must be considered when approaching matters of diction.

In general, classical stage diction is the standard used in presenting IPA singing texts, except for some folk song texts. For example, because of the peculiar characteristics of the Swabian folk dialect, Brahms' arrangement of the German folk song "Da unten im Tale" presents peculiar phoneticization problems.

All foreign language song texts included in this Anthology are presented below in a simplified IPA format. In preparation for using these transcriptions, each area of concern (regarding use of IPA symbols) will be briefly discussed.

Syllabic Duration

Since most syllabic durations are determined by the manner in which the composer sets the text to music, only problematic vowel durations are indicated in this book. The [ː] symbol, indicating a prolonged vowel sound, is used only in those cases where the longer sounding vowels need emphasizing, as when two or more vowels are voiced to a word set to one note. Two examples are the Italian word *mio* ("my") which is presented as [miːɔ], and the German word *rein* ("pure") which is presented as [rɑːɪn]. This procedure helps singers avoid the common tendency of prematurely voicing second vowels in diphthongs.

Syllabic Accents

Accents of important syllables are commonly indicated by underlinings in IPA transcriptions. However, since composers normally determine syllabic accent by rhythmic and musical means, such symbols or markings are not used.

Glottal Onsets

The glottal onset symbol [/] for words beginning with a vowel is not used. In practically all circumstances, gentle glottal onsets are typically used in articulating German words beginning with vowels that occur within a sentence, as well as for certain English words that need emphasis and clarity. However, except in very rare instances of dramatic expression, glottal onsets are not used in Italian, Spanish, and French.

Elisions

Slur markings indicating word connections are used occasionally. In such cases, elisions are indicated with the slur symbol [‿] as with the two connected Italian words *è un* ("is a") which are indicated as [ɛ‿un]. Another example of using a slur indication for connecting two words is [ply‿zœ̃] for *plus un*.

Exploded and Imploded Consonants

Singers must give attention to such consonants as [k], [p], and [t] which are "exploded" (more air released) in English and German but imploded (minimal air release) in Italian, Spanish, and French.

Special IPA/Diction Matters

In most foreign languages the tongue-flipped [ɾ] is used in lieu of the general American "r." Though they are not used in the IPA transcriptions below, the rolled or trilled [r] occurs occasionally in foreign texts to indicate more vigorous speech delivery; for example, "Ich breche dich" in "Heidenröslein." Usually, "r's" are rolled at the beginning and ending of words, or in the middle of words when occurring before a consonant; for example, "tormento" in "Nel cor più non mi sento."

The Spanish songs "Niño precioso" and "Con qué la lavaré" present some special challenges with the pronunciation of e's and o's, which are generally more closed than Italian, but not as closed as German, for example. Also, "v" is pronounced more like [β], which is less precise than the American "v." The same holds true for "d's," which are pronounced somewhat similarly to the voiceless phoneme [ð]. Essentially, "v's" and "d's" will sound more authentic if they are softed.

All song texts are assigned figure numbers according to the order of occurrence in the informational notes.

SONG TEXT: IPA TRANSCRIPTIONS AND TRANSLATIONS

Figure 1   **Con qué la lavaré** (koŋ ke la laβare)

koŋ	ke	la	laβare	la	tes	de	la	mi	kara
Con	**qué**	**la**	**lavaré**	**la**	**tez**	**de**	**la**	**mi**	**cara,**
With	*what*	*it*	*will wash*	*the*	*skin*	*of*	*-the*	*my*	*face,*

koŋ	ke	la laβare	koŋ	ke	la laβare
Con	**qué**	**la lavaré,**	**con**	**qué**	**la lavaré,**
With	*what*	*it will wash,*	*with*	*what*	*it will wash*

ke	biβo	mal	penaða
que	**vivo**	**mal**	**penada.**
That	*I live*	*badly*	*punished.*

laβanse	las	kasaðas	kon	aɣa	de	limones
Lávanse	**las**	**casadas**	**con**	**agua**	**de**	**limones;**
Wash	*the*	*matrons*	*with*	*water*	*of*	*lemons;*

(The married women wash themselves with lemon water.)

laβome	jo	kwitaða	kon	penas	i	dolores
lávome	**yo,**	**cuitada,**	**con**	**penas**	**y**	**dolores.**
I wash	*myself,*	*I sorrowful*	*with*	*pain*	*and*	*sufferings.*

Figure 2   **Da unten im Tale** (dɑ ʊntən ɪm tɑlə)

da	ʊntən	ɪm tɑlə	lɔːyfts	vasər	zo	tryp
Da	**unten**	**im Tale**	**lauft's**	**Wasser**	**so**	**trub**
There	*below*	*in the valley*	*runs*	*water*	*so*	*gloomy*

ʊnt	i	kan	dirs	nɛt	zagən	i	hap	di	zo	lip.
Und	**i**	**kann**	**dir's**	**net**	**sagen,**	**i**	**hab**	**di**	**so**	**lieb.**
and	*I*	*can*	*you-it*	*not*	*say,*	*I*	*have*	*you*	*so*	*dear.*

ʃpriçst	alvaːɪl	fon	lip	ʃpriçst	alvaːɪl	fɔn	trɔːy
Sprichst	**all'weil**	**von**	**Lieb,**	**sprichst**	**all'weil**	**von**	**Treu,**
Speak-you	*always*	*of*	*love,*	*speak*	*always*	*of*	*faith,*

ʊnt	a	bisɛlə	falʃhaːɪt	ɪs	aːʊ	vol	dabaːɪ
Und	**a**	**bissele**	**Falschheit**	**is**	**au**	**wohl**	**dabei!**
and	*a*	*bit-of*	*falsehood*	*is*	*also*	*indeed*	*with-it!*

ʊnt	vɛn	i	dirs	tsenmal	zak	das	i	di	lip
Und	**wenn**	**i**	**dir's**	**zehnmal**	**sag',**	**dass**	**i**	**di**	**lieb',**
And	*if*	*I*	*to-you*	*ten-times*	*say,*	*that*	*I*	*you*	*love,*

ʊnt	du	vɪlst	nit	fɛrʃteən	mʊs	i	halt	vaːɪtər	gen
Und	**du**	**willst**	**nit**	**verstehen,**	**muss**	**i**	**halt**	**weiter**	**geh'n.**
And	*you*	*want*	*not*	*to-understand,*	*must*	*I*	*just*	*away*	*go.*

fyɾ	di	tsaːɪt	vo	du	glipt	mi	hast	da	daŋk	i	dir	ʃøn
Für	**die**	**Zeit,**	**wo**	**du**	**g'liebt**	**mi**	**hast,**	**da**	**dank'**	**i**	**dir**	**Schön,**
For	*the*	*time,*	*when*	*you*	*loved*	*me*	*have,*	*then*	*thank*	*I*	*you*	*kindly,*

ʊnt	i	vynʃ	das	dɪrs	andərsvo	bɛsər	mak	gen
Und	**i**	**wünsch,**	**dass**	**dir's**	**anderswo**	**besser**	**mag**	**geh'n.**
And	*I*	*wish,*	*that*	*for-you*	*elsewhere*	*better*	*may*	*go.*

Figure 3 Niño precioso (niɲo presjoso)

niɲo	presjoso	mas	kel	armiɲo
Niño	**precioso,**	**mas**	**que el**	**armiño,**
Baby boy	*precious,*	*more*	*than*	*ermine,*

riswɛɲo	niɲo	djos	del	amor
Risueño	**niño,**	**Dios**	**del**	**amor.**
Sleep	*baby boy,*	*God*	*of*	*love.*

dwerme	traɲkilo	dwerme‿entretanto	
Duerme	**tranquilo,**	**duerme**	**entretanto**
Sleep	*peacefully,*	*sleep*	*meanwhile*

eleβa	un	kanto	mjumilde	βos
Eleva	**un**	**canto,**	**mi humilde**	**voz.**
Lifts	*a*	*song,*	*my humble*	*voice.*

dwerme	tʃikitito	ke	o	jase	friːɔ
Duerme,	**chiquitito,**	**que**	**hoy**	**hace**	**frio.**
Sleep,	*little one,*	*that*	*today*	*is*	*cold.*

dwerme	tʃikitito	jo	βelɑre
Duerme,	**chiquitito,**	**jo**	**velaré.**
Sleep,	*little one,*	*I*	*will watch.*

Figure 4 Star vicino (star vitʃinɔ)

star	vitʃinɔ‿al	bɛl	idɔl	kɛ	sɑma	e il	pju	vago	dilɛtːtɔ	damor
Star	**vicino al**	**bel**	**idol**	**che**	**s'ama,**	**È il**	**piu**	**vago**	**diletto**	**d'amor!**
To be	*near the*	*beautiful*	*idol*	*one*	*loves,*	*Is the*	*most*	*charming*	*delight*	*of love!*

star	lɔntano	kɔlɛːi	kɛ	si	brama	ɛ	damore‿il	pju	mɛstɔ	dɔlor
Star	**lontano**	**colei**	**che**	**si**	**brama,**	**È**	**d'amore il**	**più**	**mesto**	**dolor!**
To	*be far*	*from her*	*that*	*one*	*desires,*	*Is*	*of love*	*the most*	*sad*	*affliction!*

Figure 5 **Toglietemi la vita ancor** (tɔʎɛtɛmi la vita‿ankɔr)

tɔʎɛtɛmi	la	vita‿ankɔr	krudɛli	tʃɛli
Toglietemi	**la**	**vita ancor,**	**crudeli**	**cieli**
Take away	*the*	*life from me,*	*cruel*	*heavens*

sɛ	mi	vɔlɛtɛ	rapi	rɛːil	kɔr
se	**mi**	**volete**	**rapire**	**il**	**cor.**
If	*from me*	*you wish*	*to steal*	*the*	*heart.*

nɛgatɛmi	i	raːi	dɛl	di	sɛvɛrɛ	sfɛrɛ
Negatemi	**i**	**rai**	**del**	**di,**	**severe**	**sfere,**
Deny to me	*the*	*light*	*of*	*day,*	*severe*	*stars,*

sɛ	vagɛ	sjɛtɛ	dɛl	miːɔ	dɔlor
se	**vaghe**	**siete**	**del**	**mio**	**dolor.**
If	*glad*	*you are*	*of*	*my*	*sorrow.*

Figure 6 **Bist du bei mir** (bɪst du baːɪ mir)

bɪst	du	baːɪ	mir	ge	ɪç	mɪt	frɔːydən
Bist	**du**	**bei**	**mir,**	**geh**	**ich**	**mit**	**Freuden**
Are	*you*	*with*	*me,*	*go*	*I*	*with*	*joy*

tsʊm	ʃtɛrbən	ʊnt	tsu	maːɪnər	ru
zum	**Sterben**	**und**	**zu**	**meiner**	**Ruh!**
to	*dying*	*and*	*to*	*my*	*rest!*

ax	vi	fɛrgnʏkt	ver	zo	maːɪn	ɛndə
Ach,	**wie**	**vergnügt**	**wär**	**so**	**mein**	**Ende,**
Ah,	*how*	*pleasant*	*would be*	*thus*	*my*	*end,*

ɛs	drʏktən	daːɪnə	ʃønən	hɛndə	mir	di	getrɔːyən	aːʊgən	tsu
es	**drückten**	**deine**	**schönen**	**Hände**	**mir**	**die**	**getreuen**	**Augen**	**zu!**
it	*closed*	*your*	*beloved*	*hands*	*me*	*the*	*faithful*	*eyes*	*to (shut)!*

Figure 7   **Lascia ch'io pianga** (laʃa kiːɔ pjaŋga)

laʃa	kiːɔ	pjaŋga	la	dura	sɔrtɛ	e	ke	sɔspiri	la	libɛrta
Lascia	**ch'io**	**pianga**	**la**	**dura**	**sorte**	**e**	**che**	**sospiri**	**la**	**libertà;**
Allow	*that I*	*weep*	*the*	*harsh*	*fate*	*and*	*that*	*I sigh (for)*	*the*	*liberty;*

il	dwɔlɔ‿infraŋga	kwestɛ	ritɔrtɛ	de	mjeːi	martiri	sol	pɛr	pjɛta	si
Il	**doulo infranga**	**queste**	**retorte,**	**de**	**miei**	**martiri**	**sol**	**per**	**pietà,**	**si, (etc.)**
The	*grief shatter*	*these*	*chains,*	*of*	*my*	*torments*	*if only*	*for*	*pity,*	*yes, (etc.)*

Figure 8   **Non lo dirò col labbro** (nɔn lɔ dirɔ kɔl labːbrɔ)

nɔn	lɔ	dirɔ	kɔl	labːbrɔ	ke	tanto	ardir	nɔn‿a
Non	**lo**	**dirò**	**col**	**labbro**	**che**	**tanto**	**ardir**	**non ha.**
Not	*will*	*I say*	*with*	*(the) lips*	*which*	*so much*	*risk*	*not have.*

fɔrsɛ	kɔn	lɛ	favilːle	del	avidɛ	pupilːle
Forse	**con**	**lé**	**favillé**	**dell**	**avidé**	**pupillé,**
Perhaps	*with*	*the*	*sparks*	*of*	*avid*	*pupils,*

pɛr	dir	kɔme	tutːto	ardɔ	lɔ	zgwardɔ	parlɛra
per	**dir**	**comé**	**tutto**	**ardo**	**lo**	**sguardo**	**parlerà:**
to	*speak*	*how*	*everything*	*flames*	*the*	*look*	*will tell:*

Figure 9   **Nel cor piu non mi sento** (nɛl kɔr pju nɔn mi sɛntɔ)

nɛl	kɔr	pju	nɔn	mi	sɛntɔ	brilːlar	la	dʒɔventu
Nel	**cor**	**più**	**non**	**mi**	**sento**	**brillar**	**la**	**gioventù;**
In the	*heart*	*more*	*not*	*myself*	*feel*	*sparkle*	*the*	*youth;*

kadʒon	del	miːɔ	tɔrmentɔ	amor	seːi	kɔlpa	tu
Cagion	**del**	**mio**	**tormento,**	**amor**	**sei**	**colpa**	**tu.**
Cause	*of*	*my*	*torment,*	*Love,*	*are*	*guilty*	*you.*

mi	pitːtsiki	mi	stutːtsiki	mi	pundʒiki	mi	mastiki
Mi	**pizzichi,**	**mi**	**stuzzichi,**	**mi**	**pungichi,**	**mi**	**mastichi;**
Me	*you pinch,*	*me*	*you tease,*	*me*	*you prick,*	*me*	*you bite;*

ke	kɔza‿ɛ	kwesta‿ɔːimɛ	pjɛta
Che	**cosa è**	**questa, ohimè?**	**Pietà!**
What	*thing is*	*this, alas?*	*Pity!*

amo	rɛ‿un	tʃɛrtɔ	kɛ	ke	disperar	mi	fa
Amor	**è un**	**certo**	**che,**	**che**	**disperar**	**mi**	**fa!**
Love	*is a*	*certain*	*something,*	*which*	*despair*	*me*	*makes!*

Figure 10 *Ridente la calma* (ridɛntɛ la kalma)

ridɛntɛ	la	kalma	nɛl‿	lalma	si	dɛsti,
Ridente	**la**	**calma**	**nell'**	**alma**	**si**	**desti,**
Smiling	*the*	*calm*	*in the*	*soul*	*itself*	*awaken,*

ne	rɛsti	un	seɲɔ	di	zdeɲo‿	e	timor.
ne	**resti**	**un**	**segno**	**di**	**sdegno**	**e**	**timor.**
nor	*let remain*	*a*	*trace*	*of*	*anger*	*and*	*fear.*

tu	vjɛni	fratːtantɔ	a	strindzɛr	miːɔ	bɛnɛ
tu	**vieni**	**frattanto**	**a**	**stringer,**	**mio**	**bene,**
You	*come*	*meanwhile*	*to*	*tighten,*	*my*	*beloved,*

lɛ	doltʃɛ	katenɛ	si	gratɛ‿al	miːɔ	kɔr
le	**dolce**	**catene**	**si**	**grate al**	**mio**	**cor.**
the	*sweet*	*chains*	*so*	*welcome*	*to*	*my*	*heart.*

iɛ = e e

ei = i

Figure 11 *Ich liebe dich* (ɪç libə dɪç)

ɪç	libə	dɪç	zo	vi	du	mɪç	am	abənt	ʊnd	am	mɔrgən
Ich	**liebe**	**dich,**	**so**	**wie**	**du**	**mich,**	**am**	**Abend**	**und**	**am**	**Morgen,**
I	*love*	*you,*	*so*	*as*	*you*	*me,*	*in*	*evening*	*and*	*in*	*morning,*

nɔx	var	kaːin	tak	vo	du	ʊnt	ɪç	nɪçt	taːiltən	ʊnzrə	ʒɔrgən
noch	**'war**	**kein**	**Tag,**	**wo**	**du**	**und**	**ich**	**nicht**	**theilten**	**uns're**	**Sorgen.**
there	*was*	*no*	*day,*	*where*	*you*	*and*	*I*	*not*	*shared*	*our*	*sorrows.*

aːox	varən	zi	fyr	dɪç	ʊnt	mɪç	gɛtaːilt	laːiçt	t͡su zu	ɛrtragən
Auch	**waren**	**sie**	**für**	**dich**	**und**	**mich**	**getheilt**	**leicht**	**zu**	**ertragen;**
Also	*were*	*they*	*for*	*you*	*and*	*me*	*shared*	*easy*	*to*	*endure;*

du	trøstətəst	ɪm	kʊmmər	mɪç	ɪç	vaːint	ɪn	daːinə	klagən
du	**tröstetest**	**im**	**Kummer**	**mich,**	**ich**	**weint'**	**in**	**deine**	**Klagen,**
you	*comforted*	*in*	*sorrow*	*me,*	*I*	*cried*	*in*	*your*	*laments,*

drʊm	gɔtəs	zegən	ybər	dir	du	maːinəs	lebəns	frɔːydə
D'rum	**Gottes**	**Segen**	**über**	**dir,**	**du**	**meines**	**Lebens**	**Freude,**
Therefore	*God's*	*blessings*	*upon*	*you,*	*you,*	*my*	*life's*	*joy.*

gɔt	ʃytsə	dɪç	ɛrhalt	dɪç	mir	ʃyts	ʊnt	ɛrhalt	ʊns	baːidə
Gott	**schütze**	**dich,**	**erhalt'**	**dich**	**mir,**	**schütz'**	**und**	**erhalt'**	**uns**	**beide!**
God	*protect*	*you,*	*keep*	*you*	*me,*	*protect*	*and*	*keep*	*us*	*both!*

Figure 12 **Vaga luna** (vɑɡɑ lunɑ)

vɑɡɑ	lunɑ	ke	inɑrdʒɛnti	kwɛstɛ	rivɛ	e	kwɛsti	fjɔri
Vaga	**luna**	**che**	**inargenti**	**queste**	**rive**	**e**	**questi**	**fiori**
Lovely	*moon,*	*that*	*silvers*	*these*	*bands*	*and*	*these*	*flowers*

ed	inspiri‿ɛd‿inspiri‿	ɑʎi‿	ɛlɛmenti	il	lingwadːʒɔ	dɛlːlamor
Ed	**inspiri, ed inspiri**	**agli**	**elementi,**	**il**	**linguaggio**	**dell'amor,**
And	*breathes, and breathes*	*into the*	*elements,*	*the*	*language*	*of the love,*

tɛstimɔnjo‿or	seːi	tu	solɑ	dɛl	miːɔ	fɛrvidɔ	dezir
Testimonio	**or**	**sei**	**tu**	**sola**	**del**	**mio**	**fervido**	**desir,**
Witness	*now*	*are*	*you*	*alone*	*of-the*	*my*	*fervid*	*desire,*

ed‿ɑ	lɛi	ke	minːnamorɑ	kontɑ‿i	palpiti‿e‿	i	sɔspir
Ed a	**lei**	**che**	**m'innamora**	**conta i**	**palpiti e**	**i**	**sospir.**
And to	*her*	*who*	*me-makes-fall-in-love*	*tell the*	*tremblings and*	*the*	*sighs.*

dilːlɛ	pur	ke	lɔntanantsa	il	miːɔ	dwɔl	non	pwɔ	lɛ	dir
Dille	**pur**	**che**	**lontananza**	**il**	**mio**	**duol,**	**non**	**può**	**le**	**dir,**
Tell her	*only,*	*that*	*distance,*	*the*	*my*	*grief,*	*not-I*	*can*	*to-her*	*say,*

kɛ	sɛ	nutrɔ‿	unɑ	spɛrantsa	ɛlːlɑ‿ɛ	sol	si	nɛlːlavːvɛnir
Che	**se**	**nutro**	**una**	**speranza,**	**ella è**	**sol,**	**si,**	**nell'avvenir.**
That	*if I*	*nourish*	*one*	*hope,*	*she is*	*only,*	*yes,*	*in-the-future.*

dilːlɛ	pur	ke	dʒɔrno‿e	sera	kontɔ	lorɛ	dɛl	dɔlor
Dille	**pur**	**che**	**giorno e**	**sera**	**conto**	**l'ore**	**del**	**dolor;**
Tell-her	*just*	*that*	*day and*	*evening*	*I-count*	*the-hours*	*of-the*	*sadness;*

kɛ‿	unɑ	spɛmɛ	luziŋgjɛrɑ	mi	kɔnfɔrtɑ	nɛlːlamor
Che	**una**	**speme**	**lusinghiera**	**mi**	**conforta**	**nell'amor.**
That	*a*	*hope*	*enticing*	*me*	*comforts*	*in-the love.*

Figure 13 **An die Musik** (an di muzik)

du holdə kʊnst ɪn vifil graːʊən ʃtʊndən
Du holde Kunst, in wieviel grauen Stunden,
You lovely art, in how many gray hours,

vo mɪç dɛs lebəns vɪldər kraːɪs ʊmʃtrɪkt
Wo mich des Lebens wilder Kreis umstrickt,
Where me the life's wild ring around-binds,

hast du maːɪn hɛrts tsu varmər lip ɛntsʊndən
Hast du mein Herz zu warmer Lieb' entzunden,
Have you my heart to warm love kindled,

hast mɪç ɪn aːɪnə bɛsrə vɛlt ɛntrʏkt
Hast mich in eine bessre Welt entrückt!
Have me into a better world wafted away!

ɔft hat aːɪn zɔːyftsər daːɪnər harf ɛntflɔsən
Oft hat ein Seufzer, deiner Harf' entflossen,
Often has a sigh, your harp flowed away,

aːɪn zysər haːɪligər akɔrt fɔn dir
Ein süsser, heiliger Akkord von dir,
A sweet, holy chord from you,

den hɪmməl bɛsrər tsaːɪtən mir ɛrʃlɔsən
Den Himmel bessrer Zeiten mir erschlossen,
The heavens a better time to-me show (open up),

du hɔldə kʊnst ɪc daŋkə dir dafʏr
Du holde Kunst, ich danke dir dafür!
You lovely art, I thank you for that!

Figure 14 **Heidenröslein** (haːɪdənrøzlaːɪn)

zɑ	aːɪn	knap	aːɪn	røzlaːɪn	ʃten	røzlaːɪn	aʊf	der	haːɪdən
Sah	**ein**	**Knab'**	**ein**	**Røslein**	**stehn,**	**Røslein**	**auf**	**der**	**Heiden,**
Saw	*a*	*boy*	*a*	*little rose*	*standing,*	*little rose*	*on*	*the*	*meadow,*

vɑɾ	zo	jʊŋ	ʊnt	mɔrgənʃøn	lif	er	ʃnɛl	ɛs	nɑ	tsu	zen
War	**so**	**jung**	**und**	**morgenschön,**	**Lief**	**er**	**schnell**	**es**	**nah**	**zu**	**sehn,**
It was	*so*	*young*	*and*	*morning-beautiful,*	*ran*	*he*	*quickly*	*it*	*near*	*to*	*see,*

zɑs	mɪt	filən	frɔːydən
sah's	**mit**	**vielen**	**Freuden.**
saw-it	*with*	*many*	*joys.*

røzlaːɪn	røzlaːɪn	røzlaːɪn	rot	røzlaːɪn	aʊf	der	haːɪdən
Røslein,	**Røslein,**	**Røslein**	**rot,**	**Røslein**	**auf**	**der**	**Heiden.**
Little rose,	*little rose,*	*little rose*	*red,*	*little rose*	*on*	*the*	*meadow.*

knabə	ʃprɑx	ɪç	brɛçə	dɪç	das	du	eviç	denkst	ɑn	mɪç
Knabe	**sprach:**	**"Ich**	**breche**	**dich,**	**dass**	**du**	**ewig**	**denkst**	**an**	**mich,**
Boy	*spoke:*	*"I*	*(will) break*	*you,*	*so that*	*you*	*forever*	*think*	*about*	*me,*

ʊnt	ɪç	vɪls	nɪçt	laːɪdən
Und	**ich**	**will's**	**nicht**	**leiden."**
and	*I*	*will it*	*not*	*suffer."*

ʊnt	der	vɪldə	knabə	brɑxs	røzlaːɪn	røzlaːɪn	vertə	zɪç	ʊnt	ʃtɑx
Und	**der**	**wilde**	**Knabe**	**brach's**	**Røslein...**	**Røslein**	**wehrte**	**sich**	**und**	**stach,**
and	*the*	*wild*	*boy*	*broke the*	*little rose...*	*Little rose*	*defended*	*itself*	*and*	*pricked;*

half	im	dɔx	kaːɪn	ve	ʊnt	ɑx	mʊst	ɛs	ebən	laːɪdən
Half	**ihm**	**doch**	**kein**	**Weh**	**und**	**Ach,**	**musst'**	**es**	**eben**	**leiden.**
Helped	*it*	*but*	*no*	*pain*	*and*	*"ah,"*	*must*	*it*	*just*	*suffer.*

Figure 15 **Seligkeit** (zelɪçkaːɪt)

frɔːydən	zəndər	tsal	blyn	im	hɪməlszal
Freuden	**sonder**	**Zahl**	**blühn**	**im**	**Himmelssahl!**
Joys	*without*	*number*	*bloom*	*in*	*Heaven's hall!*

eŋəln	ʊnt	fɛrklɛrtən	wi	di	fɛtər	lertən
Engeln	**und**	**Verklärten,**	**wie**	**die**	**Väter**	**lehrten,**
Angels	*and*	*(the) transfigured,*	*as*	*the*	*fathers*	*taught.*

o	da	møçht	ɪç	zaːin	ʊnt	mɪç	eviç	frɔːyn
O,	**da**	**möcht**	**ich**	**sein,**	**und**	**mich**	**ewig**	**freun!**
O	*there*	*would*	*I*	*be,*	*and*	*to me*	*eternally*	*joyful!*

jedəm	lɛçhelt	traːʊt	aːɪnə	hɪmɛlsbraːʊt
Jedem	**lächelt**	**traut**	**eine**	**Himmelsbraut;**
Upon	*all smiles*	*trustingly*	*a*	*heavenly bride.*

harf	ʊnt	psaltər	kliŋət	ʊnt	man	tanst	ʊnt	ziŋət
Harf	**und**	**Psalter**	**klinget,**	**und**	**man**	**tanzt**	**und**	**singet.**
Harp	*and*	*psalter*	*sound,*	*and*	*people*	*dance*	*and*	*sing.*

o	da	møçt	ɪç	zaːin	ʊnt	mɪç	eviç	frɔːyn
O,	**da**	**möcht**	**ich**	**sein,**	**und**	**mich**	**ewig**	**freun!**
O	*there*	*would*	*I*	*be,*	*and*	*to me*	*eternally*	*joyful!*

libər	blaːɪp	ɪç	hir	lɛçelt	laːʊra	mir
Lieber	**bleib**	**ich**	**hier,**	**lächelt**	**Laura**	**mir,**
Rather	*remain*	*I*	*here,*	*smiles*	*Laura*	*to me,*

aːɪnən	blɪk	der	zagət	das	ɪç	aːʊsgɛklagət
Einen	**Blick,**	**der**	**saget,**	**dass**	**ich**	**ausgeklaget.**
A	*look*	*which*	*says*	*that*	*I*	*need not worry.*

zelɪç	dan	mɪt	ir	blaːɪp	ɪç	eviç	hir
Selig	**dann**	**mit**	**ihr,**	**bleib**	**ich**	**ewig**	**hier!**
Blissful	*then*	*with*	*her*	*remain*	*I*	*eternally*	*here!*

Figure 16 **Du bist wie eine Blume** (du bɪst vi aːɪnə blumə)

du	bɪst	vi	aːɪnə	blumə	zo	ʃøːn	zo	raːɪn	ʊnt	hɔlt
Du	**bist**	**wie**	**eine**	**Blume,**	**so**	**schön,**	**so**	**rein,**	**und**	**hold;**
You	*are*	*as*	*a*	*flower,*	*so*	*lovely,*	*so*	*pure,*	*and*	*tender;*

ɪç	ʃaːʊ	dɪç	an	ʊnt	vemut	ʃlaːɪçt	mir	ɪns	hɛrts	hɪnaːɪn
Ich	**schau'**	**dich**	**an,**	**und**	**Wehmuth**	**schleicht**	**mir**	**in's**	**Herz**	**hinein.**
I	*gaze*	*at*	*you,*	*and*	*sadness*	*fills*	*me*	*in the*	*heart*	*herein.*

mir	ɪst	als	ɔp	ɪç	di	hɛndə	aːʊfs	haːʊpt	dir	legən	zɔlt
Mir	**ist,**	**als**	**ob**	**ich**	**die**	**Hände**	**auf's**	**Haupt**	**dir**	**legen**	**sollt',**
To me	*is*	*as*	*though*	*I*	*the*	*hands*	*on the*	*head*	*of yours*	*lay*	*should,*

betənt	das	gɔt	dɪç	ɛrhaltə	zo	ʃøːn	zo	raːɪn	ʊnt	hɔlt
betend,	**dass**	**Gott**	**dich**	**erhalte**	**so**	**schön,**	**so**	**rein,**	**und**	**hold.**
praying	*that*	*God*	*you*	*will keep*	*so*	*lovely,*	*so*	*pure,*	*and*	*tender.*

Figure 17 **Le Charme** (lə ʃɑrm)

kɑ̃	tɔ̃	surirə	mə	syrpri	ʒə	sɑ̃ti	frɛmir	tu	mɔ̃‿nɛtrə
Quand	**ton**	**sourire**	**me**	**surprit,**	**Je**	**sentis**	**fremir**	**tout**	**mon être,**
When	*you*	*smile*	*me*	*surprised,*	*I*	*felt*	*to-quiver*	*all*	*my being,*

mɛ	sə	ki	dɔ̃te	mɔ̃‿nɛspri	ʒə	nə	py	dabɔr	lə	kɔnɛtrə
Mais	**ce**	**qui**	**domptait**	**mon esprit,**	**Je**	**ne**	**pus**	**d'abord**	**le**	**connaître.**
But	*that*	*which*	*tamed*	*my spirit,*	*I*	*not*	*could*	*at first*	*it*	*to-know.*

kɑ̃	tɔ̃	rəgar	tɔ̃ba	syr	mwa	ʒə	sɑ̃ti	mɔ̃‿namə	sə	fɔ̃drə
Quand	**ton**	**regard**	**tomba**	**sur**	**moi,**	**Je**	**sentis**	**mon âme**	**se**	**fondre,**
When	*your*	*glance*	*fell*	*upon*	*me,*	*I*	*felt*	*my soul*	*itself*	*to-melt,*

mɛ	sə	kə	sərɛ	sɛ‿temwa	ʒə	nə	py	dabɔrd‿ɑ̃	repɔ̃drə
Mais	**ce**	**que**	**serait**	**cet émoi**	**Je**	**ne**	**pus**	**d'abord en**	**répondre.**
But	*this*	*what*	*would be*	*this emotion*	*I*	*not*	*could*	*at once to it*	*respond.*

sə	ki	mə	vɛ̃ki‿	ta	ʒamɛ	sə	fy‿	tœ̃	ply	dulurø	ʃarmə
Ce	**qui**	**me**	**vainquit**	**à**	**jamais,**	**Ce**	**fut**	**un**	**plus**	**douloureux**	**charme;**
That	*which*	*me*	*conquered*	*for*	*ever,*	*That*	*was*	*a*	*more*	*painful*	*charm;*

e	ʒə	nɛ	sy	kə	ʒə‿tɛmɛ	kɑ̃	vwajɑ̃	ta	prəmjɛrə	larmə
Et	**je**	**n'ai**	**su**	**que**	**je t'aimais,**	**qu'en**	**voyant**	**ta**	**première**	**larme.**
And	*I*	*only*	*knew*	*that*	*I you loved,*	*when*	*seeing*	*your*	*first*	*tear.*

Figure 18 **Romance (rɔmãs)**

lame	vapɔre	e	sufrãtə	lamə	dusə	la‿	mɔdɔrãtə
l'âmé	**évaporée**	**et**	**souffrante,**	**l'âme**	**douce,**	**l'âme**	**odorante,**
The soul	*fleeting*	*and*	*suffering,*	*the soul*	*gentle,*	*the soul*	*fragrant,*

dɛ	lis‿	divẽ	kə	jɛ	kœji	dã	lə	jardẽ	də	ta	pãse
Des	**lis**	**divins**	**que**	**j'ai**	**cueillis**	**dans**	**le**	**jardin**	**de**	**ta**	**pensée,**
Of (the)	*lilies*	*divine*	*that*	*I have*	*gathered*	*in*	*the*	*garden*	*of*	*your*	*thought,*

u	dɔ̃	lɛ	vã	lɔ̃	til	ʃase	sɛ‿	ta‿	madɔrablə	dɛ	lis
Où	**donc**	**les**	**vents**	**l'ont-ils**		**chassée,**	**cette**	**âme**	**adorable**	**des**	**lis?**
Where	*then*	*the*	*winds*	*it have they*		*chased,*	*this*	*soul*	*adorable*	*of the*	*lilies?*

nɛ‿	til	ply‿	zœ̃	parfœ̃	ki	rɛstə	də	la	syavite	selɛstə
N'est-il	**plus**	**un**	**parfum**	**qui**	**reste**	**de**	**la**	**suavité**	**céleste,**	
Is there no	*longer*	*a*	*perfume*	*that*	*remains*	*of*	*the*	*sweetness*	*celestial,*	

dɛ	jur‿	zu	ty	m‿ãvɛlɔpɛ	dynə	vapœr	syrnatyrɛlə
Des	**jours**	**où**	**tu**	**m'enveloppais**	**d'une**	**vapeur**	**surnaturelle,**
O the	*days*	*when*	*you*	*me enveloped*	*in a*	*vapor*	*supernatural,*

fɛtə	dɛspwar	damur	fidɛlə	də	beatityd	e	də	pe
Faite	**d'espoir,**	**da'mour**	**fidèle,**	**de**	**béatitude**	**et**	**de**	**paix?**
Made	*of hope,*	*of love*	*faithful,*	*of*	*beatitude*	*and*	*of*	*peace?*

Adventures in Singing

Figure 19 **Ah! quel diner je viens de faire** (ɑ kɛl dine ʒə vjɛ̃ də fɛrə)
from *La Périchole* (lɑ perikɔl)

ɑ	kɛl	dine	ʒə	vjɛ̃	də	fɛrə	e	kɛl	vɛ̃‿nɛkstrɑɔdinɛrə
Ah!	**quel**	**diner**	**je**	**viens**	**de**	**faire,**	**Et**	**quel**	**vin extraordinaire,**
Ah!	*What*	*dining,*	*I*	*come*	*to*	*make,*	*And*	*what*	*wine extraordinary,*

ʒɑ̃‿	ne	tɑ̃	by	mɛ	tɑ̃	tɑ̃	tɑ̃	kə	ʒə	krwa	bjɛ̃	kə	mɛ̃tənɑ̃
J'en	**ai**	**tant**	**bu,**	**mais**	**tan,**	**tant,**	**tant,**	**Que**	**je**	**crois**	**bien**	**que**	**maintenant.**
That	*so*	*much*	*drink,*	*but*	*so much,*	*much,*	*much,*	*as*	*I*	*cross*	*well*	*which*	*at present.*

ʒə	sɥi‿	zɶ̃	pø	gri‿zɶ̃	pø	grizə	mɛ	ʃyt
Je	**suis**	**un**	**peu**	**grise**	**un**	**peu**	**grise,**	**Mais**	**chut!**
I	*am*	*a*	*little*	*tipsy,*	*a*	*little*	*tipsy,*	*but*	*hush!*

fo	pa	kɔ̃	lə	dizə	ʃyt	fo	pa	fo	pa	ʃyt
faut	**pas**	**qu'on**	**le**	**dise,**	**chut!**	**faut**	**pas,**	**faut**	**pas.**	**Chut!**
Want	*walk*	*which*	*the*	*-say,*	*hush*	*want*	*walk,*	*want*	*walk.*	*Hush!*

si	ma	parɔlə	ɛ‿	tɶ̃	pø	vagə	si	tu‿	tɛ̃	marʃɑ̃	ʒə	zig	zagə
Si	**ma**	**parole**	**est**	**un**	**peu**	**vague,**	**Si**	**tout**	**en**	**marchant**	**je**	**zig**	**zague,**
If	*my*	*speech*	*is*	*a*	*little*	*vague,*	*If*	*all*	*like*	*tradesman*	*I*	*zig*	*zag.*

e	si	mɔ̃‿	nø‿	jɛ	tegriʎar	il	nə	fo	sɑ̃‿	netɔne	kar
Et	**si**	**mon**	**oeil**	**est**	**égrillard,**	**Il**	**ne**	**faut**	**s'en**	**étonner**	**car.**
And	*if*	*my*	*look*	*is*	*lewd,*	*It*	*not*	*you*	*astonish*	*because.*

ʒə	sɥi‿	zɶ̃	pø	gri‿zɶ̃	pø	grizə	mɛ	ʃyt
Je	**suis**	**un**	**peu**	**grise**	**un**	**peu**	**grise,**	**Mais**	**chut!**
I	*am*	*a*	*little*	*tipsy,*	*a*	*little*	*tipsy,*	*but*	*hush!*

fo	pa	kɔ̃	lə	dizə	ʃyt	fo	pa	fo	pa	ʃyt
faut	**pas**	**qu'on**	**le**	**dise,**	**chut!**	**faut**	**pas,**	**faut**	**pas.**	**Chut!**
Want	*walk*	*which*	*the*	*say,*	*hush*	*want*	*walk,*	*want*	*walk.*	*Hush!*

Row, Row, Row Your Boat
(Traditional)

Traditional: Row,   row,   row   your boat   Gen - tly down   the   stream;
Vocalise: Sing,   sing,   sing   a song   with   a ring - ing   tone.

Mer - ri - ly, mer - ri - ly,   mer - ri - ly, mer - ri - ly,   Life   is but   a   dream.
mee-mee-mee, may-may-may,   mah-mah-mah, moh-moh-moh,   I   am not   a - lone!

Make New Friends
(American)

Make   new   friends   but   keep _____ the _____ old; _____

One   is   sil - ver   and   the   oth - er   gold.

O How Lovely Is the Evening
(Traditional)

O   how   love - ly   is   the   eve - ning,   is   the   eve - ning,

When   the   bells   are   sweet - ly   ring - ing,   sweet - ly   ring - ing,

Ding!   Dong!   Ding!   Ding!   Dong!   Ding!

Orchestra Song

(Estonian)

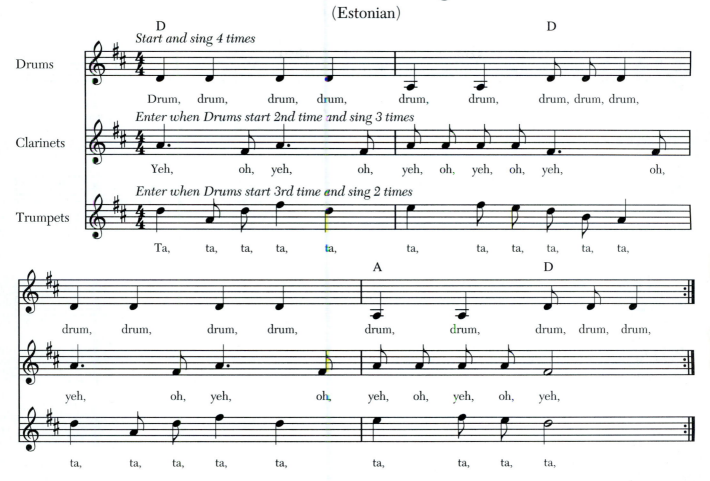

Let Us Sing Together

(Adapted from Czech Folk Tune)

Music Alone Shall Live
(Die Musici–German)

1. G — Am — D — G
All things shall per - ish from un - der the sky;
Him - mel und Er - de müs - sen ver - gehn;

2. Am — D — G
Mu - sic a - lone shall live, mu - sic a - lone shall live,
a - ber die Mus - i - ci, a - ber die Mus - i - ci,

3. Am — D — G
Mu - sic a - lone shall live, nev - er to die.
a - ber die Mus - i - ci, blei - ben be - stehn.

Shalom, Chaverim!
(Farewell, Good Friends–Palestinian)

(2 parts)

1. Dm — **2.**
Sha - lom, cha - ve - rim! Sha - lom, cha - ve - rim! Sha -
Fare - well, my friends! Fare - well, my friends! Fare -

Gm — C7 — F — Dm
lom, sha - lom! Le - hit - ra - ot, le -
well, fare - well! We'll meet a - gain, we'll

Gm — A7 A7 — Dm
hit - ra - ot, sha - lom, sha - lom.
meet a - gain, fare - well, fare - well.

Vive L'Amour

(Long Live Love–College Song)

Dona Nobis Pacem
(Traditional)

(handwritten annotations: "breathe at punctuation, legato", "(meaning?)", "vary tempo")

Do - na no - bis pa - cem pa-cem; Do - na— no - bis pa - cem.

Do - na no - bis pa - cem; Do - na no - bis pa - cem.

Do - na no - bis — pa - cem; Do - na no - bis pa - cem.

Zum Gali Gali
(Palestinian)

1. He-cha-lutz le 'man a - vo - dah; _____ A - vo-dah le 'man he-cha-lutz.
2. A - vo-dah le 'man he-cha-lutz; _____ He-cha-lutz le 'man a - vo-dah.
3. He-cha-lutz le 'man ha-b'tu-lah; _____ Ha-b'tu-lah le 'man he-cha-lutz.
4. Ha-sha-lom le 'man ha 'a - mim; _____ Ha 'a-mim le 'man ha-sha-lom.

Zum ga - li ga - li ga - li, Zum ga - li ga - li. Zum ga - li ga - li ga - li, Zum ga - li ga - li.

Approximate translation of the Hebrew text:

Verses: 1. and 2.: The pioneer's purpose is labor; labor is for the pioneer.

3. The pioneer is for his girl; his girl is for the pioneer.

4. Peace is for all the nations; all the nations are for peace.

Pronunciation of Hebrew: a = "ah"; he = "hay"; le = "leh"; i = "ee"; o = "aw"; u = "oo"; ch = German "ach".
tz = "ts"

Adventures in Singing

Amazing Grace

Text by John Newton

English/American Folk Hymn
Arr. by Bettye Ware

'Twas grace that taught my
heart to fear and grace my fears relieved; How precious did that grace appear the hour I first believed!

Through man - y __ dan - gers, toils, and snares I have al -
read - y __ come; _____ 'Tis grace ____ that __ brought me safe ___ thus __
far, And grace will __ lead me home. _____

All through the Night

Text Traditional

Welsh
Arr. by Bettye Ware

Sleep my love, and
Though I roam a

peace at-tend thee All through the night;
min-strel lone-ly, All through the night;

Guard-ian an-gels God will send thee,
My true harp shall praise thee on-ly

Adventures in Singing

Balm in Gilead

Text Traditional

African-American Folk Hymn
Arr. by Bettye Ware

Adventures in Singing

Da unten im Tale
(Below in the Valley)

Traditional Swabian Folk Dialect
English Text by Clifton Ware

Johannes Brahms (1833–1897)
Op. 97, No. 8

lieb.
bei!
dear.
too.

3. Und __
4. Für __
3. And __
4. For __

wenn   i   dirs zehn - mal sag,   das   i   di   lieb, _____   Und du
Zeit,   wo   du g'liebt   mi hast,   dank   i   dir   schön, _____   Und i
if   *I*   *say ten - fold it's*   *you*   *I love*   *so, _____*   *And you*
time   *you*   *have   loved   me, I*   *thank   you my*   *dear _____*   *And I*

willst nit   ver - ste - hen,   muss   i   halt wei - ter   gehn.
wünsch, dass   dirs an - ders-wo   bes - ser mag   gehn.
will not   be - lieve me,   per - haps   I should   go.
hope that   a - no-ther life   is   bet - ter than   here.

Down in the Valley

American Folksong
Arr. by Bettye Ware

Text Traditional

Drink to Me Only with Thine Eyes

Text by Ben Jonson

Old English Air
Arr. by Bettye Ware

Greensleeves
(What Child Is This)

English Folksong
Arr. by Bettye Ware

Text Traditional

*Christmas Carol verses

Adventures in Singing

Long Time Ago

Text Traditional

American Folksong
Arr. by Bettye Ware

158

Niño precioso
(Precious Child)

Text Traditional

Nicaraguan Folksong
Arr. by Bettye Ware

O Shenandoah

Text Traditional

Traditional American Folksong
Arr. by Bettye Ware

Simple Gifts

Text Traditional

American Shaker Tune
Arr. by Lawrence Henry

love and de-light. When true sim-plic-i-ty is gain'd, to bow and to bend we ___ shan't be a-sham'd, to turn, turn will be our de-light, 'Till by turn-ing, turn-ing we come 'round right.

'Tis the love and de-light.

Sometimes I Feel like a Motherless Child

Text Traditional

African-American Spiritual
Arr. by Bettye Ware

166

The Water Is Wide
(O Waly, Waly)

Text Traditional

British Folksong
Arr. by Bettye Ware

Adventures in Singing

Con qué la lavaré
(Oh, What Can Wash Away)

Spanish Text Unknown
English Text by Clifton Ware
and Bettye Ware

Spanish Folk Song
Arr. by Bettye Ware

vi - vo mal pe - na - da?
tor - tured life of pen - ance?

Lá - van - se las ca - sa - das con a - qua de li -
The wives of ev - 'ry vil - lage use lem - on scent ed

mo - nes; lá ___ vo - me yo, ___ cui - ta - da, lá -
wa - ter; I ___ wash my griev - ing sor - row, I

con   pe - nas   y   do - lo - res.
with   pain   and   end - less   suf - fring.

Over the Meadows

Original Textual Source Unknown
Text by Clifton Ware and Bettye Ware

Czechoslovakian Folksong
Arr. by Bettye Ware

O - ver the mea - dows green and wide,
O - ver the fields we stroll a - long,

We go a - roam - ing side by side.
Blen - ding our voi - ces in a song.

Melt - ing from win - ter's snow, stream - lets from moun - tains flow,

174

It Was a Lover and His Lass

Text Attributed to
William Shakespeare

Thomas Morley (1557–1603)
Ed. by C. W.

1. It was a lov-er and his lass,
2. Be-tween the a-cres of the rye, With a
3. This car-ol they be-gan that hour,
4. Then, pret-ty lov-ers, take the time,

hey, and a ho, and a hey no-ni-no, and a hey_____ no-ni no-ni-no,

That
These
For

o'er the green corn-field did pass
pret-ty coun-try fools did lie
How that life was but a flow'r In spring-time, in spring-time, in spring-time, The on-ly pret-ty
love is crown-ed with the prime

Now Is the Month of Maying

Text Anonymous

Thomas Morley (1557–1603)
Ed. by C.W.

°Each verse may be sung by a different singer, and the fa-la-la chorus sung by all

Adventures in Singing

with his bon - ny lass,   A - danc - ing on the grass,   Fa la
to the bag - pipes' sound,   The nymphs tread out their round
dain - ty nymphs, and speak,   Shall we play bar - ley - break?

la la la!   Fa la la la la la la   la la la la!

Come Again, Sweet Love

John Dowland (1563–1626)
Arr. by Lawrence Henry

Text Anonymous

Adventures in Singing

To see,   to hear,   to touch,   to kiss,   to die _____
I sit,   I sigh,   I weep,   I faint,   I die _____

poco rit. (2nd Time)   D.S. 2nd verse

With thee a - gain   in   sweet - est sym - pa - thy,
In dead - ly pain   and   end - less mis - er - y.

poco rit. (2nd Time)   D.S. 2nd verse

Star vicino
(To Be Close)

Anonymous
(Formerly Attributed to Salvator Rosa)
(1615–1673)
Ed. by C.W. & B.W.

Italian Text Anonymous
English Text by Clifton Ware

If Music Be the Food of Love

Text Attributed to H. Heveningham

Henry Purcell (1659–1695)
Arr. by Lawrence Henry

Moderato (♩ = 84–92)

If
mu - sic — be — the — food — of — love, Sing on, sing on, sing on, sing on till

I — am — fill'd — am — fill'd — with — joy; For then my list - 'ning soul — you — move, For

Adventures in Singing

Toglietemi la vita ancor
(Oh, Take Away My Breath, My Life)

Italian Text Unknown
English Text by Clifton Ware

High Key

Alessandro Scarlatti (1660–1725)
Ed. by B.W. & C.W.

Toglietemi la vita ancor
(Oh, Take Away My Breath, My Life)

Italian Text Unknown
English Text by Clifton Ware

Alessandro Scarlatti (1660–1725)
Ed. by B.W. & C.W.

Low Key

le - te ra - pi - re il cor.
sie - te del mio do - lor.
sire to en-slave   my heart.
hap-py to see   me grieve

Se mi vo - le - te ra - pi - re il cor.
Se va - ghe sie - te del mio do - lor.
If   you de-sire to en-slave   my heart.
If   you are hap-py to see   me grieve.

To - glie-te-mi la vi - ta an-cor.
Oh, take a-way my breath, my life.

To - glie - te - mi
Oh,   take   a - way

To - glie - te - mi
Oh, take   a - way

To - glie - te-mi la vi - ta an-cor.
Oh, take   a-way my breath, my life.

To - glie - te-
Oh, take   a-

poco rit. (second time)   D.S.

mi la vi - ta an-cor.
way my breath,   my life.

a tempo (second time)

rit. (second time)

D.S.

poco rit. (second time)

I Attempt from Love's Sickness to Fly

Text by John Dryden

Henry Purcell (1659–1695)
Arr. by Lawrence Henry

190

Bist du bei mir
(If You Are Near)

Anonymous
(Attributed to Johann Sebastian Bach)
(1685–1750)

German Text Anonymous
English Text by Clifton Ware

Ed. by C.W.

Bist du bei mir, geh ich mit Freu - den zum Ster - ben __
If you are near I go with glad - ness to death __ and __

und zu mei - ner __ Ruh', zum __ Ster - ben und zu mei - ner Ruh'.
to e - ter - nal __ rest, to __ death and to e - ter - nal rest.

Bist du__ bei__ mir, geh' ich mit Freu - den zum Ster - ben__
If you__ are__ near, I go with glad - ness to death__ and__

und zu mei - ner__ Ruh', zum _____ Ster - ben und zu mei - ner Ruh'.
to e - ter - nal__ rest, to _____ death and to e - ter - nal rest.

Ach, wie ver - gnügt wär so mein End - de: Es drück - ten__
Ah, plea - sant thought would be my end - ing: By touch - ing__

dei - ne schö - nen___ Hän - de mir___ die ge-treu - en Au - gen zu.
with your lov - ing___ hands___ my___ faith - ful eyes to gent - ly close.

Ach, wie ver - gnügt wär so mein End - de: Es drück - ten___
Ah, plea - sant thought would be my end - ing: by touch - ing___

D.S. al Fine

dei - ne schö - nen___ Hän - de mir___ die ge-treu - en Au - gen zu.
with your lov - ing___ hands___ my___ faith - ful eyes to gent - ly close.

D.S. al Fine

Lascia ch'io pianga
(Let Me in Weeping)
[O Lord, I Pray Thee]

Italian Text by Giacomo Rossi
English Texts by Clifton Ware

George Frederic Handel (1685–1759)
Ed. by C.W.

Non lo dirò col labbro
(At Evening)

Italian Text by Nicola Haym
English Text by Clifton & Bettye Ware

George Frederic Handel (1685–1759)
Arr. by Lawrence Henry

Adventures in Singing

Oh, Sleep, Why Dost Thou Leave Me?

from *Semele*

(O Lord, Hear My Prayer)

Original Text by W. Congreve
Sacred Text by Clifton Ware

George Frederic Handel (1685–1759)
Ed. by C.W.

d'ring love, re - store my wan-d'ring love a-gain de - ceive me, oh _____ sleep!

d'ring soul, re - store my wan-d'ring soul! Now I be - seech Thee, oh _____ Lord!

to my arms, to my arms re - store _____ my wan - d'ring

Hear the prayer of my heart, re - store _____ my wan - d'ring

love!

soul!

Flocks Are Sporting
(Christ Is Risen)

Text by Henry Carey
Sacred Text by Clifton Ware

Henry Carey (1689–1743)
Ed. by C.W. & B.W.

Joyfully ♩ = (138–152)

mf

5

mf

1. Flocks are   sport   -   ing,   doves are   court   -   ing,   Warb-ling   lin   -   nets
2. Flocks are   bleat   -   ing,   rocks re   -   peat   -   ing,   Val - leys   e   -   cho
1. Christ is   ri   -   sen,   from death's   pri   -   son,   In His   vic   -   t'ry
2. From Christ's   teach   -   ing,   and His   preach   -   ing,   All who   know Him

mf

11

(tr)   *f*

sweet-ly   sing,   Ah! _____
back the   sound,
now re   -   born,   A   -   le   -   lu   -   jah!
shall be   free,   A   -   le   -   lu   -   jah!

joy and plea - sure with - out mea - sure, Kind - ly
danc - ing, sing - ing, pip - ing, spring - ing, Nought __ but
Joy - ful sing - ing, prai - ses bring - ing, As __ we
Heav'n - ly trea - sure, with - out mea - sure, We __ shall

hail __ the glo - rious spring. Kind - ly hail the glo - rious
mirth __ and joy __ goes round, Nought but mirth and joy __ goes
hail __ the glo - rious morn. As we hail the glo - rious
live __ e - ter - nal - ly. We shall live e - ter - nal -

1. spring. **2.** round. _____
morn. ly. _____

My Lovely Celia
(O, My Beloved)

Textual Source Unknown

George Monro (1680–1731)
Ed. by C.W.

°Alternate words

Preach Not Me Your Musty Rules

Text by John Dalton
From: *Comus* by John Milton

Thomas A. Arne (1710–1778)
Arr. by Lawrence Henry

Adventures in Singing

sen - ses al - ways rea - son well.

If short my span I less can spare to

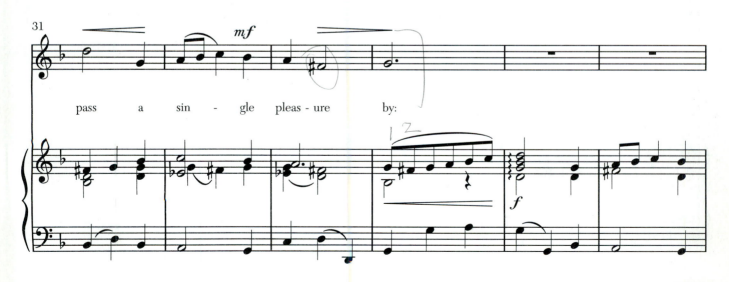

pass a sin - gle plea - sure by:

Ich liebe dich
(I Love You Dear)

German Text by Karl Friedrich Herrosee
English Text by Clifton Ware

Ludwig van Beethoven
(1770–1827)

Andante ($\quad$ = 48–52)

Ich lie - be dich, so wie du mich, am A - bend und am
I love you dear, as you love me, to - day and all to -

Mor - gen, noch war kein Tag, wo du und ich nicht theil - ten uns' - re Sor - gen.
mor - rows, we share each day with sim - ple joy, and al - so share life's sor - rows.

Auch wa - ren sie für dich und mich ge - theilt leicht zu er
Each mo - ment of our days we fill with grace - ful love and

Nel cor più non mi sento
(My Heart Has Lost Its Feeling)

Italian Text by Giuseppe Paloma
English Text by Clifton Ware

Giovanni Paisiello (1740–1816)
Ed. by C.W.

piz - zi - chi,   mi stuz - zi - chi,   mi pun - gi - chi,   mi
pinch me,   you ex - cite me,   you prick me and you

mas - ti - chi;   che co - sa è que - sta ohi - mè?   pie - tà, pie - tà, pie -
bite me;   what spite - ful things you do!   Have mer - cy, have pi - ty, be

tà! A - mo - re è un cer - to che, che di - spe - rar mi
fair!   Oh Love it's sure - ly you! Oh why do you drive me to de -

fa.
spair.

Ridente la calma
(May Calm Joy Awaken)

Italian Text Unknown
English Text by Clifton Ware

Joseph Mysliveček (1737–1781)
W.A. Mozart (1756–1791)
Ed. by C.W.

al - ma si de - sti; ne re - sti più se - gno di sde - gno e ti -
quiet, peace - ful spi - rit. *nor let there re - main here no an - ger or*

mor, ___ ne re - sti più se - gno di sde - gno e ti - mor, di
fear. ___ *nor let there re - main here no an - ger or fear, no*

sde - gno e ___ ti - mor.
an - ger ___ or ___ fear.

Tu vie - ni frat -
Then, come ___ my be -

tan - to a strin - ger mio be - ne, le dol - ce ca - te - ne si
lov - ed to join ___ now in rap - ture, In sweet - est com - mu - nion, to

calma nell' al - ma si de - sti, ne re - sti più se - gno di
wa - ken my quiet _ peace - ful spi - rit, nor let _ there re - main _ here no

sde - gno e ti - mor, _ ne re - sti più se - gno di sde - gno e ti -
an - ger or fear. _ Nor let _ there re - main _ here no an - ger or

mor, di sde - gno e ti - mor.
fear, no an - ger _ or _ fear.

Vaga luna
(Lovely Moon)

Text Anonymous
English Text by Clifton Ware

Vincenzo Bellini (1801–1835)
Based on version by Pauline Viardot-Garcia

Andante cantabile (= 66–69)

dolce

1. Va - ga lu - na __ che i - nar - gen - ti Que - ste ri - ve e que - sti
   Love-ly moon that __ co - vers with sil - ver all these banks and __ flow'rs re-
2. Dil - le pur, che lon - tan - nan - za, Il mio duol non __ può le-
   Tell my love who __ longs __ so __ far a-way that my grief I __ can - not

fio - - ri. Ed in spi - ri, ed in-spi-ri a-glie-le - men - ti, Il lin-
splen - dent, brea-thing life in - to all of na-ture's won - ders, the pure
nir __ Che se nu - tro, se nu-tro u-na spe - ran - za, El-la è
share, __ that I nour - ish and nur-ture ev - er - last - ing hope, that u-

An die Musik
(To Music)

German Text by F. von Schober
English Text by Clifton Ware

Franz Schubert (1797–1828)
Op. 88, No. 4
Ed. by C.W.

D. 547

war - mer Lieb' ent - zun - den, hast mich in ei - ne bess' - re Welt ent-
heart with love and gladness, and shown to me a bet - ter world and

rückt in ei - ne bess' - re Welt ent - rückt!
life a bet-ter world, a bet - ter life!

Oft hat ein Seuf - zer
Strains from your harp come

dei - ner Harf ent - flos - sen, ein süss - er, hei - li - ger Ak-
sigh - ing of - ten 'round me a sweet - er, ho - lier sound I've

Adventures in Singing

kord _ von _ dir
ne - ver _ heard,

den Him - mel bess' - rer _
the hea - vens o - pen _

Zei - ten mir er - schlos-sen,
wide to show _ such _ beau - ty

du hol - de Kunst ich _ dan - ke dir da-
O won - drous Art my _ thanks to you I

für, _ du hol - de Kunst, _ ich dan - ke dir!
sing _ O won-drous Art, _ my thanks _ I sing!

Seligkeit
(Bliss)

German Text by Ludwig Heinrich
Christoph Hölty
English Text by Clifton Ware

High Voice

Franz Schubert (1797–1828)
Ed. by C.W.

Seligkeit
(Bliss)

German Text by Ludwig Heinrich
Christoph Hölty
English Text by Clifton Ware

Franz Schubert (1797–1828)
Ed. by C.W.

Low Voice

Du bist wie eine Blume
(You Are So Like a Flower)

German Text by Heinrich Heine
English Text by Clifton Ware

Robert Schumann (1810–1856)
"Myrthen," Op. 25, No. 24

ist _____ als ob ich die Hän - de auf's Haupt dir le - gen
hands _____ will gen - tly hold you, and stroke your long _____ flow-ing

sollt',
hair
be - tend dass Gott dich er - hal - te
pray - ing that God ev - er keep you

so schön, so rein und hold.
so love - ly pure and fair.

Le Charme
(The Charm)

French Text by Armand Silvestre
from "Chanson des heures"
English Text by Clifton Ware

Ernest Chausson (1855–1899)
Op. 2, No. 2

Romance
(Romance)

French Text by Paul Bourget
English Text by Clifton Ware

Claude Debussy (1862–1918)
Ed. by C.W.

Moderato ♩ = 66–72

mp

L'âme é - va - po - rée et souf - fran - te, L'â-me
Soul so frail and fleet - ing, so va - grant, soul so

dou-ce, l'âme o - do - ran - te, Des lis di - vins_____ que j'ai cueil-lis Dans le jar - din de ta pen-
ten-der, a soul as ra - diant as lil-lies fair _____ that grow with-in the gar - den-ways of your rich

sée,
thoughts,

Où donc les vents l'ont-ils chas - sée
Where blow the winds this fra-grance sweet,

Cette âme a - do - ra - ble des
A - dor - a-ble soul of the

Adventures in Singing

Heidenröslein
(The Hedgerose)

German Text by Johann Wolfgang von Goethe
English Text by Clifton Ware

Franz Schubert (1797–1828)
Op. 3, No. 3

Weep You No More, Sad Fountains

Text Anonymous

Roger Quilter (1877–1953)

sets? _____ Rest you, then, rest, sad eyes! Melt not in weep - ing,

While she lies sleep - ing, Soft - ly now

soft - ly lies sleep - ing, sleep - ing.

The Call

Text by George Herbert

Ralph Vaughan Williams (1872–1958)

Adventures in Singing

Feast, as mends in length: Such a Strength, as makes his

guest. Come, my Joy, my Love, my Heart: Such a

Joy, as none can move: Such a Love, as none can

part: Such a Heart, as joys in love.

poco animato

Tempo primo tranquillo.

rall.

Dream Valley

Text by William Blake

High Voice

Roger Quilter (1877–1953)

Adventures in Singing

Dream Valley

Text by William Blake

Low Voice

Roger Quilter (1877–1953)

Adventures in Singing

The Singer
(An Unaccompanied Song)

Text by Bronnie Taylor

Michael Head (1900–1976)
Ed. by C.W.

*May be sung in any comfortable key

Adventures in Singing

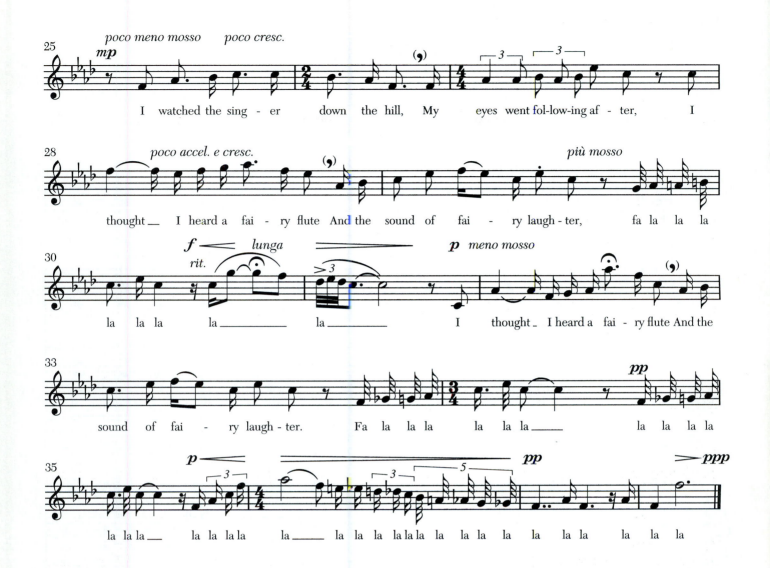

I watched the sing - er down the hill, My eyes went fol-low-ing af - ter, I

thought __ I heard a fai - ry flute And the sound of fai - ry laugh - ter, fa la la la

la la la la _____ la _____ I thought __ I heard a fai - ry flute And the

sound of fai - ry laugh - ter. Fa la la la la la la _____ la la la la

la la la __ la la la la la _____ la la la la la la la la la la la la la la la la la la la

A Memory

Text by Minnie K. Breid

Rudolph Ganz (1877–1972)

how I feel Thine eyes rest-ing on mine, Though look-ing, naught do I

see; Some-how I feel the touch of Thy hand:

Ah! _____ 'Tis but a mem - o - ry!

The Daisies

Text by James Stephens

Samuel Barber (1910–1981)
Op. 2, No. 1

High Voice

wan-dered hap-p'ly, to and fro, I kissed my dear on ei-ther cheek, In the

bud of the morn-ing O! A lark sang up, from the

breez-y land; A lark sang down, from a cloud a-far; As she and (he)

I went, hand in hand, In the field where the dais-ies are.

The Daisies

Text by James Stephens

Samuel Barber (1910–1981)
Op. 2, No. 1

Low Voice

Adventures in Singing

The Pasture

Text by Robert Frost

Charles Naginski (1909–1940)

Adventures in Singing

wait   to watch the   wa - ter   clear, _____ I   may):

I   sha'n't be gone   long.—   You   come   too.

I'm go - ing out   to   fetch   the lit - tle   calf   That's stand - ing   by   the

Program notes page 121

Heavenly Grass

Text by Tennessee Williams

Paul Bowles (b. 1910)

feet   took a walk   In   heav - en - ly grass.   All __ night   while the lone - some

stars   rolled   past,   Then my   feet come down   to   walk on earth   And my

moth - er   cried   When she   give me   birth.

Adventures in Singing

Now my feet walk far And my feet walk fast, But they still got an itch for heav-en-ly grass. But they still got an itch for heav'n-ly grass.

It's All I Bring Today

Text by Emily Dickinson*

Ernst Bacon (1898–1990)

Andante ♩ = 60–66

mp smoothly and with quiet warmth

It's all I have to bring to-day,

This, and my heart be-side, This, and my heart, and

all the fields, And all the mead-ows wide. Be

*Words printed by special permission

Copyright © 1944 (Renewed) by G. Schirmer, Inc. (ASCAP)
International Copyright Secured. All Rights Reserved. Reprinted by Permission.

sure you count,_____ should I for - get,
Some - one the sun could tell,— This, and my heart, and all_____ the
bees_____ Which in the clo - ver dwell._____

richly

poco rit.

pp

rit.

Program notes page 121

Infant Joy

Text by William Blake
from *Songs of Innocence*

David Evan Thomas (b. 1958)

Adventures in Singing

"I hap-py am, Joy, _____ sweet Joy, _____ Joy, _____ is my name."

Thou _____ dost smile, I sing, _____ I sing, _____ I sing _____ the while,

Sweet joy be - fall _____ thee! Sweet joy, Sweet joy, _____ sweet joy be -

fall thee! _____ fall thee. _____

Tipsy Song
(from *La Périchole*)

French Text by Ludovic Halévy
English Text by Clifton Ware

Jacques Offenbach (1819–1880)
Ed. by C.W.

High Voice

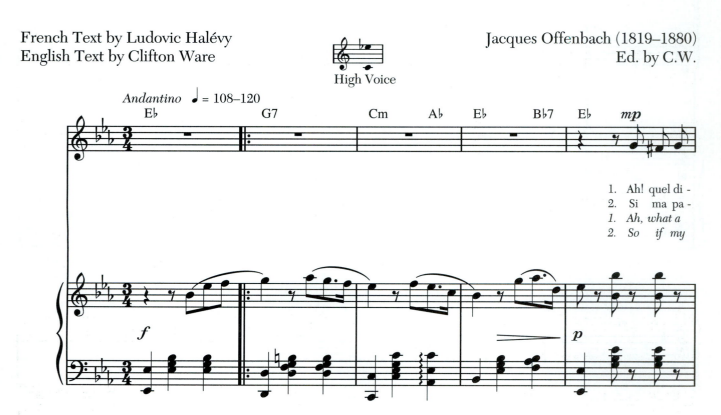

Tipsy Song
(from *La Périchole*)

French Text by Ludovic Halévy
English Text by Clifton Ware

Jacques Offenbach (1819–1880)
Ed. by C.W.

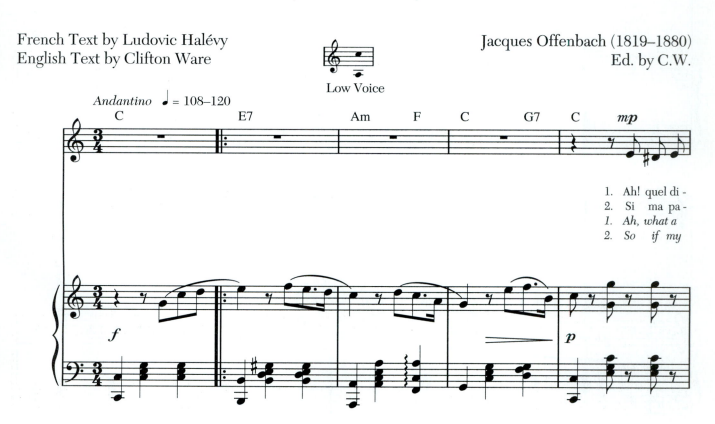

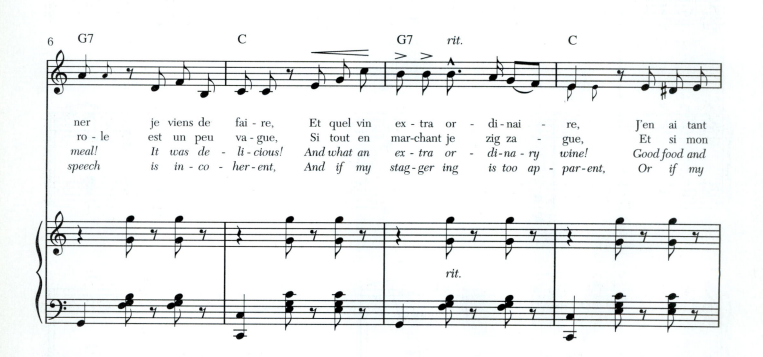

Adventures in Singing

Oh, What a Beautiful Morning
(from *Oklahoma!*)

Text by Oscar Hammerstein II

Music by Richard Rodgers

Adventures in Singing

On a Clear Day
(from *On a Clear Day You Can See Forever*)

Text by Alan Jay Lerner

Music by Burton Lane

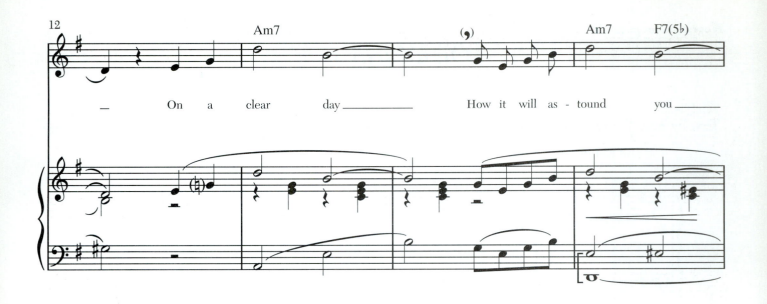

On a clear day _____ How it will as - tound you _____

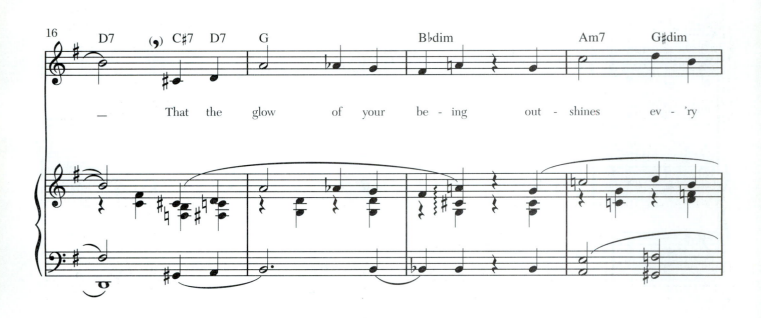

That the glow of your be - ing out - shines ev - 'ry

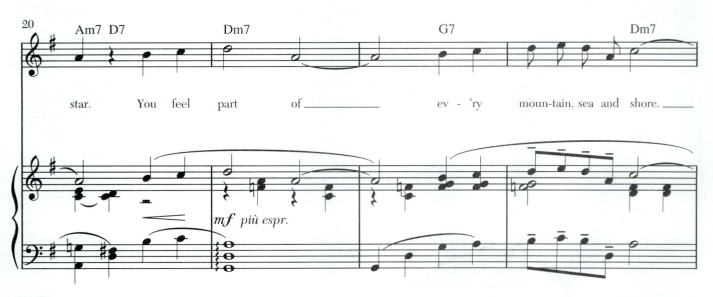

star. You feel part of _____ ev - 'ry moun-tain, sea and shore. _____

Adventures in Singing

Almost Like Being in Love
(from *Brigadoon*)

Text by Alan Jay Lerner

Music by Frederick Loewe

Adventures in Singing

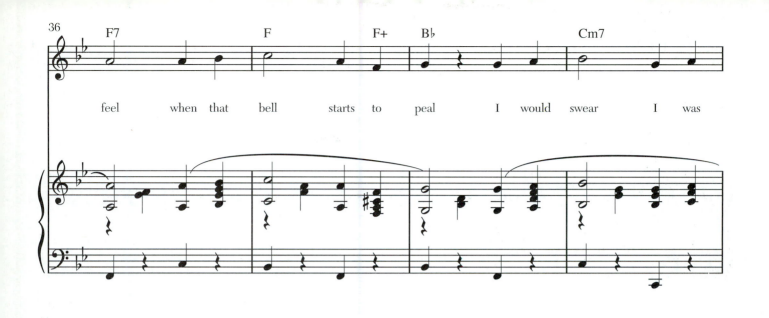

feel   when that   bell   starts to   peal   I   would   swear   I   was

fall - ing,   I   could   swear   I   was   fall - ing,   It's   al - most   like

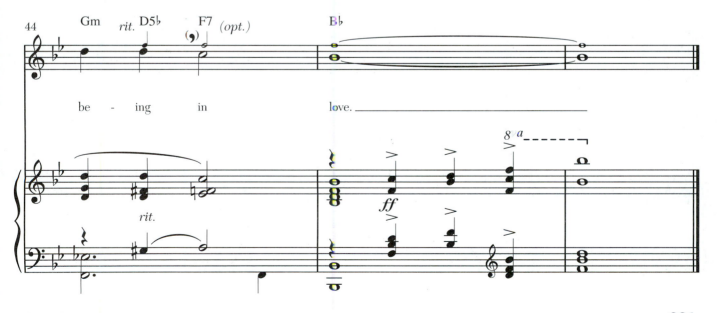

be - ing   in   love.

'S Wonderful

Text by Ira Gershwin

Music by George Gershwin

Note: If both verses are sung, observe the repeat sign.
If one verse is sung, use the second ending only.

Till There Was You
(from *The Music Man*)

Text and Music by Meredith Willson

Adventures in Singing

music and there were won-der-ful ros - es, they

tell me in sweet fra - grant mea - dows of

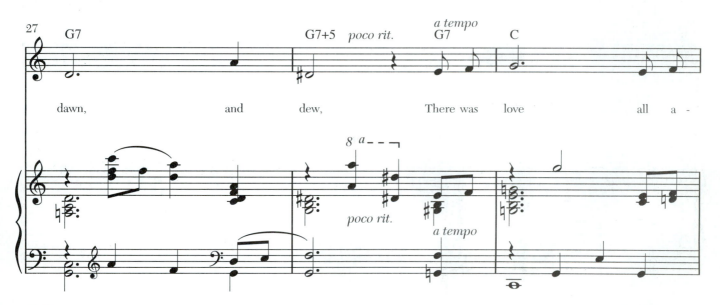

dawn, and dew, There was love all a -

Adventures in Singing

Try to Remember

(From *The Fantasticks*)

Text by Tom Jones

(High Voice)

Music by Harvey Schmidt

Try to Remember
(From *The Fantasticks*)

Text by Tom Jones

(Low Voice)

Music by Harvey Schmidt

Adventures in Singing

Any Dream Will Do
(from *Joseph and the Amazing Technicolor Dreamcoat*)

Text by Tim Rice

Music by Andrew Lloyd Webber (b. 1948)

Adventures in Singing

The world was wak - ing, a - ny dream will do.

A crash of drums, _ a flash of light, _ my gol - den coat flew

out of sight, _ The col - ours fad - ed in - to dark - ness, I was left a -

lone. May I re - turn

Put On a Happy Face
(from *Bye, Bye, Birdie*)

Text by Lee Adams

Music by Charles Strouse

Glossary

Some terms in this glossary are referenced in the text;
others are mentioned on the sheet music in the Song Anthology.

A

a cappella: Singing without instrumental accompaniment; originated with choral church music performed in sixteenth-century Europe.

a tempo: Indicates return to normal tempo after an interruption or temporary change of tempo.

abdomen (abdominal area): Portion of the body lying between the pelvis and the thorax (chest cavity), with the exception of the back.

abduction: Drawing apart of the vocal folds from the midline position or opening of the glottis, as occurs with breathing.

accelerando: Becoming faster.

accent: Emphasis on one note or chord.

accompaniment: Separate part or parts that accompany a solo or ensemble, such as a keyboard (piano) instrument.

acoustics: Science of audible sound, including its production, transmission, and effects.

ad libitum, ad lib.: At liberty, freely, and usually slowly.

adagio: A tempo slower than andante.

Adam's apple: Common term for the visible protrusion of the larynx (thyroid cartilage) in the neck, mostly observable in males.

adduction: Drawing together of the vocal folds or closing of the glottis in the act of phonation.

agonist: Anatomically, a prime mover muscle that is opposed in action by another muscle called the antagonist.

al fine: To the end, that is, repeat until reaching the word *fine.*

alla breve: Performed with one beat per half note, usually two beats to a measure.

allargando: Becoming broader and slower.

allegretto: In a somewhat lively tempo but less quick than allegro.

allegro: In a lively tempo.

alto: Low female voice, usually used in choral music.

alveolar ridge: Upper dental ridge where speech sounds occur when the apex of the tongue touches it, for example "d," "l," and "t."

amplitude: Magnitude or range of movement of a vibrating object.

anatomy: Scientific study of the structure of the human body.

andante: In a slow tempo, similar to a moderate walking pace.

andantino: In a moderately slow tempo but usually faster than andante.

animando: Becoming faster (animated).

antagonist: Anatomically, a muscle or muscle group that opposes the primary countermovement of the agonist muscle or muscle group.

appoggiatura: In modern practice, a rhythmically strong dissonant note that resolves to a consonant note, usually to emphasize dramatic intent of the text.

appoggio: Development of a coordinated, dynamic balance among the processes of respiration, phonation, and resonation in singing.

aria (air): Refers primarily to Italian vocal composition; a solo composition for voice in an opera, oratorio, or cantata.

arpeggio (arpeggi): Notes comprising a chord played or sung in succession in ascending or descending order.

art song: Vocal composition that combines voice, text, and instrumental accompaniment in an artistic manner and style.

articulation: Physiological process of producing consonants in speech and singing.

articulators: Speech organs—jaw, tongue, lips, teeth, soft palate, and hard palate—which work to modify the acoustic properties of the vocal tract.

arytenoid cartilages: Derived from the Greek word *ladle,* the two matching pyramidal-shaped cartilages connecting the larynx and the arytenoid muscle and acting as primary activators in phonation.

aspirate: Articulation of a speech sound with audible friction, for example, the use of the consonant "h" to induce airflow.

aspirato: Singing style based on using "h's" to articulate fast moving notes.

assai: Very much.

B

baritone: Male voice of medium range and vocal color, between bass and tenor.

baroque: Musical style that existed from approximately 1600–1750, represented by such composers as Monteverdi, Purcell, Scarlatti, Bach, and Handel.

bass: Lowest male voice type; also used to describe both the lowest note in a chord and the low-pitched string instrument by that name.

bel canto: Literally translated as "beautiful singing" in reference to a vocal style that emphasizes purity of tone and flexibility; originated in seventeenth-century Italy and remained strong through the first part to the nineteenth century with such composers as Bellini, Rossini, and Donizetti.

belting: Style of pop singing where the chest voice is pushed upward beyond its natural limits without gradual blending with the head voice.

bleat: Fast, tremulous tone (nine or more pulses per second) resembling the sound of a goat and possibly caused by pharyngeal constrictor tensions.

breath management: Efficient handling of the breath cycle in producing vocal tone.

bronchi: Bifurcation of the trachea into two branches leading to the lungs.

bronchiole: Smallest division of the bronchial tree within the lungs, branching off from the bronchi.

C

cadenza: Elaborate ornamental musical passage exhibiting the skills of a solo performer; usually appears at the end of an aria.

cantabile: In a lyric, legato style.

cantata: Literally meaning "sung"; a chamber-sized secular or sacred vocal composition for solo instrument with other musical forces, for example, chorus and/or instrumentalists.

cartilage: Nonvascular body tissue more flexible than bone.

catch breath: Quick, partial intake of air, usually in fast tempo music.

chest register (chest voice): Heavy voice mechanism (register) existing primarily in the low vocal range and marked by sensations of vibrations in the chest.

chiaroscuro: "Bright-dark" tonal characteristics of a dynamically coordinated and balanced voice.

chord: Two or more pitches sounded simultaneously.

chorus (choir): Composed of many singers, usually balanced between sopranos, altos, tenors, and basses.

classical (classicism): Musical style of clarity, dignity, and balanced form that existed from approximately 1750–1825, represented by such composers as Haydn, Mozart, and Beethoven; also refers to music of high artistic intent and permanence.

coda: Literally meaning "tail"; concluding section of a composition.

cognates: Consonants produced with the same place and manner of articulation, differing only by unvoiced or voiced characteristics, e.g., [p] or [b].

coloratura: Elaborate ornamentation or embellishment, including fast passages and trills, both written and improvised.

con anima: With soul and spirit.

con espressione: With expression.

con moto: With movement.

consonant: Speech sound created when articulating organs obstruct breath flow.

continuant: Speech sound sustained with a single breath, for example "m," "n," "ng," "z," and "s."

continuo (basso continuo): In baroque music, a bass part written in shorthand notation for an accompaniment to be filled in with chords; usually played by a keyboard instrument (organ or harpsichord) and a bass instrument (cello).

contralto: Lowest and rarest female voice used in solo singing.

costal: Pertaining to rib or costa.

crescendo (cresc.): Becoming louder.

cricoid cartilage: Lower circular cartilage of the larynx located at the top of the trachea.

D

da capo (D.C.): Literally meaning "from the head" or "beginning"; return to the beginning and then continue to *fine* (end).

da capo aria (form): Three sections consisting of two contrasting sections (A and B) and a repetition of the first (A), usually with embellishments of the melodic line.

dal segno (D.S.): Return to the D.S. sign (𝄌) and continue to the end.

decibel: Acoustical unit for measuring the relative loudness of sound, the 1 unit is the smallest degree of intensity perceived by the human ear and 130 marks the threshold of pain toleration.

declamatory: An impassioned dramatic style of rhetorical speech and singing.

decrescendo (decresc.): Gradually getting softer.

diaphragm: Large dome-shaped partition comprising muscle tendon and sinews; facilitates breathing and separates the abdomen (stomach) from the thorax (chest).

diaphragmatic-costal breathing: Combined involvement of the abdominal muscles, diaphragm, and intercostal (rib) muscles in breathing.

diction: Comprehensive manner and style in which language is rendered according to established standards of word usage and pronunciation.

diminuendo: Becoming softer.

diphthong: Combination of two vowel sounds on one syllable, for example "sigh," "night," and "say."

dolce: Sweetly.

dramatic voice: Heavy in quality and large in size.

duet: Musical composition for two performers.

dynamics: Degrees of loudness and softness.

E

energy: The biological force or power that expands one's physical and mental capacity for living.

ensemble: Group of performing musicians.

enunciation: Act of pronouncing syllables, words, or sentences in an articulate manner; also associated with definite statements, declarations, or proclamations.

epigastrium: Triangular portion of the high abdominal area at the base of the sternum and directly below the ribs.

epiglottis: Leaf-shaped cartilage located between the root of the tongue and the entrance to the larynx; responsible for protecting the larynx from foreign matter (food) that could otherwise get into the lungs.

exhalation (expiration): That part of the breath cycle when air is expelled.

expression: Act of communicating thoughts and feelings to others.

extrinsic: Meaning "external" or "on the outside"; for example, neck muscles that support and influence laryngeal action.

F

falsetto: Associated primarily with the high register and light quality of the male voice; produced by using only the medial compression of the vocal folds.

fermata: Pause, hold, or wait on a note, chord, or rest sustaining the duration longer than normal for dramatic effect; sometimes called a "bird's eye" (𝄐).

fine (Italian): End, close.

flute/whistle register: Highest vocal range in the female voice, sometimes referred to as "squeak" or coloratura register.

focus: Term borrowed from optics, referring to the concentration and clarity of tone.

folk song: Familiar song of simple musical and textual content, created and modified through person-to-person transmission without being written down.

form: (See **song form**)

formants: Regions of prominent energy distributions (overtones) in a vocalized tone that determine the characteristic qualities of vowels, as well as individual vocal quality.

***forte* (f):** Loudly.

***forte-piano* (fp):** Playing or singing loudly, immediately followed by a softer dynamic.

***fortissimo* (ff):** Very loud.

frequency: Number of vibrations or cycles per second that determine pitch; the faster the vibrations per second, the higher the pitch.

fundamental: Lowest frequency of a complex sound wave, the frequency of which usually determines what is perceived by the listener as pitch.

G

glide: Vocal sounds caused by the movement or "gliding" of either the tongue or the lips or both, for example, "w," "r," and "l."

glottals: Vowels voiced with a sharp onset (attack) by building up breath pressure and releasing it abruptly in either a gentle or harsh manner.

glottis: Space between the vocal folds.

H

hard palate: Anterior bony portion of the roof of the mouth.

harmony: Chordal, or vertical, structure of a musical composition.

head register (voice): Adjustment of the laryngeal mechanism that produces a lighter tonal quality, with sensations experienced in the head; suitable for soft singing and for the upper part of the voice range.

hertz (Hz): Unit of measurement of cycles per second, for example, 440 Hz (A_4); named for the physicist Gustav Hertz.

hymn: Simple religious song of praise, thanks, or plea.

hyoid bone: U-shaped bone located at the base of the tongue and at the top of the larynx.

I

inhalation (inspiration): That part of the breath cycle when air is taken into the lungs.

intensity: Amplitude of pressure variations resulting from vibratory impulses passing through an elastic medium such as air or water; magnitude of loudness or volume; depth of emotional expression.

intercostal muscles (external and internal): Three sets of muscles between the ribs that control their raising and lowering.

intercostal: The short external and internal muscles between the ribs.

interpretation: Performer's personal artistic re-creation and realization of a composer's musical and dramatic intentions.

interval: Distance in pitch between two tones.

intonation: Degree of accuracy in producing pitches.

intrinsic: Meaning "internal" or "on the inside"; for example, intrinsic muscles of the larynx.

K

key: Main ("key") note or tonal center of a composition to which all its notes are related and on which the work normally ends.

L

largo: Broadly.

larynx: An organ of the respiratory tract situated in the throat and neck above the trachea (windpipe); composed of cartilage and muscles and containing a pair of vocal folds which vibrate to produce voice.

legato: Smoothly and connected, without a discernable break in sound.

leggiero: Lightly.

lied: German word for "song," used in reference to art songs by such German composers as Schubert, Schumann, Brahms, and Wolf.

lieder (plural for lied): German art songs.

ligament: Strong band of tissue connecting the articular extremities of bone.

lyric voice: Light in quality and moderate in size.

M

ma non troppo: Meaning "but not too much."

major scale: Musical scale with a major third interval between the first and third notes.

marcato: Stressed, accented.

melody: Succession of tones perceived as a musical line.

messa di voce: To crescendo (increase) and decrescendo (diminish) a sustained pitch (tone) from soft-to-loud-to-soft dynamic levels.

meter: Division of music into measures or bars, each with a specific number of beats or pulses, for example, $\frac{2}{2}, \frac{2}{4}, \frac{4}{4}, \frac{3}{4}, \frac{6}{8}$

metronome: Mechanical device that maintains a steady beat at any tempo, slow to fast.

***mezzo forte* (mf):** Moderately loud; less loud than *forte*.

mezzo-soprano: Female voice of medium range and somewhat darker tone color, usually found in the performance of opera and oratorio.

minor scale: Musical scale with a minor third interval between the first and third notes.

mixed (middle) register: Blending and dynamic balancing of chest and head register mechanisms in the middle range of the voice.

moderator: Medium tempo.

molto: Very much.

morendo: Dying.

muscular antagonism: Anatomically, a balanced tension created when a muscle or muscle group opposes the primary countermovement of the agonist muscle or muscle group.

musicology: Professional study of all aspects of music history, literature, theory, and philosophy.

N

nasal cavity port: Passage from the pharynx into the nasal cavity at the point where the velum (soft palate) is capable of touching the back wall of the nasopharynx.

notation: System of symbols used for writing music.

O

octave: Eight-note interval between a note and the nearest note above or below of the same name.

onset: Initiation of vocal-fold vibration in response to airflow.

opera buffa: Comic opera.

opera: Theatrical work using scenery, props, costumes, lighting, dance, text, and vocal and instrumental music with staged dramatization; usually sung throughout.

operetta: Theatrical work similar to an **opera** (see above), but shorter and lighter in subject matter and musical substance; uses spoken dialogue.

opus (Op.): Used to indicate the chronological position of a composition within a composer's entire output, for example, Op. 1, no. 4.

oratorio: Large composition based on a religious text for soloists, chorus, and instrumentalists and usually concertized rather than staged.

ornament: Extra notes serving to decorate or embellish a melody.

ossify: To become bone; for example, when cartilage turns into bone.

overtones: Upper harmonics that, in conjunction with the fundamental, make up a complex musical tone.

P

palate: Roof of the mouth, divided into hard (front) and soft (back).

passage zone *(zona di passaggio):* Series of pitches in the middle voice wherein several tones can be sung by varying register principles.

pharynx (throat): That portion of the vocal tract and alimentary canal situated immediately behind the mouth and esophagus, comprising three connecting chambers: (1) the laryngopharynx, which is the space immediately above the vocal folds, (2) the oropharynx, which extends from the hyoid bone to the terminal point of the soft palate, and (3) the nasopharynx, which lies directly behind the nose and above the soft palate.

phonation: Vibration of the vocal folds to produce sound.

phonemes: Small unit of speech sounds (vowels or consonants) that collectively comprise a linguistic or phonetic system.

phrase: Series of notes sung or played as a single musical and expressive unit, analogous to a clause or sentence in verbal language.

phrasing: Art of shaping a musical phrase expressively, including places for breathing.

physiology: Scientific study of the functioning of the parts of the human body.

piano: Softly; also used as a name for the pianoforte keyboard instrument.

pitch: Property of tone resulting from frequency of vibrations; for example, 440 vibrations per second will produce the pitch A_4.

più: More.

pivotal zone *(zona di passaggio):* Approximate point or pitches of register transition.

placement: Subjective term used to describe vibratory sensations experienced during singing, usually in the facial mask.

plosive: Speech sound caused by a complete stop, closure, and release of air by either the glottis or the organs of articulation, for example, some forms of "b," "p," "t," "d," "k," and "g."

poco a poco: Little by little.

poco meno mosso: A little less motion, slower.

portamento: Connection between two pitches produced by maintaining the vowel performed on the first pitch while slurring, usually at the last moment, to the second pitch.

presto: Very fast; faster than *allegro*.

pulse (beat): Regular beat that is the foundation of a steady tempo.

R

rallentando (rall.): Becoming gradually slower.

range: Distance between the lowest and highest notes of a song or a person's voice.

recitative: Sung music that closely follows the inflections, tempi, and phrasings of speech and is used to convey dramatic action prior to an aria or a composition for vocal ensemble.

register: Series of consecutive, homogeneous tone qualities, the origin of which can be traced to a special kind of biochemical (muscular) action.

Renaissance: The period following the Middle Ages, approximately 1425–1600, when art, literature, and science were revived, humanism spread, and classical values restored.

repertoire: List of pieces that a musician or group of musicians have learned and are ready to perform.

resonance: Spontaneous reinforcement and amplification of tonal vibrations (energy) occurring whenever a cavity is tuned to the natural fundamental frequency (pitch).

resonator: Sympathetically vibrating surface or cavity that amplifies and dampens overtones.

respiration: Exchange of internal and external gases during the complete breath cycle.

rhythm: Whole feeling of movement in music in time, with patterns of organization according to duration, regularity, and variation of notes above the underlying meter.

ritardando (rit.): Becoming gradually slower.

ritenuto (rit.): Held back.

romantic (romanticism): Musical style during the nineteenth century based on strong subjective emotions and represented by such composers as Schumann, Verdi, and Wagner.

round: Musical piece formed by three to four voice parts repeating the same melody three to four times, entering at regular intervals, and blending into a harmonious unit.

S

scale: Series of rising pitches arranged in order of frequency of vibrations, most commonly with seven tones per octave.

sempre: Always.

soft palate: Muscular membrane (velum) in the roof of the mouth behind the hard palate.

song cycle: Group of songs with a similar subject or style, planned to be performed as a unit.

song form: Structure and organization of all elements involved in a musical composition: strophic (stanzas); two-part (AB); three-part (ABA); and through-composed (all new material) are the major song forms.

soprano: Highest female voice and highest part of a choir.

sostenuto: In a sustained, connected manner.

sound wave: Movement of air particles in concentric spheres (compression and rarefaction waves) within an elastic medium; consists of four basic elements—frequency, amplitude, duration, and form.

sound: Movement of air particles set in motion by a vibrator, transported to an ear, and perceived as tone or noise.

Sprechstimme: Type of dramatic vocalization halfway between song and speech.

staccato: Detached.

sternum: Breast bone in the center of the chest to which the ribs attach.

straight tone: Static, vibratoless tone which is caused by manipulative control of the larynx.

strap muscles: Muscles connecting the hyoid bone (above these muscles) to the sternum below, and connecting to the pharyngeal musculature behind; they function to stabilize the larynx.

strophic: Songs constructed in stanzas, each sung to the same melody, as in hymns.

subglottic: Below the glottis.

subito: Suddenly.

T

technic (technique): Procedures and methods used in acquiring skills and executing tasks; involves using exercises designed to help the necessary muscular coordination, strength, and skill for proper performance.

tempo: Rate of speed in music.

tenor: Highest male voice.

tenuto (ten.): Held, slightly lengthened.

tessitura: Particular range of a composition (song or aria) that is most consistently used, as opposed to the total range or compass of a composition; also refers to the comfortable singing range of the voice.

thorax (chest cavity): That portion of the torso situated between the neck and the abdomen which houses the breathing organs within the framework of the ribs, costal cartilages, and the sternum.

through-composed: Song form constructed of new material throughout with no repetitive material.

thyroid cartilage (Adam's apple): Largest, single cartilage of the larynx; contains the vocal folds.

timbre: Distinctive quality and character of a tone, resulting from the combined effect of the fundamental and its overtones.

tone: Musical sound of a definite pitch and quality.

trachea: Commonly referred to as the windpipe; a cartilaginous tube through which air passes to and from the lungs.

tranquillo: Peacefully.

tremolo: Vibrato with rate of speed faster and more narrow than the six to seven oscillations per second of efficiently produced tone.

trill: Intended oscillation of pitch; oscillation of a semitone or more that is produced by movement of the larynx.

triphthong: Combination of three vowel sounds on one syllable, for example, "air," "ear," and "our."

U

unison: Two or more performers sounding the same pitch.

unvoiced: Consonants produced without vocal-fold vibration; for example, "h," "f," "p," "s," "t," and "k."

V

velum: Membranous partition and muscular portion of the soft palate.

ventricle: Small cavity or pouch; for example, the laryngeal sinuses known as the ventricle of Morgani, situated between the true and false folds.

verse: Portion of a song where the music remains the same while the words change with each repetition.

vibrato: Natural pitch variant of six to seven neurological, physically produced pulses per second that occur when the voice is well-coordinated and balanced.

viscera (abdominal cavity): Soft internal organs of the body, notably those of the trunk; for example, the intestines.

vocal folds: Lower part of the thyroarytenoid muscles, or true folds (cords, bands, or lips).

vocal fry: Sometimes referred to as "the scrape of the glottis" because of the frying quality produced on the lowest vocal pitches when lacking sufficient airflow.

vocal range: The compass of pitches (low to high) capable of being performed by a particular voice type.

vocalise: Vocal exercise designed to accomplish specific vocal and musical tasks.

voiced: Vocal-fold sounds set in motion by airflow; also refers to consonants produced by vocal-fold vibration.

volume: "Loudness of sound," best measured in terms of acoustic energy or intensity.

vowel modification: Vowel adjustments made according to pitch levels throughout a singer's full vocal range; allows for tone equalization.

vowel: Speech sound produced when breath is not stopped (see consonants); for example "ee," "ay," "ah," "oh," and "oo."

W

wobble: Undesirable, slower-than-normal vibrato pattern, or oscillation of pitch.

Y

yodeling: Style of singing a melody with frequent leaps and glides mixed with normal singing, usually improvised by the performer and commonly heard in Austrian, Bavarian, Swiss, and country-western music.

Z

zart: Tender, gentle.

Bibliography

Sources of Information and Recommended Readings

A. General Resources on Voice and Singing

Alderson, R. (1979). *Complete Book of Voice Training*. West Nyack, N.Y.: Parker Publishing.

Appelman, R. (1975). *Science of Vocal Pedagogy*. Bloomington, Ind.: University of Indiana Press.

Brown, O. L. (1996). *Discover Your Voice*. San Diego, Calif.: Singular Publishing Group.

Brown, W. E. (1973). *Vocal Wisdom: Maxims of Giovanni Battista Lamperti* (enlarged ed.). Boston, Mass.: Crescendo Publishing.

Bunch, M. (1993). *Dynamics of the Singing Voice*. 2d ed. N.Y.-Wien: Springer-Verlag.

Christy, V. A. (1967). *Expressive Singing*. 3d ed., 2 vols. Dubuque, Iowa: William C. Brown.

Doscher, B. (1988, 1994). *The Functional Unity of the Singing Voice*. 2d ed. Metuchen, N.J.: Scarecrow Press.

Fields, V. A. (1984). *Foundations of the Singer's Art*. 2d ed. New York: National Association of Teachers of Singing.

Gardiner, J. (1968). *A Guide to Good Singing and Speech*. Boston, Mass.: Crescendo Publishing.

Hammar, R. (1978). *Singing, an Extension of Speech*. Metuchen, N.J.: Scarecrow Press.

Henderson, L. B. (1991). *How to Train Singers*. 2d ed. West Nyack, N.Y.: Parker Publishing.

Lawson, J. T. (1955). *Full Throated Ease*. New York: Mills Music.

Lessac, A. (1967). *The Use and Training of the Human Voice*. 2nd ed. New York: Drama Book Specialists.

Leyerle, W. (1987). *Vocal Development through Organic Imagery*. New York: Leyerle Publications.

Linklater, K. (1976). *Freeing the Natural Voice*. New York: Drama Book Specialists.

McClosky, D. B. (1972). *Your Voice at Its Best*. Plymouth, Mass.: The Memorial Press.

Miller, R. (1986). *The Structure of Singing*. New York: Schirmer Books.

Miller, R. (1993). *Training Tenor Voices*. New York: Schirmer Books.

Proctor, D. F. (1980). *Breathing, Speech, and Song*. N.Y.-Wien: Springer-Verlag.

Rama, S., Ballantine, R., & Hymes, A. (1979). *The Science of Breath: A Practical Guide*. Honesdale, Pa.: Himalayan Institute of Yoga Science and Philosophy.

Rosewall, R. B. (1961). *Handbook of Singing*. Evanston, Ill.: Summy-Birchard.

Ross, W. E. (1959). *Secrets of Singing*. Bloomington, Ind.: University of Indiana Press.

Sundberg, J. (1977). "The Acoustics of the Singing Voice." *Scientific American*, March, 82–91.

Sundberg, J. (1987). *The Science of the Singing Voice*. DeKalb, Ill.: Northern Illinois University Press.

Titze, I. R. (1994). Principles of Voice Production.

Vennard, W. (1967). *Singing: The Mechanism and the Technic*. New York: Carl Fischer.

Westermann, K. N. (1955). *The Emergent Voice*. Ann Arbor, Mich.: Edwards Brothers.

B. Self-Improvement and Awareness

Alexander, F. M. (1984). *The Use of the Self*. Reprint. Downey, Calif.: Centerline Press.

Campbell, D. (1986). *Introduction to the Musical Brain*. St. Louis, Mo.: Magnamusic-Baton.

Cooper, M. (1984). *Change Your Voice, Change Your Life*. New York: Barnes and Noble Books.

Covey, S. R. (1990). *The Seven Habits of Highly Effective People*. New York: Simon & Schuster.

Covey, S. R., Merrill, A. R., & Merrill, R. R. (1994). *First Things First*. New York: Simon & Schuster.

Csikszentmihalyi, M. (1990). *Flow: The Psychology of Optimal Experience*. New York: Harper and Row.

Edwards, B. (1979). *Drawing on the Right Side of the Brain*. New York: St. Martin's Press.

Goleman, D. (1995). *Emotional Intelligence*. New York: Bantam Doubleday Dell Publishing Group.

Green, B. with Gallwey, W. T. (1986). *The Inner Game of Music*. Garden City, N.Y.: Anchor/Doubleday.

Herrigel, E. (1964). *Zen in the Art of Archery*. New York: McGraw-Hill.

Jones, F. (1979). *Alexander Technique: Body Awareness in Action*. New York: Schocken Books.

Kuntzleman, C. T. (1981). *Maximum Personal Energy*. Emmaus, Penn.: Rodale Press.

Lakein, A. (1974). *How to Get Control of Your Time and Your Life*. New York: Signet Books, New American Library.

Leonard, G. (1992). *Mastery: The Keys to Success and Long-Term Fulfillment*. New York: Plume (Penguin Books).

Markova, D. (1991). *The Art of the Possible*. Emeryville, Calif.: Conari Press.

Moore, T. (1994). *Care of the Soul*. New York: HarperCollins.

Ornish, D. (1993). *Eat More, Weigh Less*. New York: HarperCollins.

Peck, M. S. (1974). *The Road Less Traveled*. New York: Signet Books.

Pritikin, R. (1990). *The New Pritikin Program: The Premier Health and Fitness Program for the '90s*. New York: Simon & Schuster.

Ristad, E. (1982). *A Soprano on Her Head.* Moab, Utah: Real People Press.

Seligman, M. (1991). *How to Change Your Mind and Your Life.* New York: Knopf.

C. Vocal Health, Anatomy, and Physiology

Boone, D. (1983). *The Voice and Voice Therapy.* Englewood Cliffs, N.J.: Prentice-Hall.

Boone, D. (1991). *Is Your Voice Telling On You.* San Diego, Calif.: Singular Publishing Group.

Brodnitz, F. (1987). *Keep Your Voice Healthy.* Houston, Tex.: College-Hill Press.

Creager, J. G. (1983). *Human Anatomy and Physiology.* Belmont, Calif.: Wadsworth.

Cooper, M. (1973). *Modern Techniques of Vocal Rehabilitation.* Springfield, Ill.: Charles C. Thomas.

Greene, M. C. L. & Matieson, L. (1990). *The Voice and Its Disorders.* San Diego, Calif.: Singular Publishing Group.

McCloskey, D. B. (1972). *Your Voice at Its Best.* Plymouth, Mass.: The Memorial Press.

Perkins, W. H. & Kent, R. D. (1986). *Functional Anatomy of Speech, Language and Hearing.* Waltham, Mass.: College-Hill Press.

Punt, N. A. (1979). *The Singer's and Actor's Throat.* 3d ed. London: Heinemann Medical Books.

Titze, I. R. (1993). *Vocal Fold Physiology: Frontiers in Basic Science.* San Diego, Calif.: Singular Publishing Group.

Zemlin, W. R. (1981). *Speech and Hearing Science: Anatomy and Physiology.* Englewood Cliffs, N.J.: Prentice-Hall.

D. History of Singers and Singing

Hines, J. (1974). *Great Singers on Great Singing.* New York: Simon & Schuster.

Monahan, B. J. (1978). *The Art of Singing: A Compendium of Thoughts on Singing Published between 1777 and 1927.* Metuchen, N.J.: Scarecrow Press.

Pleasants, H. (1974). *The Great American Popular Singers.* New York: Simon & Schuster.

Pleasants, H. (1966). *The Great Singers: From the Dawn of Opera to Our Own Time.* New York: Simon & Schuster.

Rushmore, R. (1971). *The Singing Voice.* New York: Dodd, Mead and Company.

E. Phonetics, Diction, and Song Texts Translations

Adler, K. (1967). *Phonetics and Diction in Singing: Italian, French, Spanish and German.* Minneapolis: University of Minnesota Press.

Coffin, B. (1964). *Phonetic Readings of Songs and Arias.* Boulder, Col.: Pruett Press.

Coffin, B. (1966). *Word-by-Word Translations of Songs and Arias.* New York: Scarecrow Press.

Colorni, E. (1970). *Singer's Italian.* New York: G. Schirmer.

Cox, R. G. (1970). *The Singer's Manual of German and French Diction.* New York: G. Schirmer.

Grubb, T. (1979). *Singing in French.* New York: Schirmer Books.

Marshall, M. (1953). *The Singer's Manual of English Diction.* New York: G. Schirmer.

Miller, P. L. (1973). *The Ring of Words, An Anthology of Song Texts.* New York: W. W. Norton.

Moriarity, J. (1975). *Diction: Italian, Latin, French and German.* New York: E. C. Schirmer.

Odom, W. (1981). *German for Singers.* New York: Schirmer Books.

Prawer, S. S. ed. (1964). *The Penguin Book of Lieder.* England: Penguin Books.

Uris, D. (1971). *To Sing in English.* New York: Boosey & Hawkes.

Wall, J. (1990). *Diction for Singers.* Dallas, Tex.: Pst. . .Inc.

F. Vocal Performance Practice, Style and Interpretation

Adler, K. (1965). *The Art of Accompanying and Coaching.* Minneapolis: University of Minnesota Press.

Balk, H. W. (1977). *The Complete Singing Actor.* Minneapolis: University of Minnesota Press.

Balk, H. W. (1985). *Performing Power.* Minneapolis: University of Minnesota Press.

Balk, H. W. (1989). *The Radiant Performer.* Minneapolis: University of Minnesota Press.

Bernac, P. (1970). *The Interpretation of French Song.* New York: Praeger.

Caldwell, R. (1990). *The Performer Prepares.* Dallas, Tex.: PST. . . Inc. (video also available)

Emmons, S. & Sonntag, S. (1979). *The Art of the Song Recital.* New York: Schirmer Books.

Fischer-Dieskau, D. (1977). *The Fischer-Dieskau Book of Lieder.* Gerge Bird and Richard Stokes, trans. New York: Alfred A. Knopf.

Gelineau, P. (1992). *Understanding Music Fundamentals.* 2d ed. New York: Prentice-Hall.

Greene, H. P. (1912). *Interpretation in Song.* London: MacMillan (2d ed., 1956) New York: St. Martin's Press.

Gorrell, L. (1993). *The Nineteenth-Century German Lied.* Portland, Oreg.: Amadeus Press.

Lehmann, L. (1972). *Eighteen Song Cycles: Studies in Interpretation.* New York: Praeger.

Lehmann, L. (1945). *More Than Singing.* New York: Boosey-Hawkes.

Meister, B. (1980). *An Introduction to the Art Song.* New York: Taplinger Publishing.

Moore, G. (1954). *Singer and Accompanist.* New York: Macmillan.

Schiøtz, A. (1970). *The Singer and His Art.* New York: Harper and Row.

G. Solo Vocal Repertoire

Coffin, B. (1956–1962). *The Singer's Repertoire.* 5 vols. New Brunswick, N.J.: Scarecrow Press.

Coffin, B. & Singer, W. (1962). *Program Notes for the Singer's Repertoire.* Vol. 5. New Brunswick, N.J.: Scarecrow Press.

Emmons, S. & Sonntag, S. (1979). *The Art of the Song Recital.* New York: Schirmer Books.

Espina, N. (1977). *Repertoire for the Solo Voice.* Metuchen, N.J.: Scarecrow Press.

Friedberg, R. (1981). *American Art Song and American Poetry:* Vol. 1, *America Comes of Age.*; Vol. 2, *Voices of Maturity;* Vol. 3, *The Century Advances.* Metuchen, N.J.: Scarecrow Press.

Goleeke, T. (1984). *Literature for Voice: An Index of Songs in Collections and Source Book for Teachers of Singing*. Metuchen, N.J.: Scarecrow Press

Kagen, S. (1968). *Music for the Voice*. Bloomington, Ind.: Indiana University Press.

Nardone, T. (1976). *Classical Vocal Music in Print*. Philadelphia, Pa.: Music Data.

Stevens, D. (1962). *A History of Song*. New York: W. W. Norton.

Whitton, K. (1984). *An Introduction to German Song*. London: Julia MacRae.

H. Solo Vocal Music Collections

Art Song, Oratorio, and Opera Solo Vocal Repertoire

A Heritage of Twentieth Century British Song. 2 vols. Boosey-Hawkes.

A New Anthology of American Song. 2 vols. (high & low). G. Schirmer.

Anthology of Modern French Song. M. Spicher, ed. 2 vols. (high & low). G. Schirmer.

The Art Song. Vol. 25 (Music for Millions Series). Consolidated Music Publishers.

Best of Pathways of Song. F. LaForge & Earhart. Vols. 1–2 (high) and Vols. 3–4 (low). Warner Bros.

Contemporary American Art Songs. B. Taylor. 2 vols. (high & low). Ditson.

50 Art Songs from the Modern Repertoire. G. Schirmer.

50 Selected Songs by Schubert, Schumann, Brahms, Wolf, & Strauss. 2 vols. (high & low). G. Schirmer.

56 Songs You Like to Sing. G. Schirmer.

The First Book of Tenor/Soprano/Mezzo-Soprano/Bass/Baritone Solos. J. F. Boytin, ed. 6 vols. G. Schirmer.

Great Art Songs of Three Centuries. B. Taylor, ed. 2 vols. (high & low). G. Schirmer.

G. Schirmer Operatic Anthology. R. Larson, ed. 5 vols. (soprano, mezzo-soprano, tenor, baritone, & bass). G. Schirmer.

The New Imperial Edition. S. Northcote, ed. 6 vols. (soprano, mezzo-soprano, contralto, tenor, baritone, & bass). Boosey-Hawkes.

Song Anthology One and Two. A. L. & W. D. Leyerle, eds. Leyerle Publications.

Songs by 22 Americans. 2 vols. (high & low). G. Schirmer.

Songs through the Centuries. B. Taylor, ed. 2 vols. (high & low). Carl Fischer.

26 Italian Songs and Arias. J. G. Paton, ed. 2 vols. (medium high & medium low). Alfred Press.

Popular Music Repertoire (Broadway, Standards, and Country)

The Big Book of Standards. Hal Leonard Publishing.

Broadway Repertoire. 5 vols. (soprano, mezzo-soprano, tenor, bass-baritone, & duets). Hal Leonard Publishing.

The Top 50 Country Hits. Columbia Pictures Publications.

The Top 100 Popular Songs. Columbia Pictures Publications.

I. General Voice Texts with Song Anthologies (Art Song, Folk, and Other)

Christy, V. A. (1990). *Expressive Singing Song Anthology*. Rev. by J. G. Paton. 5th ed. Dubuque, Iowa: William C. Brown.

Christy, V. A. (1997). *Foundations in Singing*. Rev. by J. G. Paton. 6th ed. Dubuque, Iowa: William C. Brown.

Harlow, B. (1985). *You, the Singer*. Chapel Hill, N.C.: Hinshaw Music.

Kenny, J. (1987). *Becoming a Singing Performer*. Dubuque, Iowa. William C. Brown.

Lindsley, C. E. (1985). *Fundamentals of Singing for Voice Classes*. Belmont, Calif.: Wadsworth Publishing Co.

Miller, K. E. (1990). *Principles of Singing*. 2d ed. Englewood Cliffs, N.J.: Prentice-Hall.

Schmidt, J. (1993). *The Basics of Singing*. 3d ed. New York: Schirmer Books. (audiocassette accompaniment available)

Stanton, R. (1983). *Steps to Singing for Voice Classes*. Belmont, Calif.: 3d ed. Wadsworth Publishing.

Name and Subject Index

Adventures in Singing

Adventures in Singing